INTERNATIONAL PERSPEC[
YUGOSLAV CONFLICT

For Maureen
to complete the set
alex
1996

International Perspectives on the Yugoslav Conflict

Edited by

Alex Danchev
Professor of International Relations
Keele University

and

Thomas Halverson
Credit Officer
European Bank for Reconstruction and Development

Introduction by
Michael Ignatieff

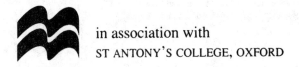

in association with
ST ANTONY'S COLLEGE, OXFORD

First published in Great Britain 1996 by
MACMILLAN PRESS LTD
Houndmills, Basingstoke, Hampshire RG21 6XS
and London
Companies and representatives
throughout the world

This book is published in the *St Antony's Series*
General editor: Alex Pravda

A catalogue record for this book is available
from the British Library.

ISBN 0–333–60452–0 hardcover
ISBN 0–333–65775–6 paperback

First published in the United States of America 1996 by
ST. MARTIN'S PRESS, INC.,
Scholarly and Reference Division,
175 Fifth Avenue,
New York, N.Y. 10010

ISBN 0–312–15838–6

Library of Congress Cataloging-in-Publication Data
International perspectives on the Yugoslav conflict / edited by Alex
Danchev and Thomas Halverson.
p. cm.
Includes bibliographical references and index.
ISBN 0–312–15838–6 (cloth)
1. Yugoslav War, 1991– —Congresses.   I. Danchev, Alex.
II. Halverson, Thomas E.
DR1313.I586   1996
949.702'4—dc20   95–43679
                                                              CIP

10   9   8   7   6   5   4   3   2   1
05   04   03   02   01   00   99   98   97   96

Printed Great Britain by
Ipswich Book Co. Ltd, Ipswich, Suffolk

Contents

Acknowledgements

This book grew out of an international conference on the ongoing Yugoslav conflict, held under the aegis of the Department of International Relations at Keele University in September 1994. One of the aims of that conference, like its predecessors on the Falklands and the Gulf, was to bring together, not only different ethnicities and nationalities – especially important in this conflict – but also different affiliations and experiences: participants, diplomats, officials, journalists and academics all rubbed shoulders round the conference table. The debate among them is reflected in the following pages.

The conference was made possible by financial support from the Ministry of Defence, the Foreign and Commonwealth Office, the Esmée Fairbairn Charitable Trust, the British Academy and, at Keele, the Bruce Centre and Research Development and Business Affairs. A number of our students volunteered to act as temporary unpaid administrative assistants: Mike Bell, Debbie Durrant, Tamara Ismail, Sion Lloyd-Jones, Ashten Regan, Paul Roe, Sue Taylor, Greg Thompson and Adam Whittaker. Maureen Groppe and Pat Thompson provided essential secretarial support before and after the event. Richard Devetak played an invaluable part in preparing the proceedings for publication. We are much indebted to them all. We are also grateful to Peter Howson, who went to Bosnia as an official war artist, for generously allowing his work to be reproduced on the cover, and to Sam Chatterton Dickson of Flowers East for making this possible.

There are perhaps two tests of a successful conference – that it is interesting and even enjoyable to attend; and that it has a long scholarly half-life. This conference, like its predecessors, appears to have passed the first of those tests. It is about to take the second.

ALEX DANCHEV and TOM HALVERSON
Keele and London, 1995

Notes on the Contributors

Marie-Janine Calic is a Researcher at the Stiftung Wissenschaft und Politik in Ebenhausen. She has worked as an observer for the (then) CSCE in Macedonia and as an adviser to the UN Special Representative in the former Yugoslavia. She is the author of *The Social History of Serbia 1815–1941* (1994) and *The War in Bosnia-Herzegovina* (1995).

Christopher Cviic is Associate Research Fellow in the European Programme of the Royal Institute of International Affairs (Chatham House) in London, and Editor of *The World Today*. He is the author of *Remaking the Balkans* (2nd edn, 1995) and *An Awful Warning: The War in Ex-Yugoslavia* (1994).

Andrei Edemskii is a Researcher at the Slavic and Balkan Studies Institute of the Russian Academy of Sciences in Moscow. In 1992 he was the coordinator of a team of experts briefing the Gaidar government on the transformation of Central and Eastern Europe. He is working on a study of Russian policy on the Yugoslav conflict.

Misha Glenny is a writer and broadcaster, and a former Central Europe correspondent of the BBC World Service, stationed in Yugoslavia from June 1991. He is the author of *The Rebirth of History* (2nd edn, 1993) and *The Fall of Yugoslavia* (2nd edn, 1993).

James Gow is Lecturer in War Studies at King's College, London, and Research Associate in the Centre for Defence Studies. He is the author of *Legitimacy and the Military: The Yugoslav Crisis* (1992) and *Triumph of the Lack of Will: International Diplomacy and the Yugoslav War of Dissolution* (1995).

Françoise Hampson is Reader in Law at the University of Essex. She has been on fact-finding visits to the former Yugoslavia on behalf of both Amnesty International and the International League for Human Rights. She is the author of numerous articles in the fields of human rights law and the law of armed conflicts, among them 'Liability for War Crimes', in Peter Rowe (ed.), *The Gulf War in International and English Law* (1993).

Michael Ignatieff is a writer and broadcaster, and former Fellow of King's College, Cambridge. He first saw *ancien régime* Yugoslavia in the late 1950s, when his father was serving in the Canadian Embassy in Belgrade. He is the author of *The Needs of Strangers* (1984) and *Blood and Belonging* (1993).

Olivier Lepick is a Research Fellow at CREST, at the Ecole Polytechnique in Paris, and a former student at the Graduate Institute for International Relations in Geneva.

Adam Roberts is Montague Burton Professor of International Relations and Fellow of Balliol College, Oxford, and a Fellow of the British Academy. Among many other works, he is the editor (with Benedict Kingsbury) of *United Nations, Divided World: The UN's Roles in International Relations* (2nd edn, 1993).

Ivan Vejvoda is a Research Fellow in the European Institute at the University of Sussex, and a former Research Fellow in the Institute for European Studies in Belgrade. He is the author of 'Yugoslavia and the Empty Space of Power', in *Praxis International* (1994), and editor (with David Dyker) of *Yugoslavia and After* (forthcoming).

Introduction: Virtue by Proxy
Michael Ignatieff

For ordinary citizens in the West, 'doing something' about Yugoslavia has meant getting someone else to do it for us. Peace-keepers, relief workers, United Nations (UN) negotiators have intervened on our behalf and because they are our 'proxies', we bear some responsibility – how much is not clear – if they get hurt doing our bidding.

There have been dozens of lives lost among the UN peace-keeping contingent and countless more serious injuries. At Camp Pleso hospital in Zagreb, I have watched American doctors trying to save the lives of UN soldiers injured either by enemy fire or by mines. These soldiers – from Canada, Denmark, France, Bangladesh, Nepal and a host of other countries – are the modern mercenaries of our conscience. It was sobering to discover, in this military hospital, that my own personal desire for intervention has resulted, among other things, in these men losing their legs and hands.

To be sure, there are countless additional reasons why they have lost their arms and legs, and my personal intentions do not rank high on the list. Still, by virtue of the fact that they are mandated by the UN, and by virtue of the fact that I – and millions of other people – have wanted them doing this job, I bear an indeterminate portion of responsibility for their injuries.

The indirectness of an ordinary citizen's moral implication in the interventions of the postwar era makes it difficult for us to discipline our moral wishes with a due sense of their consequences. In the Second World War, if you wished to stop Hitler, you went to a recruiting post and volunteered. You 'did your bit'. It is one thing to volunteer to repel aggression; quite another to volunteer other people to do so. The characteristic of most interventions in the post-Cold War era is that someone else 'does your bit' for you. The ironies of good intentions are not borne by those who happen to have them.

Having such intentions turns out to be an easy matter if you are shielded from their consequences. It is noticeable that the desire to intervene appears to bear an inverse relation to a person's distance from the costs. Throughout the Yugoslav conflict, the demand for intervention has come from intellectual and cultural figures who, in the nature of things, could not either 'intervene' themselves or directly order intervention. The political leaders who hesitated to intervene did so because they would have had to bear the political costs of failure more directly than most of those counselling intervention. It was customary for the 'interveners' to claim the reverse: to argue on the basis of a sojourn in Sarajevo, that it was they who were closest to the implications of intervention or nonintervention, while it was the politicians, far away, who were taking refuge in their distance to refuse to face the catastrophe. Yet if intervention at the level desired by the 'interveners' did not occur, it was not because those charged with the decisions were in moral flight from the realities, but because they were only too cognisant of the risks.

Thus far, I have been talking about the problem of moral proxy as it relates to ordinary citizens who 'demand' intervention. American foreign policy itself could be regarded as a case of the problems of moral action by proxy. Because of its policy of avoiding battlefield casualties at all costs, America has willed moral action by proxy, that is, without wishing to share the consequences. Thus at Camp Pleso, the Americans sew up the wounds of the UNPROFOR soldiers, but have not committed troops to walk those same minefields. American policymakers may indeed wish to achieve certain moral objectives – peace and security in Yugoslavia – but to have such intentions and then to shy away from their costs is to commit yourself to moral actions which must, in the nature of things, fail. A cynic might remark that what matters about an intervention, for American policymakers, is neither its success nor failure in real terms, but sustaining the appearance of moral concern and the semblance of global leadership.

The chief moral problem in willing intervention by proxy is justifying the deaths of those who intervene on one's behalf or who die as a result of intervention. Such justifications usually take the form of setting the actual deaths incurred by intervention against the potential deaths saved by such actions. This moral accounting, troubling at all times, is especially unsettling in Yugoslavia because it is simply not clear that intervention has saved very many lives. Hence, the lives that have been lost or maimed by intervention seem especially unredeemed. Even if we do think their sacrifice was worthwhile, we are back to the troubling indirectness of 'our' relation to intervention – the sense that whether intervention works or fails, it is not 'we' who pay the costs, but someone else – the mercenary soldiers employed by the UN, or the peoples of the region themselves.

When intervention does not seem to have worked, as in the case of Yugoslavia, those who have called for 'intervention' can deal with failure in a number of ways. Moral disgust with 'Europe', with the 'UN', with 'politicians' is an especially seductive avenue, since it leaves the whole enterprise of virtue by proxy unexamined. Moral disgust is in fact a strategy of disengagement, a means of liquidating a moral commitment instead of renewing it.

The Yugoslav war continues, and yet for most of those who made intervention a *cause célèbre*, it is already 'over'. It is certainly over as a cause, as a political project, as a moral issue. The caravan has moved on to other causes, other issues. And yet the war continues.

If 'intervention' has been a failure, moral disgust should be resisted. Instead, those who called for intervention should re-examine both our language of appeal and our motives behind intervention in order to take the measure of failure, and if possible, avoid a repetition.

THE NARCISSISM OF INTERVENTION

Was it appropriate, for example, to believe that intervention, of any kind, was a defence of European values? One of the grimly useful results of the Yugoslav débâcle surely is to make everyone more humble and precise in their reference to values. It was macabrely appropriate that after all the empty rhetoric about Europe standing for tolerance and civility, the concentration camp should have made its return, to remind us that such institutions are part of 'our' heritage too. Only a Europe infatuated with its own image of itself should have been particularly surprised by the return – so soon – of what it had so studiously repressed.

The whole interventionist project had an incorrigibly narcissistic motivation. European intellectuals were chiefly interested in Yugoslavia as theatre for the display of their own moral profile. Putting the matter perhaps too bluntly, we intervened to save ourselves. We wanted to show that Europe 'meant' something, stood for toleration within a peaceable and civilised civil society. This imaginary Europe, this narcissistic image of ourselves, we believed was incarnated in the myth of a multiethnic, multiconfessional Bosnia.

This discovery of an ideal image of ourselves in a part of Europe in which no Western European intellectual had taken the slightest interest before the war had its peculiar aspects. It was not clear, for example, whether Bosnia did in fact approximate our dream image of it as a tolerant, multiconfessional place. The few experts there disagreed as to whether a multiethnic polity was ever viable in Bosnia. The fact that the Bosnian Serbs set out to dismember this polity from its inception was taken, not as proof that a multiethnic polity could not work, but that it had been strangled at birth by nationalists. This thesis – which sought to salvage the dream of a multiethnic Bosnia from its evident collapse – dismissed the Bosnian Serbs, who had genuine fears and grievances, as tools of nationalistic demagogues. The desire to intervene may just have caused us to rewrite the history of Bosnia to make it conform to our ideal of a redeemable place. In the psychology that led to demands for intervention, the complex and ambiguous ethnic realities of Bosnia were converted into a screen on which Europe projected its multicultural fantasy of itself. Truly we intervened to save ourselves.

It was ironic, of course, that a Western Europe which had happily ghettoised its own Muslim *gastarbeiter* minorities suddenly discovered in Muslim–Christian co-existence in Bosnia the very picture of its own multicultural dreams. Intellectuals, especially in France, who had absolutely nothing to say about the treatment of the Muslim minority in France or about the compatibility of ethnic difference with the centralising Jacobin tradition of the republic suddenly found themselves taking up the cause of multiethnic society in Bosnia. Why in Bosnia if not in Boulogne Billancourt? Why in Sarajevo if not in Berlin or Leicester?

THE ETHICS OF DISPLACEMENT

It was observable that intervention in Yugoslavia offered a foreign cause to intellectuals who had lived through the liquidation, throughout the 1970s and 80s, of all viable domestic commitments. Bosnia became the latest *bel espoir* of a generation that had tried ecology, socialism, anti-totalitarianism and antiracism, only to find all of these causes absorbed into the banality of bourgeois politics. This was most noticeable the case in France, where intellectuals like Bernard Henri-Lévy seemed to see the Bosnian cause chiefly as an opportunity for a self-dramatising public role. What was rescued in Bosnia, by this politics, was not Bosnia, but the image of the committed intellectual of the Left. Results were secondary. Indeed, failure either did not matter at all, or was understood as belonging to a line of noble failure stretching back to the Spanish republican cause of the 1930s.

Again the point is not to criticise the individuals involved, but to understand that the success or failure of intervention in Bosnia itself become secondary to the dramatics of 'taking a stand' as public intellectuals. This is a moral seduction to which intellectuals are perhaps especially prone. Cut off from the actual exercise of power, enraptured by the role of serving as moral witness, intellectuals found themselves, in the case of Bosnia, seduced into believing that it was commitment itself to the Bosnia cause which mattered. The seductiveness of ineffective moral witness was all the more alluring in the context of a general depoliticisation attendant upon the end of the Cold War and the collapse of French socialism as an ideological project.

Bosnia became a theatre of displacement, in which political energies that might otherwise have been expended at home – in struggling to create a multicultural, multiethnic society in Western Europe – were directed instead at defending the mythic multiculturalism of embattled Bosnia. This displacement might not have occurred had there been a mobilised and effective political party structure at home to absorb and canalise the restless moral energies of educated people.

Of course, political activism at home never precludes moral activism abroad. Internationalism has always gone hand in hand with most kinds of socialist politics. The difficulty was that the collapse of a political project at home left internationalism without any of the institutional supports necessary to make it effective: political parties, trade unions, student organisations, clubs and so forth. The institutions of the new politics – Greenpeace, aid charities like *Médecins sans Frontières* or Amnesty International – proved to be either too weak, organisationally, or too divided from each other by their single-issue focus to be able to mobilise a domestic constituency behind international intervention. This critical organisational weakness at home helps to explain why the demand for intervention in Bosnia joined the doleful list of lost causes of the left.

DID INTERVENTION MAKE THINGS WORSE?

It is no disservice to the devotion and courage of the peace-keepers, relief workers, journalists, negotiators who intervened on our behalf to ask whether, in the end, they not did not make things worse.

We should ask, for example, whether the attempt to deliver humanitarian relief convoys to civilians in the midst of war zones did not, in the end, prolong the war by sustaining the civilian hinterlands on which militias depend. This might be true, but it might also be only another way of saying that international relief prevented the total defeat of the Muslim population. Thus while prolonging the war, we did prevent one side from being annihilated and possibly exterminated. Yet although we fed the victims, we refused to arm them, and by failing to arm them, we denied them effective means of resistance.

The Bosnian situation exposed all the dilemmas of attempting to maintain moral neutrality in a war zone. We sought, in principle, to bring relief to innocent civilian victims on all sides. Inevitably some victims were not so innocent, and inevitably much aid found its way into the hands of belligerents. Moreover, most of the victims were from one side, and so attempts to relieve them drew us into conflict with the other side, the major aggressor.

The futility of humanitarian relief and peace-keeping in a war zone became apparent, while European efforts to broker a negotiated settlement appeared to ratify aggression and ethnic

cleansing. With the moral implications of these forms of intervention becoming more unpleasant, many Americans became
tempted by intervention by proxy, that is to say, arming the
Muslims and enabling them to reconquer lost territory. At
least, then, it was argued, they could achieve on the battlefield
what could not be won at the negotiation table – their survival.
Most European governments found it too much of a Machiavellian paradox to believe that sending arms to Yugoslavia was
the best way to bring the war to a livable conclusion. It seemed
impossible to expect virtue to flow from the arming of vice.
If Americans believed in such Machiavellian strategies, it was
because they believed that 'the Muslims' were innocent victims. Hence it followed that innocent victims could put arms
solely to good purposes. That they might well put the arms to
bad purposes, namely ethnic cleansing, only seemed inevitable
to those who thought it unwise to divide the Bosnian populations into neat moral categories of praise and blame.

The intervention strategy which was adopted – to protect
the Muslims in safe havens, to keep Sarajevo from falling while
doing virtually nothing to stop Serb bombardment – was per-
fectly consistent with the conviction that we could not and
should not commit ourselves to a land war in the Balkans
against the Serbians. In effect, the West's policy consisted in
saying: we will not fight the chief aggressor, and we will not
enable the victims to resist; but we will try to prevent the victims from being wiped out.

Yet by failing to stop and reverse Serbian aggression, the
West became complicit in the destruction of Bosnia and its
capital city. The UN allowed itself to become the administrator of the Serbian siege of Sarajevo. The UN both prevented
the city from starving to death and yet, by doing nothing to
break the siege, it helped to prolong the city's suffering. Moral
results could hardly be more ambiguous than this.

The best one can say is that outside intervention helped to
retard Serbian achievement of its goals of a Greater Serbia.
Had Croatia not been recognised in late December 1991, it is
possible that it would have been conquered entirely. Had UN
detachments not gone into Sarajevo, it is possible that it would
have fallen, and if it had fallen, all of Bosnia would now be in
the hands of the Bosnian Serbs. When Western diplomats claim
that our intervention has fulfilled its limited mandate, they

mean, in effect, that we prevented the full realisation of Serbian war aims.

Yet the manner in which this was done should give us all pause for thought. The Yugoslav case seems to illustrate the maxim that the best is sometimes the enemy of the good. The interventions we took not only did not succeed; they made it impossible to adopt ones that could have done better. By deploying peace-keepers on the ground, the West offered their lightly armed troops as potential hostages to local warlords. This then precluded sustained use of air power as a dissuasive tool, and as an instrument of coercive diplomacy. The peace-keeping strategy also precluded the lift and strike option: lifting the arms embargo and striking at the Serbs.

One conclusion to draw from all of this is that one should never send humanitarian aid or peace-keepers to a war zone where the parties refuse conciliation or refuse to abide by the resolutions of the UN. Such 'interventions' actually reduce the incentives to end conflict while compromising the authority, effectiveness and integrity of the 'interveners'. Moreover, to engage in melioristic half-measures in such a situation is to preclude the possibility of escalating military or diplomatic action later on.

THE PROBLEM OF HINDSIGHT

Intervention is both a problem of knowing what to do and when to do it. The issue of timing haunts all retrospective looks at the Yugoslav catastrophe.

As late as 1986, maintaining the unity of federal Yugoslavia was a plausible goal for international policy in the Balkans. By 1990, it was no longer so. Yet, both European and American policy proclaimed support for a unified Yugoslavia until June 1991. Such support from outside helped to legitimise the Serb invasion of Croatia in June of that year.

In hindsight, it seems clear that by 1990, Europe and America should have tried to help the parties towards a peaceful divorce with minority rights guarantees. All sides should have been issued with clearly stated dissuasive threats against the forcible transfer of populations or the rectification of borders. There is no guarantee, however, that such a policy would have prevented catastrophe. The problem then and now is that Western threats of the use of force lacked credibility.

Both Western interventionists and the Yugoslav victims who begged for intervention seriously overestimated the capacity of outside governments to affect outcomes. The NATO powers had one weakness which all of the extremists in the area clearly understood: no outside power was willing to commit itself to a full-scale invasion or imperial policing operation in the area. In practice, the only conceivable military action was the air strike, and all the major actors, in Belgrade, Pale, Zagreb and in NATO headquarters, understood how limited its effectiveness was bound to be. Such air strikes could dissuade Serbian militias from attacking UN units, but they could not reverse Serbian territorial gains.

This is not to claim that air power is useless. The key issue is one of timing. If NATO had announced that it was prepared to defend Croatia against Yugoslav People's Army (JNA) attack in July 1991 with air strikes to back up Croatian land forces, it is possible that Serbian expansionism in the Balkans could have been stopped. Once again, we confirm the old adage that early intervention is better than late. Moreover, short, sharp, dissuasive intervention is more effective against aggression than humanitarian relief of the victims coupled with negotiations. Yet it is easy to be wise after the event. At the time, in June 1991, the JNA assault on Croatia was supported in many quarters in the West as a federal state's legitimate response to secession. Hence intervention faced policymakers with a choice between competing principles. Were we to support the Croatians' right to self-determination, or the territorial integrity of a nation-state? Once again, what might have seemed the right choice of action as late as 1989 was no longer the right choice for Western policymakers in 1991.

IMPERIAL GUILT

Yugoslavia illustrates the besetting weakness of any imperial power that decides to renounce imperial means. If the chief issue in any intervention is how to devise a rapid-exit strategy, interventions are bound to fail. There are very few problems in the post-Cold War world which can be solved by quick-exit interventions. The critical issue is why so many of the former imperial powers are unwilling to contemplate intervention as a commitment over the long haul.

Most of the problems of the post-Cold War world concern the collapse of states, and the resulting collapse of the capacity of the civilian populations to feed and protect themselves, either against famine, climate or internecine warfare. In a world in which nations once capable of imperial burdens are no longer willing to shoulder them, it is inevitable that many of the states created by decolonisation should prove unequal to the task of maintaining civil order. Such nations have achieved self-determination on the cruellest possible terms. Either they are torn apart by ethnic conflict, or they are simply too weak to contend with the poverty of their people.

Yugoslavia belongs to a growing category of states, in the southern rim of the former Soviet Empire and in Africa, which have collapsed leaving their citizens in the Hobbesian war of all against all, or as Michael Walzer has it, some against some.

What these societies need, desperately, is internal peace followed by the patient reconstruction of the infrastructure of civil society: institutions – schools, hospitals, courts, police stations – in which the rule of law rather than the rule of the gun prevails. This is work which is totally ill-suited to the post-Cold War style of instant intervention and quick exit. What is needed is long-term, unspectacular, commitment to a molecular rebuilding of society itself. Obviously, such work can only be undertaken by the people themselves, but long-standing and long-suffering commitment by outsiders can help.

In the nineteenth century, this work was 'the white man's burden': the building of the infrastructure of imperial rule and administration. In the Balkans, it was the work of the Ottomans, and then of the Austro-Hungarians. Shattered traces of their work still dot the landscape. At least in retrospect, imperial rule has a certain logic: those who cannot agree to rule themselves may be able to submit to rule by strangers.

This logic did not survive the rise of nationalism and the doctrine of self-determination. We are now living with the consequence of the modern axiom that rule by strangers is worse than rule by your own; that it is better for people to govern themselves, even if they make a mess of it, than to be ruled by foreigners, even if these foreigners do a passable job.

For democrats, there is no return from the truth of these axioms, and no point whatever in indulging nostalgia for the heyday of imperial division of the globe. Yet the question remains, what is to be done when self-determination fails, when civil war or famine destroys a polity? Once the immediate crisis has been resolved, who is to do the rebuilding? Who is to re-create the institutions necessary for self-determination to function? Even if some form of peace or permanent truce can be brokered in the Balkans, it will take a generation or two to rebuild the institutions on which civic trust and a functioning polity depend. Who is ready to shoulder this burden?

It is at this point that the idea of trusteeships and protectorates becomes plausible. For once states have imploded, once trust among ethnic groups has been destroyed by violence, someone must come in and administer the society on a day-to-day basis, not just for months, but for years, until ordinary people can shake off the fear and loathing which divide them. This means rule by strangers. Yet such exercises are a potential incitement to insurrection unless they have the legitimacy of an international mandate and a firm time limit. In other words, the next task facing the international community is to devise a form of trusteeship which reproduces the benefits of imperial rule (benefits, that is, for the indigenous population), without reproducing the dynamic of revolt which will destroy what such exercises set out to achieve: a stable and self-determining polity.

1 American Perspectives
Thomas Halverson

Why did the world's most powerful nation, which adroitly assembled an international coalition to destroy decisively Iraq's occupation army in Kuwait, demonstrate a hesitant, limited commitment to resolving the worst conflict in Europe since the Second World War? Moral indignation and exhortations to 'do something' which might stop the humanitarian, political and military disaster of the former Yugoslavia often obscure the search for an answer. The Yugoslav conflicts have been a complex problem for the United States. Washington policymaking – messy at the best of times – has emerged from a constantly shifting and complicated milieu of interests and imperatives. Domestic politics, changing perceptions and the dynamic of events on the ground have at different times seemed to drive decisions. Yet policy at bottom has been founded on an identifiable understanding and definition of American national interests. A sound analysis of America's Yugoslav policy must therefore comprehend and understand the debate about US interests and the appropriate role of American military forces in furthering those interests. There are many strands in the rope of interests which bind American actions to Balkan security, and their strength has changed repeatedly. So have the perceptions of the costs versus benefits of using force to influence the conflict. This chapter therefore begins by identifying the basic factors which have shaped Yugoslav policy. Those will then be weighed and investigated through combination and recombination as the US has backed spasmodically away from four broad strategic positions, or phases, since the Yugoslav wars of succession began.

INTERESTS AT STAKE

Definitions of national interests provide few insights into actual security policy; what matters is the price a country will pay to secure them. Yet interests remain central to explaining security policies. Unfortunately, the Yugoslav dissolution came at a time of transition in which America had begun to reassess its post-Cold War roles and missions. Neither a serious debate nor a sound government assessment of developing European security problems had emerged by June 1991. So Yugoslav policy must be placed within a context of global flux in American policy thinking.

The American debate on Yugoslavia since the wars began, both within and without government, has emphasised two themes: discrete US interests and systemic interests (that is, norms of state behaviour shared generally by the international community). It is always easier to justify military intervention when clear, demonstrable, and discrete national interests are threatened. Since 1991 several American interests have been affected by the Yugoslav war. The least important was economic. American investments and financial exposure in Yugoslavia, though sizeable, could not be safeguarded regardless. The weightier interests reflected political/strategic considerations. During the Cold War a Balkan war would have been gravely dangerous, threatening to entangle the US and the Soviet Union. But even before the Soviet collapse Washington understood that a more relaxed attitude was warranted. Fighting in the Balkans no longer automatically constituted a threat requiring the use of military force. Nevertheless, America retains a strong national interest in peace and security in the region.

Political interests loomed large, and among the most important has been the objective of facilitating continued security cooperation with old allies in NATO and new friends to the East. America has sought, wisely, to protect its European interests through NATO, to secure its continued critical role in ensuring European security and protect its own credibility. America has also developed an interest in building a cooperative security/political relationship, first with the Soviet government, and then with Russia. This interest has powerfully influenced America's Balkan policy. These then are the main demonstrable American interests at stake in the former Yugoslavia (FY). What then of the systemic interests?

Disintegration and ethnic conflict within an internationally recognised state present many threats to established laws and precedents of international state behaviour. Events in the FY have challenged numerous international principles and presented impulses for American intervention which contradict established rules of state behaviour. Human rights have been systematically violated, international borders rearranged by force, and aggression accepted by default. Protection of established norms of state behaviour involves systemic interests which America shares with all states, but in this case, European states in particular. America also shares a collective interest in containing the destruction of war, helping to alleviate human suffering and minimising the threat to the normative principles of international relations and security. These interest are easily identified, perhaps mundane. But Washington's perception of the threat to these general interests versus threats to America's particular interests, demonstrably explains much American policy.

Interest definitions have inevitably flavoured the American debate for and against military intervention in the FY. Whatever one's understanding of the interests at stake, debate about their appropriate price (interventionists will pay more, noninterventionists less, to secure them) has revealed clear themes. Interventionists argued that force was appropriate to stop ethnic cleansing, to prevent or roll back aggression, to set proper state behaviour precedents for the post-Cold War era, and to show that NATO and American military forces remain credible and necessary. Those opposed usually opined that intervention should be left to the EU which has a direct interest and anyway seeks greater foreign and defence policy power; would risk excessive American human casualties and material cost; had no clear identifiable political objective and thus constituted a quagmire; risked ruining more important possibilities for cooperation with Moscow; would involve an inappropriate match between the geographic and strategic strengths and weaknesses of American versus Serb strategy and weapons. This argument has bubbled away, percolating in a great pot with arguments about America's interests. Behind this argument, clear phases of debate and government policy can be discerned. They are characterised by an identifiable balance among these interests and a 'fair' price to protect them, a calculation which largely explains US policy.

PHASE 1: PRESERVATION OF THE YUGOSLAV FEDERATION

US–Yugoslav relations had been amicable and businesslike for several decades as Washington valued Tito's independence from Moscow and his demonstration of divisions within international communism. After Tito's death America paid less attention to the country. But with the fall of the Berlin Wall, the unification of Germany, the collapse of East European communism, and then the Iraqi invasion of Kuwait, things changed. Obvious issues of high politics crowded out threatening developments in Yugoslavia in the period 1989–90. Overall European political changes markedly lowered the strategic importance of Yugoslavia and the threat of regional European conflict generally as a motivator for American intervention. While Slovenes, Croats, Bosnians and Serbs were busily unravelling the fabric holding their federation together, the very time when wise, concerted outside actions could possibly have averted war, Washington was too busy elsewhere (literally) fighting other fires. Besides, America needed Soviet cooperation for more pressing problems, particularly during the Gulf crisis, and thus considered Moscow's sensitivities when pondering Yugoslavia. Basically, the convenient description of a 'multiethnic communist federation with a history of civil war', summarised loosely the career of both Yugoslavia and the Soviet Union. So the Bush administration was keenly aware that Yugoslav policy had implications for internal and external Soviet policy. Encouraging ethnic division in Yugoslavia might encourage it in the USSR, something George Bush greatly feared.

Few remember the heady Euro-enthusiasm of 1990 when European Community (EC) leaders and pundits alike discussed European 'architectures', charting in the Maastricht intergovernmental conference a robust increase in European diplomatic influence leading to a serious EC foreign and security policy. These sentiments were welcomed by Washington. The President believed that a stronger Europe and a confident unified Germany could together shoulder more of America's traditional European security burden within a continued NATO alliance. Until Slovene and Croat independence in June 1991, Washington happily ceded the Yugoslav crisis to the EC and viewed it as a test case for the Community's budding foreign policy. Yugoslavia was seen as a localised 'European' problem which affected the European allies directly and which they themselves should try to resolve.

Slovene and Croat declarations of independence altered the situation irreversibly. The US was bound and determined to preserve the Yugoslav federation. It is important to note that in this period there was virtually no public debate and the administration was more or less free to make policy without pressure. The President clearly favoured Yugoslav unity; if that proved impossible, then dissolution could only be countenanced if done by the mutual, peaceful, agreement of all the participants. Bush's underlying attitude was demonstrated in a heavily criticised speech delivered in Kiev (still then Soviet Ukraine) on 1 August 1991, only five weeks into the fighting in Croatia and Slovenia. While his speech addressed the Soviet case, its logic applied amply to his Yugoslav policy. Discussing the problematic relationship between central government and independence-seeking Soviet republics, Bush said: 'Freedom is not the same as independence. Americans will not support those who seek independence in order to replace a far off tyranny with a local despotism. They will not aid those who promote a suicidal nationalism based upon ethnic hatred.' Bush hoped that 'republics will combine greater autonomy with greater voluntary interaction – political, social, cultural, economic – rather than pursuing the hopeless course of isolation'.[1] What relevance to Yugoslavia? Deputy Secretary, later Secretary of State, Lawrence Eagleburger, a Serbo-Croat speaker and influential Yugoslav policy participant, fundamentally believed that there was little that outsiders could do to avoid war in Yugoslavia.

I personally do not believe that violence could have been avoided under any circumstances. But I do remain convinced that the republics' unilateral and uncoordinated declarations of independence, which we unsuccessfully opposed, led inexorably to civil war. Then, as now, the only alternative to perpetual bloodshed was for the parties to negotiate their separation from each other, and meanwhile to guarantee respect for pluralism and the rights of minorities within their borders. And the only responsible policy for the United States was the one we followed: namely to discourage unilateral acts intended to avoid such negotiations and such guarantees.[2]

Here we have the explanation for American policy in Phase One: despite the market economic and democratic reforms under way in the Yugoslav republics, their relations with the communist federal government and the procedures through which they pursued their independence were seen by the administration as sowing the seeds of ethnic conflict and undermining regional stability. Combined with Washington's lack of attention to Yugoslavia, the desire to see Europe take the lead, and the importance of not poisoning relations with or setting unhelpful precedents for the Soviet Union, the explanation emerges.[3] Thus we see Secretary of State James Baker visiting Belgrade in June 1991 to lobby for Yugoslav unity, trying, as in Moscow, to prop up a crumbling communist federation being undermined by democracy-seeking, market-orientated nationalists who might otherwise have expected Washington's support. Here we have what Jonathan Eyal called 'The Original Sin' when American policy gave the wrong message to both sides: a green light to the Serbs to attack and a strong motive to the Slovenes and Croats to declare independence before America and the West took stronger measures to stop them.[4] There was no intervention debate in Phase One, nor much of a debate about American interests. Such arguments usually follow rather than precede wars. Unfortunately, during the only phase of the conflict when forceful outside policy might have averted the impending catastrophe, the administration's analysis of the problem and overall judgment of costs and benefits dictated a policy supporting the preservation of a liberalised Yugoslav federation.

PHASE 2: UNTIL RECOGNITION: PRESERVING A LOOSE FEDERATION

Once wars erupt an entirely new menu of political–military problems inevitably emerges. Croat and Slovene wars for independence forced America to formulate a new policy and to decide: whether to recognise independence; what borders were legitimate international boundaries; whether America should provide economic, political, or military support; and to whom? In the heat of summer 1991 Washington happily let the EC and its appointed mediator, Lord Carrington, take the diplomatic lead. Safe haven problems in Northern Iraq and continued instability in Moscow reinforced existing administration proclivity to stand back. Presidential and administration attention was further hijacked by Soviet problems with the coup against Gorbachev in August 1991. The Soviet crisis dominated Washington's attention, justifiably, until the dissolution of the Soviet Union in December 1991.

Events on the ground in Yugoslavia drove policy debate in this period. Slovenia achieved territorial control relatively quickly. But in Croatia the balance of forces did not correspond to federation political boundaries, or to ethnic distribution. While the EC and UN affected to reach a negotiated solution, Washington engaged in increasingly acrimonious debate with her allies about whether, and under what conditions, to recognise Croatia and Slovenia. The issue demonstrated what was to become a paramount interest in American policy: the need to act, or at least be seen to act, in concert with allies rather than unilaterally. As the EC controlled the only diplomatic initiative, President Bush would not undermine their leverage by recognition, even had Washington then wished to – which it did not. The Bush administration was populated with a number of highly competent strategic thinkers who believed it essential to protect and expand the community of principles and purpose which bound the Western allies together during the Cold War. If large disasters were to be avoided in future, the great powers, including as they hoped a reforming and liberalising USSR/Russia, would have to cooperate and show restraint in regional conflicts like the FY. It was competitive strategies in the Balkans and elsewhere which had proved so disastrous in the past and which President Bush wanted to ensure against in the future.[5] But when unity is top priority, real differences produce lowest common denominator policies. Thus in autumn 1991 Washington demurred over recognition, while within the EC Germany forced her partners' hands into recognising Slovene and Croat independence.

During Phase One Washington and her allies all understood the threat to systemic interests which the escalating fighting embodied. Once war broke out Washington and her allies were keen to isolate and contain it and agreed with relative ease on the first moderate and riskless steps like a trade and arms embargo. Accurate analyses of causation and lines of authority within FY were not always apparent, but the consensus explanation in Washington and in the EC pinned the label of 'aggressor' on the Serbs and the Yugoslav People's Army (JNA). Nevertheless, economic sanctions were placed on the whole of what was still Yugoslavia by the US on 6 December 1991.

Once the EC resolved its acrimonious recognition debate, America followed, recognising Slovene, Croat and Bosnian independence within pre-crisis Yugoslav federation borders on 7 April 1992; only four days after EC recognition of Bosnia.[6] This step was taken only after Washington was convinced that these states met the requisite criteria for recognition and had some evidence that it was the peaceful and democratically expressed will of their own peoples. As Croat–Serb fighting had continued and expanded in scope and intensity, for example along the Adriatic coast (Dubrovnik) and in the Vukovar region, a public debate about the wisdom or unwisdom of intervention began to emerge in America. The administration had increasingly to clarify and defend its definition of American interests, its analysis of the conflict and its policy of non-intervention. Until the Bosnian government referendum of 1 March 1992 and declaration of independence in April, the administration could feel justifiably comfortable that it was doing no more than the American public would support or expect. Only when seemingly weak, vulnerable, innocent or helpless people in Croatia and particularly Bosnia were threatened and killed – as vividly portrayed in the media – did the intervention brigade begin demanding that a higher price be paid to correct the problem.

PHASE 3: FROM RECOGNITION TO CLINTON

While there was debate about what more America should do about an essentially Croat–Serb conflict, the real 'do something' impulse came after the newly recognised Bosnia-Herzegovina was attacked from within and without. Bosnia's particular ethnic mix and population distribution left the weak multiethnic state between the hammer of the Serbs and the anvil of the Croats. It was the relentless display of ethnic cleansing, devastation and victimisation of innocents which stimulated domestic pressure for America to go beyond economic sanctions. Many argued in frustration that Europe demonstrably lacked the leadership and power to handle the crisis effectively; America should therefore take the lead by default. Pictures in August 1992 of emaciated Bosnian prisoners in Bosnian Serb concentration camps only demonstrated the pathetic inadequacy of the EC and the UN. Yet President Bush was unmoved, despite the increasing threat of conflagration which the intensified fighting represented.

Bush administration policy reflected a set of conclusions about American and international interests generally in FY, and resulted from military analysis pointing to the inappropriateness of force as a solution. Bush's inclination was clearly against intervention irrespective of military advice. Nevertheless, his own, and the Pentagon's military thinking reinforced his caution about American participation in any sort of military intervention in the FY. Stated simply, the nature of civil wars, Yugoslav geography, topography, weather and other military factors left the Pentagon convinced that nothing short of a massive intervention on the ground and in the air would produce meaningful results. Any such intervention would entail serious political and military risks and costs which would, the administration believed, be out of all proportion to America's interests in the region.[7] Given this military logic, the main strand of American policy reflected Washington's intention to 'accept any resolution arrived at peacefully, democratically, and by negotiation'.[8] Coercive measures such as the arms embargo and economic sanctions were adjuncts to a negotiating strategy, not preliminaries to a military intervention strategy. President Bush's ideas for a Bosnian settlement mirrored earlier preferences for an overall Yugoslav deal: support for a negotiated agreement backed by all the constituent groups which would preserve a unified Bosnian government within existing Bosnian borders.

Washington cooperated with her allies in supporting the first deployment of UN peace-keeping forces to Croatia which was agreed in February 1992. Nevertheless, the administration refused to participate. Aware that its attitude would in future cripple or make impossible any potential intervention, or peace-keeping force for Bosnia, the administration agreed in principle to participate in a future UN peace-keeping force there. But only to enforce an agreement freely entered into by all sides in which all parties desired an American presence.

Public pressure for military action only became serious when fighting worsened markedly in Bosnia, bringing the bombardment of Sarajevo with its destruction and civilian deaths vividly to public attention. Shaken from its previous torpor by increasing moral outrage, the administration began publicly to castigate EC countries for handling the problem poorly. Secretary of State Baker began to pursue a more forceful line, pushing for a comprehensive array of sanctions against Serbia to pressure Belgrade into a settlement. Were it not for a presidential election, American policy would probably have remained firmly against any use of American military force of any kind, even in Bosnia. For President Bush believed firmly that at no point in 1992 was it clear 'that the application of limited amounts of force by the United States and its traditional friends and allies would have had the desired effect given the nature and complexity of that situation'.[9] Nevertheless, while administration analyses of interests and appropriate policies remained relatively constant, American policy began to move, influenced by the rhetorical challenge of the Democratic candidate Bill Clinton, who used Bosnia as a vehicle to contest President Bush's image as a foreign policy specialist. On Yugoslavia, Clinton had this to say:

> A year ago last June, Mr. Bush sent his secretary of state to Belgrade, where in the name of stability, he urged the members of the dying Yugoslav federation to resist dissolution. This would have required the peoples of Bosnia, Croatia and Slovenia, to knuckle under to Europe's last communist strongman. When instead these new republics asserted their independence, the emboldened Milosevic regime launched the bloodiest war in Europe in over 40 years.[10]

Clinton clearly implied that as President he would be more forceful in supporting democracy-seeking states fighting for independence from a communist Yugoslav federation. Specifically he called for air power to be used to protect humanitarian aid convoys.

As the United Nations increased its involvement in Bosnia during summer 1992, deploying troops to Sarajevo and organising humanitarian aid, Washington still offered only political and humanitarian support. Few opposed generous humanitarian assistance but the administration refused to risk American personnel as part of the UN's deployments in Croatia or Bosnia. Deployment of British, French and other national UN contingents changed the array of possible policy options. It markedly increased the influence of London and Paris over Yugoslavia policy and placed UN forces as potential hostages. Both of these points remained important factors as Washington debated with her allies about appropriate next steps. Public and election pressure had its effects on President Bush. When French troops arrived in Sarajevo in July 1992, Washington wanted to increase its responsibility proportionately and instituted aid flights into Sarajevo airport and participated in the joint NATO/WEU naval sanctions enforcement in the Adriatic. In October 1992 American and other NATO forces began monitoring flights in the airspace of Bosnia-Herzegovina in response to UN Security Council Resolution 781 which requested member states to monitor the ban on military flights.

Interestingly, the Bush administration took perhaps its most forceful and risky steps after the election. Secretary of State Eagleburger publicly identified Serbian officials who, the US Government believed, were implicated in war crimes and accountable to a future war crimes tribunal. Recognising that preventing the spread of the conflict was at once one of the highest priorities, and perhaps achievable without use of American force, President Bush in December 1992 wrote to Serbian President Milosevic warning the Serbs that any attack on the Albanians of Kosovo would meet a stern American response. This was the most direct and serious military threat yet made by the US. Before Bush left office, the Vance–Owen peace plan was completed to be dropped on the desk of the incoming administration. It violated most of Washington's stated settlement objectives but became the starting point for debate within the new administration.

PHASE 4: SLOWLY ACCEPTING THE FACTS

In phase four President Clinton and his Yugoslav policy could be caricatured as a baseball player stepping up to bat, striking out, then retiring to the dugout for a time before trying again; each time with less determination. Every successive swing at what came to be known in the State Department as the 'problem from hell' shrank the belief that America could or should employ significant military force to influence the outcome.

After the November 1992 election the clear expectation was that Bill Clinton's words meant action in Bosnia. The administration set to work with vigour, the State and Defense Departments drafting a comprehensive list of policy options.[11] Nearly a year of fighting in Bosnia had irreparably changed the balance of political and military forces, and the ethnic dispositions on the ground; reformulating the equation of interests at stake, but also, circumscribing the array of reasonably priced policy responses – particularly military ones. The low-risk options had been tried to no avail, while the price of reversing ethnic cleansing, or Serbian gains, let alone imposing a settlement militarily, had escalated significantly.

FIRST CRACK AT THE BALL

In truth the new President had been dealt a weak hand: Bosnian Serbs had captured about 70 per cent of Bosnia; UNPROFOR forces were vulnerable to retaliatory attack, the civilian population required humanitarian aid simply to survive; and the military geography was a nightmare, with isolated Muslim enclaves surrounded by Serbian troops and not protectable with limited applications of force. Worse, initially the warring sides indicated willingness to accept the Vance–Owen plan whose conception of cantonisation (within a weak unified government) the administration had claimed rewarded Serbian aggression. Clinton was as opposed to the creation of ethnically based mini-states as Bush had been.[12] There were no easily identifiable options offering reasonable hopes of 'success', even if 'success' could be defined. After several weeks of internal debate Secretary of State Warren Christopher went to bat for the President. Protestations that the conflict 'is not distant to our concerns', and that America 'cannot afford to ignore it' did not mask the Clinton–Bush policy continuity. Christopher defined the interests at stake: moral outrage at ethnic cleansing and human rights abuse; threat to 'direct strategic concerns' like the principle that 'internationally recognised borders should not be altered by force'; and the possibility of geographic escalation. All these would set bad precedents for the post-Cold War era. The US interests under threat were systemic: they were no more important to America than to the former Yugoslavia's European neighbours. Christopher could easily have uttered President Bush's words of January 1993: 'It is unreasonable to expect the United States to bear the full financial burden of intervention when other nations have a stake in the outcome.'[13]

President Clinton's purportedly more muscular swing at the war constituted six steps: (1) America to 'engage actively and directly' in peace negotiations through a special envoy; (2) communication with all parties that war will only end through negotiation; (3) tighten sanctions and increase pressure on Serbia, including US commitment to respond to Serbian aggression in Kosovo or Macedonia; (4) steps to alleviate humanitarian suffering; (5) commitment to share the burden of enforcing a peace agreement. 'If there is a viable agreement containing enforcement provisions, the US would be prepared to join with the United Nations, NATO, and others in implementing and enforcing it, including possible US military participation', and (6) closer consultation with Russia.[14] Despite the hype, this initiative represented only marginally more American engagement. Washington would, however, invest more political prestige and capital. Clinton's policy boiled down to two basic points: no unilateral actions, and no US ground troops 'except to carry out a peace agreement that had been entered into in good faith between the parties'.[15] It quickly became clear that only serious application of military force would provide effective influence; in this Clinton had no more interest than Bush. So the administration began quite soon to describe Bosnia as a quagmire once more, and to speak less about moral imperatives.[16] Torn between the moral urge to intervene and a rational temptation to keep out, the Clinton policy moved only slightly towards the former; nothing like the distance that a thoroughgoing interventionist policy would have required. American policy remained extremely important on the ground, however, as Washington's noisy debate constantly influenced the warring parties, particularly the Bosnian government, which resisted serious negotiation in the naive belief that Washington would employ significant military force on its behalf against the Serbs.

Within the context of limited military commitment (that is to say no ground troops), the US did harness together a number of incremental initiatives in the first three months of Clinton's presidency to push the Serbs in Serbia and Bosnia to reach an 'acceptable' settlement. Beyond continuing the Adriatic naval sanctions blockade, emergency aid drops were organised for isolated villages who could not be supplied any other way. The abandonment of escort fighters, which might have provoked the Serbs, and the inclusion of Croat and Serbian villages itself indicated the administration's unwillingness to do anything which might obviously favour one side over the other. President Clinton also began lobbying NATO and the UN Security Council to enforce the no-fly zone. Touted as a clear signal to the Serbs, this patently was not. Violations were irrelevant to developments on the ground. But diplomatic constraints were severe even for this limited measure. Russia would only agree to sanction air power under very strict conditions; as indeed Britain and France, who feared that America's aggressiveness would endanger their UNPROFOR contingents.

President Clinton evoked 'leadership', but the new rhetoric exceeded the policy reality which was bound by the same constraints perceived by President Bush. Despite a desire to demonstrate leadership, Clinton would only act multilaterally.[17] French and British force deployments as part of UNPROFOR gave their views enormous credibility in the White House; Clinton consistently refused to take unilateral steps which they opposed.[18] Moreover, Washington was loath to have its burgeoning 'strategic partnership' with Russia founder on the Bosnian rocks; and Russia's relationship with the Serbs therefore gave President Yeltsin a consistently restraining hand on US policy even if its strength was often unclear. The requirement for unity with the allies initially masked the most distinctive new Clinton conclusion: that the most practicable and moral policy would be to lift the arms embargo on the Bosnian Muslims allowing them to bolster their military power and defend their own sovereignty.[19] The Bosnian Serbs enjoyed an enormous advantage in heavy weapons from the JNA and Serbia proper which had 'the unintended consequence of freezing in place a vast disparity in arms, and of severely constraining the Bosnian government's ability to defend itself'.[20] This analysis, that the use of American forces should follow rather than precede military assistance allowing a friendly government to defend itself, was widely though not universally shared in America.

There was another, subtler, difference with the Bush administration. President Bush, Lawrence Eagleburger, Brent Scowcroft and other key policymakers had fewer illusions about the nature of civil wars in general, and the Yugoslav war in particular. They did not see it in black and white, aggressor and victim terms. Rather, the war reflected shades of grey, where if the Serbs of Bosnia, Serbia and Croatia were often the aggressors, they were also sometimes the victims. Bosnian and Croat forces were understood also to engage periodically in ethnic cleansing, cynically shell their own people, and manipulate outsiders' perceptions so as to lure them into intervention on their behalf. Initially at least the Clinton inner circle tended to see the Bosnian situation as outright Serb aggression – with all the connotations the word evokes against the internationally recognised, weak, liberal and virtuous Bosnian government.[21] Administration statements in early 1993 reflect inadequate understanding of the nature of the conflict and the complicated facts on the ground.[22] Britain and France, by contrast, had a fuller appreciation of the complexities gained through direct experience with UNPROFOR. As the administration gained in experience, so its understanding deepened.

Without the administration's desire, or public pressure, to intervene seriously in the conflict by deploying ground forces, much of the debate gravitated towards arguments about what could be achieved by the low-risk, cut-price method of using air forces alone. This reflected an implicit consensus that air power would be proportionate in cost and risk to America's interests; and was anyway to America's comparative military advantage. Stimulated by the Gulf War experience, many argued that a judicious use of smart bombs could provide the incentive that the Serbs needed to stop their attacks on innocent villages and agree what Washington would consider a 'just' peace.[23] Although the administration received considerable domestic political criticism for its Bosnia policy in 1993, few supported anything more than the use of air power.[24] Some, however, opposed air strikes as tokenism or pure gesture, which would create unwanted new American responsibilities without achieving anything worthwhile.[25]

Military advice from the Joint Chiefs of Staff (JCS) continually restrained military intervention supporters, particularly those supporting troop deployments. Even on the subject of a peace-keeping deployment subject to the President's conditions, the Chairman of the JCS, Colin Powell, was deeply cautious.[26] Even Supreme Allied Commander Europe (SACEUR) Shali-kashvili and the Chairman of NATO's Military Committee doubted that air power would accomplish what its proponents believed possible.[27] In terms of intervention on the ground, Secretary Christopher himself exclaimed: 'It's a morass, it's a quagmire.'[28] Given cautious military advice, the administration carefully operationalised the criteria which any deployment of US forces must meet. In April 1993 Christopher identified four tests that any American use of force must pass: Had the goal been clearly stated to the American people?; Was there a strong likelihood that force would be successful?; Was there an 'exit strategy'; Was there a programme which could attract the support of the American people?[29] These military criteria created a high barrier against American military intervention. Few could envisage how American deployments in Bosnia, even under UN auspices to police a universally acceptable ceasefire, could surmount it. Indeed, these criteria ensured that the only direct use of American military power would be air power.

Nevertheless, military contingency plans were undertaken and the Joint Chiefs of Staff analysed requirements for US participation in a UN peace-keeping deployment. NATO discussions cited a notional figure of 50 000–60 000 UN troops of which perhaps a half to a third would be American, but only to enforce a 'fair' and 'enforceable' peace agreement.[30] Such a deployment would only occur as part of a NATO-directed, UN-authorised operation, and not directly under UN command. The administration believed that only NATO could undertake an operation of this size and complexity. Throughout 1993 the stated American commitment to contribute to a peace-keeping force confused other governments and observers who took it at face value; in fact, it was always highly conditional, particularly in respect of the need for Congressional and public support. Indeed, defining a 'fair' agreement was a loophole big enough to drive a tank through. Polls consistently showed weak public support for military intervention. In late April 1993, after weeks of Serbian shelling of Srebrenica, a CNN/*USA Today*/Gallup poll found 62 per cent opposed even to US air strikes.[31] Congressional opinion exhibited an interesting array of liberals for intervention and conservatives against.[32] House of Representatives Speaker Thomas Foley laid out his own five conditions for any intervention: (1) no use of US ground troops to end the war; (2) must be a clear policy in concert with European allies and Russia; (3) must have UN authority; (4) must specify when and how involvement will end; (5) must seek Congressional approval.[33] Clearly there was no political consensus capable of sustaining a military intervention or peacekeeping operation involving significant human and material costs. That the White House never chose to define what Congressional approval meant indicated how far away any deployment always was. This pessimistic conclusion was only confirmed by continued failure to reach agreement in Bosnia throughout 1993; and powerfully reinforced by the rapid loss of confidence in humanitarian intervention and UN peace-keeping operations after Somalia. And of course, the President was extremely keen to prevent any foreign quagmire from destroying his domestic political priorities.[34]

Clearly the Clinton administration's additional threats had some effect, particularly the preference to end the arms embargo on the Bosnian government. Nevertheless, Serbs in Bosnia and Belgrade quickly proved adept at interpreting American resolve. Following the Serbian attacks in April 1993, for example, on the isolated pocket of Srebrenica in Eastern Bosnia, President Clinton threatened air strikes and lobbied aggressively for allied support. Washington, London and Paris tried to build a crescendo of pressure on the Bosnian Serbs to agree to the Vance–Owen plan. The threat of increased economic sanctions against Serbia, extensive air strikes and arms for the Bosnian government did the trick, if only momentarily.[35] American threats influenced the Serbs to sign up at the last possible moment to the Vance–Owen plan, at the very time the Secretary of State was visiting allied capitals seeking support for ending the embargo.[36] Despite Clinton's real commitment actually to employ air power, ultimately it proved unsuccessful when the Bosnian Serbs rejected the plan in early May; precisely after the political pressure for action had receded. Notwithstanding the President's bombing threats, the White House still opposed unilateral action, which meant that British, French and Russian opposition to lifting the arms embargo or punitive air strikes against the Serbs restrained Clinton's hand.[37]

2ND AT BAT

After the failure in April and May to reach an agreed peace in Bosnia, Clinton shouldered his metaphorical bat, stepped back from the plate, and effectively ceded Bosnia to Europe in a combination of frustration and petulance. The administration began to use different language, emphasising the broad goal of containment, the inherent complexities of civil wars, the conflict's 'European' nature and the President's belief that the public would appreciate his 'clear disciplined restraint' in the use of American military power.[38] Long-acknowledged constraints on American interests and commitments were reiterated: 'while we have clear reasons to engage and persist, they do not obliterate other American interests involving Europe and Russia, and they do not justify the extreme costs of taking unilateral responsibility for imposing a solution.'[39] This tossing of the Bosnian mess into Europe's lap was not widely criticised and received cautious support from the important papers. Yet it did open a period of increasingly acrimonious transatlantic shouting as the President turned his attentions to pressing domestic issues. Britain, Germany and France wanted firm leadership and positively required American military help to field a serious peace-keeping force, while Washington was tentative in its leadership, and when it appeared the Europeans did not like its conclusions. This discord again allowed military and political developments in Bosnia to change the policy context. Bosnian Serb attacks on Sarajevo subsequently increased steadily, as did the pressure on Muslim enclaves in eastern Bosnia which the UN had eventually declared 'safe areas'. Cynically, they were not called safe havens because the Iraq precedent would have implied a similar Western commitment to protect them with force. These enclaves were entirely surrounded and shelled incessantly, notwithstanding threats and entreaties from America and her allies.

Once again in late summer 1993 Washington stepped up to bat in response to public outrage at the massacre of innocent civilians in Sarajevo and other safe areas, and gave another go at assembling international support for the limited use of air power. President Clinton's proposal to use air power to relieve the siege and buttress diplomatic manoeuvres constituted a marginal increase in American determination to confront the Serbs. The administration had become frustrated and disenchanted with the Vance–Owen peace process and increasingly agitated for its preferred 'lift and strike' policy of arming the Muslims while using air power to protect safe areas. At a meeting of NATO's North Atlantic Council in August continued French and British resistance meant Washington was able to elicit only a warning. Appropriate military plans and command and control arrangements were prepared, but instead of action Washington was constrained to making more hollow threats.[40]

While Washington remained fearful of any actions which could entangle it in Bosnian fighting, the overriding imperative to prevent the spread of fighting motivated one of America's few forward-thinking acts of preventative diplomacy. The complexities of the Macedonia problem are legion, and the US was keen to prevent the conflict from spreading there. Advised by the CIA of a real spillover threat, which could ultimately ensnare Greece and Turkey, Washington deployed US forces to newly independent Macedonia in early July 1993.[41] Despite its open-ended nature, a clear mistake in administration criteria for participation in UN peace-keeping, additional forces were added in December to monitor the border with Serbia.[42] Formal American recognition of 'The Former Yugoslav Republic of Macedonia' came only in February 1994.[43]

Troop deployments in Macedonia were a preview of a quiet, ambitious and aggressive American diplomacy in the Southern Balkans. In order to prevent war spreading south and east, Washington constructed and cultivated a strong diplomatic relationship with the countries to the south of Serbia, notably Albania. Tirana granted Washington important military access, began to receive American weapons, and generally established a close bilateral relationship. While this quiet diplomatic work represented a heightened US interest and commitment to the area, it nevertheless conformed to the basic argument. Though willing to invest some prestige, political capital, money and occasionally take manageable military risks, Washington would never have bolstered these efforts with the application of significant military force, particularly on the ground. American troops in Macedonia would have been withdrawn at the first sight of serious fighting.

LAST INNING

By autumn 1993 the Vance–Owen plan was effectively dead. The warring parties had determined that Western threats were idle and that they could carry on with their war. Henceforth any American threats or military intervention would have to be even greater to achieve any effect. The facts on the ground made the administration's goal of a unified Bosnian state more and more unrealistic. Despite the existence of six misnamed safe areas, none of the major powers was willing effectively to defend them. The Serbs became more uncompromising, and the Bosnians less confident of international rescue. Without firm American determination to defend specified interests, employing military power in support of a well-articulated strategy, the European allies defended their own particular interests, ensuring NATO's effective impotence in the face of its first real post-Cold War test. The main problem for the US, and indirectly for any peace process, was America's continued rhetorical undermining of the UN peace negotiations, together with an unwillingness to employ its own military power to facilitate a more 'just' outcome which would not accept ethnic cleansing or countenance Serbian territorial gains from aggression.

Once the Clinton administration and its international partners had set their parameters for the use of military force, there has followed a continuous series of rows between Washington, London and Paris over how best to protect safe areas; the appropriate conditions for the use of air power in support of UN operations; the establishment of the Bosnian–Croat federation; creation of the international contact group; and arguments about the partition plan. All of these issues consumed inordinate diplomatic time and energy. All constituted limited steps beyond which the US would not go: 'The United States is doing all it can consistent with our national interest' as Christopher had said.[44] Crucially, once the Somali fiasco of September 1993 made clear that American ground troop deployments were virtually impossible in Bosnia, Washington's influence atrophied, virtually ensuring that no serious UN peace-keeping force could be fielded to support an overall Bosnian settlement.[45] As a result, developments on the ground led inexorably to a three-way partition of Bosnia reflecting the realities of military power, the consequences of conquest, and the results of ethnic cleansing. Rather than face difficult choices, the new US envoy to the peace talks, Charles Redman, began participating directly in support of the Bosnian government. The objective, he said in February 1994, was to 'produce the kind of results the Bosnians have been looking for'. Washington sought 'a good negotiated solution and surely one that takes account of the Bosnians'.[46] Unable to arm the Bosnians and unwilling to intervene militarily on their behalf, Washington finally began to take more realistic negotiating steps which would facilitate a settlement, however far removed from the Clinton administration's original goals. This involved America's brokering of a renewed alliance between the Bosnian government and their erstwhile Croatian allies, thus isolating the Serbs.[47]

Since mid-1994 the fundamental bases of American policy have not changed. All that has varied is the widening gap between what Washington sometimes said, and what it was willing to do. The new Defense Secretary, William Perry, spoke out more honestly and realistically than many of his colleagues:

> What are our national interests in Bosnia today? First of all, and I want to emphasise this point strongly, we have a compelling national security interest in preventing that war and its consequences from spreading beyond Bosnia. Indeed beyond the Balkans. At the same time, we have a humanitarian interest in trying to limit violence and relieve the suffering while we are working for a peace settlement. These are real interests, and we take them quite seriously, but they are limited interests and our actions need to be proportional to our interests.

Describing the actions appropriate to America's interests, Perry was equally realistic:

> It is not to become a combatant in the war. We are not seeking to win a military victory in Bosnia, or even to fight a war in Bosnia . . . We have three specific objectives while those peace negotiations are going on. The first of those is to limit spread of the violence; second, is to limit the effects of the violence; and the third is to mitigate the effects of the violence.[48]

There is nothing here about guaranteeing the sovereignty of a unified Bosnia within internationally recognised borders, reversing ethnic cleansing; no longer any mention of participation in a UN peace-keeping force. There have only been a couple of deviations in the gradual diminution of American engagement in the FY since. The first was the renewed drive for air strikes after the Sarajevo market massacre in February 1994. Considerable Congressional agitation for bombing ensued with the President strongly constrained by sensitivity to British and French fear of retaliation against their own troops.[49] Despite the intense activity surrounding the NATO ultimatum and exclusion zone around Sarajevo which followed, the severity of the Russian backlash and immense restraint in the use of air power to enforce it – in the face of repeated Serb provocations – served to reinforce existing policy rather than demonstrate a more active stance.[50] The situation in Sarajevo was markedly improved by NATO's ultimatum, leading to calls for exclusion zones to be employed in other areas of Bosnia, such as Gorazde. Yet the Secretary of Defense and the Chairman of the Joint Chiefs of Staff were quick to squelch such thoughts, even in the face of continued Serb assaults.[51] Again, Russian pique at not receiving advance warning of US air strikes against the Serbs around Goražde in April, together with friction over how much pressure to direct at the Bosnian Serbs in the peace negotiations, reminded the administration of Bosnia's potential to derail wider US–Russian cooperation.[52]

Frustration and belated realisation that nothing useful could be achieved while the major powers pursued moderately different policies led Washington to establish the 'contact group' of high-level diplomats from the US, Germany, Britain, France and Russia. They in turn shifted goals to a four-month ceasefire in the hope that a settlement would follow a ceasefire rather than vice versa. By May 1994 America and the contact group had moved far enough to countenance a Bosnia settlement giving the Serbs 49 per cent and the Bosnian–Croat federation 51 per cent of Bosnian territory.[53] Though this would still require considerable Serb withdrawals, it reflected the crude realities of power on the ground and a significant backtracking from all earlier US goals. Congressional pressure to allow arms to the Bosnian government further indicated that political pressure for tougher measures was directed towards helping the

Bosnians to help themselves rather than intervening directly with US forces.[54] Decreasing American commitment to Bosnia was mirrored by British and French desires to withdraw their own forces. Even the UN Secretary-General had come to believe that UNPROFOR should be withdrawn.[55] These weak threats – to pull out of UNPROFOR, lift the arms embargo or use limited air strikes to protect UN forces or safe areas – and the positive incentive of limited lifting of sanctions against Serbia constituted the entire diplomatic leverage of America and the allies. Vehement Russian and strong internal administration opposition made even the threat of arming the Bosnian government hollow.[56] Despite the contact group, there has been little seriousness behind American threats in Bosnia since the group was established. Irrespective of the engineered split between Belgrade and the Bosnian Serbs, almost nothing would provoke American military action, let alone any thought of US troops for any potential peace-keeping force.

GAME OVER?

The record to date indicates that the price President Clinton would be prepared to pay to influence a peace agreement or participate in its enforcement has fallen steadily further. Several wider factors reinforce this view. The first is the administration's extensive policy review of America's role in UN peace-keeping activities, Initially, the administration's enthusiasm for multilateral peace-keeping was considerable: it was a means of gaining legitimacy for American actions, and reducing the risks and responsibilities of actions for operations of limited importance. The Yugoslav experience itself put a dent in such thinking. But the real erosion derived from the rapid souring of the intervention in Somalia, especially after the operation in which a number of soldiers were killed and more than 70 wounded. Washington's hasty withdrawal demonstrated that in a peace-keeping scenario where casualties are likely America's staying power is highly questionable. The new peace-keeping policy confirmed a serious loss of faith and interest in such endeavours and embodied demanding criteria for US participation.[57] If this were not enough, the White House has increasingly turned its attention to problems closer to home: Haiti, Cuba, Mexico and domestic politics. These factors reduced determination and interest in the wars of the Yugoslav succession.

The Yugoslav crisis endures, but its policy context constantly changes. For Washington, the interests at stake remain fairly consistent; and few of the threats affect America alone. It should not therefore surprise others that the US has chosen to pay a relatively smaller price to protect against them than many might originally have expected, or that US 'exceptionalism' might have suggested. Given America's many other interests in Europe, the Americas and Asia it has been quite rational to expect other powerful nations with correspondingly strong interests in maintaining international order to pay more. Arguably the Bush and Clinton administrations have been right to conclude that far more damage would be done to America's interests in the long run if it intervened militarily in the FY and failed to achieve stated goals, than if it restrained its ambitions and commitments there. American policy has been both reactive and concessive, following developments on the ground and progressively abandoning stated objectives; yet this has corresponded rather well with what the American people and their elected representatives seem willing to pay to rectify a small catastrophe in the Balkans.

NOTES

1. Remarks by the President in Address to the Supreme Soviet of the Ukrainian Soviet Socialist Republic, 1 August 1991.
2. 'Eagleburger Cites Gains, Warns of Future Challenges', Official Text United States Information Service, 13 January 1993.
3. See Patrick Glynn, 'Yugoblunder', *The New Republic*, 24 February 1992, pp. 15–17.
4. Steve Coll, ' "Original Sin" and a 4-Year Tale of War', *International Herald Tribune*, 21 April 1994.
5. It was this belief that outside power should not meddle or pick sides in regional disputes – and standard UN practice – which later motivated the Clinton administration to oppose Islamic contingents such as those offered by Iran to join UNPROFOR. See 'Islamic Bloc Offers Troop Units to UN For Bosnia', *International Herald Tribune*, 14 July 1993; 'US Opposes Iran For Bosnia Mission', *International Herald Tribune*, 15 July 1993.

6. See 'Statement on United States Recognition of the Former Yugoslavia', 7 April 1992.

7. For a detailed discussion of American thinking on intervention in general and in the FY, see Thomas Halverson, 'Disengagement by Stealth: the Emerging Gap between America's Rhetoric and the Reality of Future European Conflicts', in L. Freedman (ed.), *Military Intervention in European Conflicts* (Oxford: Blackwell, 1994).

8. 'Statement on United States Recognition on the Former Yugoslav Republics', 7 April 1992.

9. George Bush, 'Remarks at the United States Military Academy in West Point, New York', 5 January 1993.

10. Democratic Presidential Candidate Gov. Bill Clinton Address on 'Democracy in America' at an Event Sponsored by the University of Wisconsin, 1 October 1992. See also Stephen Engelberg and Michael R. Gordon, 'Use of Force in Bosnia: When a President Faces a Candidate's Rhetoric,' *International Herald Tribune*, 5 April 1993.

11. These include US troop deployments as part of UNPROFOR, use of air power and more. See Stephen Engelberg and Michael R. Gordon, op. cit.

12. Although there were a few lonely dissenters in the public debate, John Mearsheimer's views in April 1993 looked ruthlessly realistic then, they have largely become fact now. John J. Mearsheimer, 'Balkan Peace: Shrink Bosnia to Rescue It, and Threaten Force', *International Herald Tribune*, 1 April 1993.

13. George Bush, 'Remarks at the United States Military Academy in West Point, New York', 5 January 1993.

14. Secretary Christopher, 'New Steps Toward Conflict Resolution in the Former Yugoslavia', US Department of State Dispatch, 15 February 1993, 4:7.

15. Warren Christopher, 'Need for American Leadership Said Greater than Ever', *European Wireless News Alert*, 1 June 1993. Also 'Clinton Shies From Solo Intervention in Bosnia', *International Herald Tribune*, 24–5 April 1993.

16. Thomas L. Friedman, 'Clinton About-Face: Bosnia as Quagmire', *International Herald Tribune*, 8 April 1993. The administration carefully avoided calling Serbian policy in Bosnia genocide, in the knowledge that it would trigger legal and moral obligations which they were keen to avoid. See Richard Johnson, 'Is It Genocide or Isn't It? Senior US Officials Are Loath to Say', *International Herald Tribune*, 15 February 1994.

17. Clinton believed that a primary American mistake in Vietnam was to conduct the war unilaterally rather than multilaterally; lack of allied willingness should have told Washington something – a lesson he kept in mind when considering Yugoslavia. See Clinton's remarks in a radio interview on 12 March 1993.

18. Radio interview remarks, 12 March 1993.

19. National Security Adviser Lake said months later that the President 'feels very strongly about this' and that 'there never should have been an arms embargo against Bosnia'. 'Senate Backs Lifting of Bosnia Embargo', *International Herald Tribune*, 13 May 1994.

20. Alan Cowell, 'Clinton Seems Committed to Lifting Bosnia Embargo', *International Herald Tribune*, 26–7 June 1993.

21. For example: 'It stemmed from aggression against an independent state' said Anthony Lake, 'Lake Says US Interests Compel Engagement Abroad', Official Text USIS, 22 September 1993.

22. For example, see the comments of US Ambassador to the UN Madeleine Albright, in Jacquelyn S. Porth, 'US Seeks Multilateral Remedy to Regional Conflicts', *European Wireless File News Alert*, 20 April 1993.

23. For example, Anthony Lake, 'America's Credibility Is at Stake in Bosnia', *International Herald Tribune*, 13 April 1993; William Safire, 'Bosnia: The Answer Is to Give Bombing a Chance', *International Herald Tribune*, 10 August 1993; editorial from *The New York Times*. 'Bomb Them to the Table' in *International Herald Tribune*, 22 April 1994.

24. 'Pressure Grows in US For Air Raids in Bosnia', *International Herald Tribune*, 21 April 1993; Richard Burt and Richard Perle, 'Think About Where the Bombs Will Fall', *International Herald Tribune*, 12–13 February 1994.

25. For example Bernard E. Trainor, 'Think Again: Bombing the Serbs Can Only Prolong the Agony', *International Herald Tribune*, 28 April 1994.

26. Elaine Sciolino, 'On Bosnia, Nunn is Unsettled', *International Herald Tribune*, 25–6 September 1993.

27. Michael R. Gordon, 'NATO General Doubts Air Raids Will Dent Serb Resolve', *International Herald Tribune*, 22 April 1994; 'Military Chiefs See Major Risk in A Yugoslav Air Campaign', *International Herald Tribune*, 28 April 1993; Elaine Sciolino, 'Air Strikes in Bosnia?', *International Herald Tribune*, 30 April 1993.

28. Warren Christopher, 'Need for American Leadership Said Greater than Ever', *European Wireless File News Alert*, 1 June 1993.

29. 'Military Chiefs See Major Risk in a Yugoslav Air Campaign', *International Herald Tribune*, 28 April 1993.

30. See the comments of President Clinton in a photo-op with President Izetbegovic, 8 September 1993. John Lancaster and Ann Devroy, 'US Troops to Lead NATO Balkan Action', *International Herald Tribune*, 5 May 1993; 'Pentagon Warns on Bosnia Troop Level', *International Herald Tribune*, 10 March 1994.

31. 'Military Chiefs See Major Risk In A Yugoslav Campaign.' CBS News found half of those surveyed opposed US air strikes with 38 per cent in support. Gallup found 55 and 36 per cent respectively, while ABC found 65 per cent approving if air strikes were conducted in conjunction with allies. Paul F. Horvitz, 'House Speaker Sets Conditions for Any US Military Action', *International Herald Tribune*, 10 May 1993.

32. The administration received severe criticism from a number of pro-intervention democrats, like Senator Joseph R. Biden, Jr, 'For A New Strategy To Preserve Bosnia', *International Herald Tribune*, 9 June 1993; Dennis De Concini, 'It Is Time to Bomb the Serbs', *International Herald Tribune*, 19 May 1993. Former Secretary of State George Shultz was a strong advocate of a more robust American policy. Anthony Lewis, 'Shultz on Bosnia: "The Ultimate End of a Disgrace"', *International Herald Tribune*, 15 February 1994.

33. Paul F. Horvitz, 'House Speaker Sets Conditions for Any US Military Action', *International Herald Tribune*, 10 May 1993.
34. R. W. Apple, 'For Clinton, Decision Time Is at Hand', *International Herald Tribune*, 9 February 1994.
35. Ann Devroy and Ruth Marcus, 'Clinton Weighs US Troops for Bosnia Enclaves', *International Herald Tribune*, 14 May 1993.
36. Paul Horvitz, 'Pressured by Belgrade, Bosnian Serb Accepts Pact', *International Herald Tribune*, 3 May 1993.
37. Eugene Robinson, 'Britain Reaffirms Opposition to Lifting Bosnia Arms Ban', *International Herald Tribune*, 20 April 1993; 'Russia to Bar Arms to Muslims', *International Herald Tribune*, 30 June 1993.
38. Paul F. Horvitz, 'Intervention in Bosnia: Clinton Mutes His Fervour', *International Herald Tribune*, 13 May 1993.
39. Anthony Lake, 'Lake Says US Interests Compel Engagement Abroad', Official Text USIS, 22 September 1993. See also Madeleine Albright, 'US To Use Diplomacy When Possible, Force When Necessary', Official Text USIS, 24 September 1993. Assistant Secretary of State for European and Canadian Affairs Oxman later noted that 'American policy has been designed to meet three goals: to try to achieve a viable peace acceptable to all parties, to provide humanitarian relief, and to prevent the conflict from spreading'. 'The United States and Europe: The Year Past, the Year Ahead', Official Text USIS, 1 February 1994.
40. White House Office of the Press Secretary, Statement by the Press Secretary, 2 August 1992; ' "Very Clearly" US Warns Serbs of Risk of Air Strikes', *International Herald Tribune*, 5 August 1993.
41. Letter from the President to the Speaker of the House of Representatives and the President pro tempore of the Senate, 9 July 1993.
42. Text of a Letter from the President to the Speaker of the House of Representatives and the President pro tempore of the Senate, 8 January 1994.
43. Statement by the Press Secretary, 'US Recognition of the Former Yugoslav Republic of Macedonia', 9 February 1994.
44. Joseph Fitchett, 'US and Europe Signal Bosnia Muslims to Seek Peace Now', *International Herald Tribune*, 22 July 1993.
45. 'NATO Bars Bosnia Action without US', *International Herald Tribune*, 15 October 1993.
46. David Ottaway, 'US Gives New Dynamism to Peace Talks', *International Herald Tribune*, 12–13 February 1994.
47. Daniel Williams and Thomas W. Lippman, 'Muslim–Croat Pact Aims to Isolate Serbs', *International Herald Tribune*, 3 March 1994.
48. Remarks by Secretary of Defense William J. Perry to the National Defense University at Fort McNair, Washington DC, 15 June 1994.
49. Remarks by the President upon Departure from the South Lawn, 6 February 1994.
50. See comments of Secretary of Defense Perry and CJCS Shalikashvili at the DOD Press Conference of 21 February 1994; Celestine Bohlen, 'Assailing NATO, Russia Calls for UN Council Meeting', *International Herald Tribune*, 11 February 1994. Russia's movement of troops from Croatia into Sarajevo was seen by many as a mischievous attempt to

give the Serbs a ladder to climb down while making NATO air strikes impossible. See 'Russians Force Serbian Pullout', *International Herald Tribune*, 18 February 1994; Daniel Williams, 'Bosnia Strains Revive US–Russia Suspicions', *International Herald Tribune*, 21 February 1994; Jim Hoagland, 'A Bosnia Test for US–Russian Entente, *International Herald Tribune*, 24 February 1994.

51.   Michael R. Gordon, 'Military Fears Bosnia Success Will Inspire More Adventure', *International Herald Tribune*, 16 March 1994; Michael R. Gordon, 'State Department Balks at Pentagon's Hands-Off View of Force in Bosnia', *International Herald Tribune*, 7 April 1994.

52.   Celestine Bohlen, 'Yeltsin, Miffed, Demands Role in Bosnia Decisions', *International Herald Tribune*, 12 April 1994; 'Using Force in Bosnia May Lead to "War Forever", Yeltsin Says', *International Herald Tribune*, 13 April 1994; Lee Hockstader, 'Russia Says Clinton Gave "Assurances" on Air Strikes', *International Herald Tribune*, 22 April 1994; Roger Cohen, 'US–Russia Rift Shakes Unity on Bosnia', *International Herald Tribune*, 19 May 1994.

53.   Daniel Williams, 'US Backing a Joint Plan on Partition of Bosnia', *International Herald Tribune*, 4–5 June 1994.

54.   Paul Horvitz, 'House Demands Clinton Allow Arms for Bosnia', *International Herald Tribune*, 10 June 1994; This was also the view of *The New York Times*, 'Lift the Arms Embargo', *International Herald Tribune*, 28 July 1994.

55.   'UN Chief Urges Balkan Retreat', *International Herald Tribune*, 26 July 1994.

56.   Margaret Shapiro, 'Bosnia Arms Could Spark "World War", Russia Says', *International Herald Tribune*, 15 June 1994.

57.   'Executive Summary: The Clinton Administration's Policy on Reforming Multilateral Peace Operations', Department of Defense, 5 May 1994.

2 Russian Perspectives
Andrei Edemskii

Russia's policy towards the Yugo-crisis needs to be analysed within the general framework of the attempt by the ruling elite to adjust the Russian Federation to the post-Cold War international environment; and as the expression of severe political struggle over the transformation in Russia waged by different parties, movements and interest groups. In this context Russian policy may be considered in the light of five problems:

(1) Russia's perceptions of the post-Cold War international order and the place of Russia in it. This new world order has two aspects. As Russian adjustment to the Western world existed and developed without the USSR after October 1917, and as the changing of the structures of the Western world itself.

(2) Russia's perceptions of 'post-Soviet space', and her policy towards the 'near abroad' including Russian-speaking minorities. The situation in the former Yugoslavia and 'the problem of the Serbian people' was considered as an unsuccessful model of post-Communist transition.

(3) The continuation of long-running Russian debates between 'Westernisers' and 'Slavophiles' under the new cover of 'Atlanticists' and 'Eurasians', and the rethinking of traditional historic ties between Russia and the Slavonic nations.

(4) The clash of 'reformers' and 'conservatives' over the speed, direction, depth and nature of the reforms, and the disagreements within the 'reformer's camp' itself.

(5) Perceptions of the political situation in the post-Yugoslav space, particularly the changing attitude of Serbian authorities towards the conflicts there.

The policy of Russia towards war in the former Yugoslavia may be divided into four phases:[1]

1st phase (Summer–Autumn 1991) – phase of disintegration of Socialist Federative Republic of Yugoslavia (SFRY) with Russia's abstention from the conflict.

2nd phase (Winter 1991–Autumn 1992) – phase of increasing insistence of Russia to participate in conflict regulation after unsuccessful attempts of the EC–UN and CSCE efforts to resolve the crisis with Russian involvement in the work of the UN Security Council.

3rd phase (Winter 1992/93–December 1993) – the attempts of Russian diplomacy to facilitate the implementation of Vance–Owen Plan at their request, and the gradual involvement of Russia in the international efforts at regulation.

4th phase (December 1993–to date) opposition to gradual unilateral military involvement of NATO (without the UN Security Council approval), and complete (actual and institutional) participation of Russia in conflict-regulation on an equal footing.

THE VIEW FROM MOSCOW

In the first instance the attempt to reform the USSR determined Gorbachev's approach to the Yugoslav crisis. The domestic situation in the Soviet Union determined decisive support by Gorbachev for the Yugoslav forces trying to keep Yugoslavia united by any means. This had been expressed in the series of statements by Soviet leaders.[2]

On 6 July 1991 Gorbachev sent a special presidential envoy, Yulii Kvitsinsky, to Belgrade, Zagreb, and Ljubljana where he tried to convince the leadership in the various republics to keep Yugoslavia united. But after Gorbachev's envoy came back to Moscow and shared his views on the future of SFRY Gorbachev believed that disintegration was inevitable because the EC, especially Germany, supported it.[3]

Moscow decided to act together with Washington to try to preserve Yugoslav unity, having in mind the dangerous exposure of the USSR along national lines. Gorbachev managed to receive the support of a US administration worried about the possibility of ethnic explosions in the USSR and the growing influence of a reunited Germany in post-Communist Eastern Europe. By 31 July 1991, on the occasion of President George Bush's visit to the USSR, the leaders of the two superpowers issued a joint declaration condemning the violence in Yugoslavia and also calling for respect for the principles of the Helsinki Accords.[4] Washington and Moscow were both alarmed about the precedent that the break-up of Yugoslavia might set for the Soviet Union, the preservation of which was central not only to Gorbachev's policies but to those of the Bush administration as well. The cooperation with America made possible a tougher approach to the war in Yugoslavia. The statement issued by Premier Pavlov's government on the eve of the August plot demonstrated how far Moscow might go. It warned 'international factions' against interference in Yugoslav internal affairs, emphasising the 'unstable boundary between goodwill services and interference in internal affairs'. Moscow rejected appeals to recognise the secession of Slovenia and Croatia. It supported 'plans for reforming the federative state'.[5] During Yugoslav Premier Ante Markovic's visit to Moscow he was encouraged to preserve unity of his state.

This policy of aiming to preserve federal unity continued after the failed August plot. Moscow tried to act in coordination with the international community. It announced the 'practical stop' of arms sales ('special deliveries') to Yugoslavia.[6] It supported the participation of the CSCE in conflict-regulation with the missions of goodwill. These were mere appeals without any clear vision. Cooperation with Washington went into shadow. In Autumn 1991 Gorbachev was still pretending to be a powerful world leader. To raise his domestic prestige he invited Milosevic and Tudjman to Moscow. The success of the meeting was considered as a pretext for domestic policy on 'renewed inter-republican Union' as the alternative to a repetition in the USSR of the 'Yugoslav finale'. But the 'Slavic deal' ended with the acceptance of a joint communiqué without any practical results.[7]

The approach of Yeltsin towards the Yugo-crises was not explicit. The Russian leader rising to power simply had no time or energy to follow events there. The leadership as a whole was totally occupied with the problems of their own survival and the development of the USSR. They left foreign policy matters to Gorbachev at that stage.[8] Over May–June 1991 Yeltsin and his followers were preoccupied with the presidential campaign and with striking a decisive blow against the Communist Party. Yeltsin's entourage had tried to find allies among national-democrats in the Baltic countries. They drew parallels between Moscow's policy of keeping the Baltic republics in the USSR and Belgrade's attitude to the secession of Slovenia and Croatia. The media supporting Yeltsin accused the Soviet leadership and Pavlov's government of pressing the secessionist republics to give up their democratic beliefs. They appealed to the West to intervene in the conflict at an early stage to prevent a bloodbath.[9]

In late 1991 the main efforts of the Russian leaders were targeted at removing Gorbachev, preventing economic collapse in their country and finding some way of organising post-Soviet space. But the attitude towards Belgrade was negative because the position taken by official Belgrade during the decisive events of August 1991 was antipathetic to the Russian approach towards the Balkans. Milosevic's silence was interpreted as support for Yeltsin's enemies because Moscow usually personified inter-state relations. Later Foreign Minister Kozyrev always characterised the Serbian leadership as 'the commun-nationalist forces in Belgrade'. It might be concluded that the Russian President during his visit to Germany in November 1991 encouraged his hosts to take a more active approach in the Balkans. A joint statement expressing 'commitment to democracy as the only legal form of ruling' was signed.[10] Bonn might have considered it indirect support to the newly elected Slovenian and Croatian leaders against Yugoslavia's centre. Towards the end of 1991 the Russian liberal media condemned the activity of Belgrade and of the JNA, interpreting them as the struggle between 'Belgrade as communist union's centre and the young democracies in the North'. They stressed that NATO had to stop the genocide conducted by the Serbs against the Croats. NATO could accomplish this task freely since after the collapse of communism in the USSR there was not even a theoretical possibility of converting the conflict into a clash between Communist East and democratic West.[11]

Phase 2 (1992). From abstention to improvisation to formulation of new goals and the means of their achievement.

In 1992 Russia's relations with the rest of the world were governed by four features: (1) the domestic political necessity of conducting a difficult post-communist transformation in a friendly international environment, in the expectation of manifold assistance from the highly developed industrialised states; (2) the desire of the new Kremlin authorities to receive recognition of Russia as successor to the USSR in world politics, pre-empting the claims of other former Soviet republics on the Soviet international heritage; all of this accompanied by the need to demonstrate a more liberal approach to international affairs than Gorbachev's team; (3) real international romanticism grounded partly on the naive assumption that Yeltsin's team as anti-communist fighters would be warmly welcomed by those who proclaimed the fight against the Communist menace in the Cold War, partly by the romantic belief in the new interconnections and interdependence of the post-Cold War order; (4) the intention to 'join the West, Europe', as it had been proclaimed by Yeltsin's entourage when Yeltsin was president of the Supreme Soviet.

The non-explicit approach to the Yugo-crises continued in the first half of 1992. Constant attention was paid to the possibly negative reaction of the population to the 'shock therapy' policy. A lot of energy was devoted to the problems with the Ukraine regarding the Black Sea fleet and 'Crimea problem'.[12] At the same time the 'Yugoslav matter' was a marginal issue in the minds of those conducting reforms in Russia in the first half of 1992. During the shock therapy period under Yegor Gaidar, under the ideological influence of Gennady Burbulis, the main foreign policy idea was the fear of being isolated from Europe by the construction of some sort of *cordon sanitaire* from Croatia to Poland, initiated by Ukraine.[13] In this context full diplomatic representation in Zagreb and Ljubljana was badly needed for the architects of Russian reforms (if there were any). At the same time Russia did not want to lose the influence in Serbia and Montenegro gained by the activity of the Russian embassy there. The Russian Foreign Ministry sent a special mission to visit Zagreb, Ljubljana and Belgrade to inform everyone of Russian intentions and perspectives before the official announcement of diplomatic recognition for Croatia and Slovenia. Yurii Deriabin, the head of the mission, called the necessity to recognise 'unfortunate'; the reality of the failure of the policy aimed at preserving Yugoslavia's unity. Deriabin named active cooperation with the states of the European Community and the three post-Yugoslav successor states as the main priorities of Russian diplomacy in the crisis.[14] Russian diplomacy considered that Russian recognition of Croatia increased Russian possibilities of assisting in a fair resolution of the Serbian minority problem in Croatia.[15] Russian diplomacy tried to keep a distance in the conflict. On the other hand Deriabin mentioned that Moscow was worried by the tendency 'to isolate artificially' the traditional friend of Russia, the Serbian nation, using religious dogmas and ideological stereotypes. He promised that Moscow would insist on taking 'a measured approach' to the conflict and understanding of the specific situation. During the talks with Serbian leaders in Belgrade the Russian delegation confirmed Russian readiness to sign a political agreement on cooperation with the Republic of Serbia.[16] The diplomatic formula for the Russian approach to the crisis was invented: Russia would respect the choice of the secessionist republics and also respect the choice of 'those who want to stay in Yugoslavia.'[17]

From that moment the uneasy balance of Russian diplomacy began, between attempting to act in accordance with Western pressure on the Serbs and avoiding the accusation of domestic opposition of a dependent pro-Western Foreign Ministry line on the Yugoslav conflict. At this time Russian leaders formally gained all the attributes of great power status. Moscow tried to take an active part in shaping international relations and sharing responsibility for the new international order. Moscow has consistently refused unilaterally to push for the total diplomatic isolation of Belgrade. On the other side, Russian diplomats wanted to stress that their activity did not mean that Russia would automatically support Serbia. During his visit to ex-Yugoslavia in May 1992 Kozyrev signed accords on exchanging diplomatic missions with Croatia and Slovenia. In Belgrade the delegation tried to explain that Russian resistance to the isolation of Serbia did not mean approval of Serbian policy in Bosnia. There were no signs that the Serb leaders were ready to meet the requests of the international community.

Kozyrev formulated the background idea for international regulation of the conflict – 'the necessity of participation of all states with their specific possibilities'. He praised the West for its skilful variation of the 'carrot and stick' for regulation, and mentioned the economic weakness of Russia and limits for participation in conflict-regulation. The single Russian trump-card at that moment was her traditional ties with the nations of the region. Kozyrev realised the need to play 'solo' more often, as the Russian delegation did in Lisbon. Mentioning the Serbian leaders' fears of losing their national roots in the new world order, Kozyrev did not reject the demand to keep 'originality', but stressed 'civilised originality according to international laws and norms'.

The preliminary result of the Foreign Minister's tour was a temporary armistice called the 'Russian peace'. It was broken just after Kozyrev's return to Moscow. After some hesitation, the Russian representative to the UN, Yulii Vorontsov, voted for imposing sanctions on rump-Yugoslavia. Several versions of the reasons for joining the international sanctions regime were aired among observers. According to the most popular one the decision to vote for punishment was mere improvisation by President Yeltsin during his meeting with the Chairman of the EC Commission, expecting financial assistance and prolongation of Soviet financial debts inherited by Russia.[18] This hypothesis might be indirectly confirmed by Yeltsin himself in his 'Presidential Notes' since he expected 'significant financial credits from the IMF'. The Russian leader was afraid of the second phase of inflation combined with the wave of strikes as a result of the shock therapy policy. Yeltsin was in 'troubled if not gloomy mood' and the promises of G-7 of large-scale financial assistance were the single source of hope.[19] On the eve of his visit to the USA, the veto on sanctions was not a good start for shaping a new international order.[20] The vote in the Security Council symbolised Russian readiness to join a great power concert in shaping the new order. Russia voted for 'legal' means of crisis resolution and not for military ones. This step was also defined by domestic politics as the logical continuation of the whole course set by the Russian leadership after Autumn 1991. Support for Belgrade could involve Russia in disputes over the process whereby the former administrative inter-republic lines might become overnight interstate borders recognised by the international community. This would waste energy badly needed for reforms.

Russia's vote 'for' sanctions against Serbia raised a wave of discussion on Russian foreign policy priorities in general and ex-Yugoslavia in particular. It gave those who were unsatisfied with the course of the domestic reforms a 'legal' chance to criticise the authorities. The pressure on those responsible for foreign policy was clear from several directions: in the opposition media, open letters, appeals to government and so on. The idea of re-creating the 'Slavonic committees'[21] of the nineteenth century was aired in Russian society. The rumours of Croatian troops from Croatia being deployed in Bosnia spread to condemn the conspiracy policy of the West and the 'betrayal' policy of Russia. The pragmatic wing of the foreign policy establishment had also criticised the Foreign Ministry insisting that a 'firm stand' for Belgrade was better 'coin' in the trade for assistance from the West. In June 1992 the Supreme Soviet discussed the matter. The head of the parliamentary international committee, Yevgeniy Ambartsumov, pointed out that it was not necessary for Russia 'as an independent state with its own national interests' to follow an American approach shaped by the interests of an American election campaign.[22] He expressed the common mood of fear that the US might think of repeating the Gulf war, this time against Slavic people.[23] Deputies were against drawing any analogy with 'Iraq's case' because in their view the problem was 'inter-ethnic conflict' not Serbian aggression. The discussion resulted in the adoption of a resolution 'on the Yugoslav matter', with recommendations to the government to take 'a more balanced approach to all parts [of the conflict]' and condemning 'armed intervention of any state or group of states in the conflict in BiH under any pretext'.[24] This resolution gave Russian diplomats more political room in their discussions with their western colleagues and stressed as a final argument the significance for countries with deep-rooted democratic traditions.[25]

The wave of criticism influenced the approach of Russian diplomacy until the end of the year. After that senior diplomats stressed that Belgrade was not the single perpetrator of the war; rejected 'regulation of the conflict by force'; and condemned appeals 'to bomb Belgrade' as irresponsible because they would lead to further destabilisation of the situation. The statement that 'ethnic cleansing in the former Yugoslavia' was conducted by 'Serbs, Croats and Muslims as well'[26] became commonplace in their speeches. Further visits of a Russian Parliamentary delegation composed of prominent former dissidents of the Communist regime but critical of Kozyrev and loyal to Yeltsin influenced a more active Russian approach and great concern with the development of events. From Summer 1992 the Yugoslav conflict became one of the major Russian instruments for shaping a new international order, at the very time when, from an institutional point of view, Russia was in fact peripheral to the international response. The UN Security Council was the only place where Russian diplomacy saw the opportunity to have influence on the international community's approach. The tribune of the UN offered the possibility of testing the new vision of the Russian leadership in organising the new world order through UN activity on the ex-Yugoslav model.

In August 1992 Russian diplomacy organised enormous activity in the UN, sponsoring or co-sponsoring Security Council resolutions at its special session. Russian diplomats tried to prevent any military action and to promote Russia's leading role as the actor responsible for the 'political solution' of crises.[27] The diplomatic capital gained in New York allowed Russia to be considered as a major player in the London conference which had been organised as an EC–UN enterprise. The Russian delegation acted as the mediator between the Serbs and the rest of the world. Another attempt was coordination with the American administration and opposition to any possible military solution which Bush might be tempted to sponsor in order to win the forthcoming election campaign. Kozyrev used the cooperation with the US to 'penetrate' the EC efforts for more active involvement in regulation on a 'day-by-day basis'.[28] In his presentation he proposed that the external borders of the former Yugoslavia be inviolable and a moratorium be imposed on the changing of internal borders, with a guarantee of the rights and special status of national minorities (in Kosovo, the Krajina and elsewhere).[29] The main principles of Russian policy after the London conference may be summarised as follows: 'equal responsibility of all sides'; active support for the London conference mechanisms providing that final decisions be discussed in the Security Council where Russia had her 'voice'; no new resolutions against Belgrade on the grounds that the previous ones should be implemented first. Russia insisted also on more secure procedures for sanctions and punishment for sanction breakers.

The essence of Moscow's policy towards Serbia was the expectation that Belgrade's regime would erode under the activity of the federal authorities (President Dobrica Cosic and Prime Minister Milan Panic). Russia tried to assist 'constructive forces' and to isolate 'aggressive forces' in Belgrade hoping for the non-violent democratic evolution of rump-Yugoslavia.[30] Moscow insisted on easing sanctions as a sign to the Serbian people of support for an alternative to Milosevic, trying to create a rift between him and the federal leadership. Yevgenii Ambartsumov in his speech at the European Parliament asked for support for 'democratic changes' in Yugoslavia. Kozyrev organised a meeting of ministers of the Big Five at Russian headquarters in New York.[31] Attempts were made to organise a meeting of Panic with Yeltsin during the visit of the latter to China.[32] In sum, Russia proposed to pressure Belgrade into cooperation with Washington.[33]

Phase 3 (1993) was characterised by tentative Russian attention to the crises and attempts to increase Russian influence in the process of conflict-regulation.

The general pattern of Russian foreign policy in 1993 was the continuation of the path towards partnership with the West,[34] yet at the same time the Russian leadership was more vocal on the necessity to reorientate the 'pro-Western shift' in its international activity. The predominant mood in the Russian establishment was that liberal internationalism had overestimated the commonality of interests in the international community. The international community was not prepared to provide huge financial assistance to Yeltsin's regime under easy conditions.[35] At the same time the romantic perceptions of the new international order were evaporating.[36] Russian initiatives regarding the conflicts in the near abroad (in Moldova and Abkhazia) were not supported in the CSCE. Yeltsin adapted to the changing political climate by moving toward the centre and pretending to play the role of 'Father of the Nation', trying to absorb and balance between different forces. The beginning of 1993 indicated a more independent course in foreign affairs as the result of opposition pressure at the end of 1992.[37] Moscow had also tried to gain momentum from the changing American administration, considering the interregnum period as suitable for a more active Russian role in world affairs. This natural tendency towards a rebirth of Russian diplomacy was accompanied by some anti-American rhetoric. Yeltsin criticised American attempts to 'dictate' the rules.[38]

The beginning of 1993 marked the start of a 'diplomatic attack' in the Balkan direction, and attempts to convince the world of the existence of Russian interests in the Balkan region. After the electoral defeat of Panic, Milosevic was legitimised in

Moscow's view as leader through democratic elections. Since December 1992 the Russian attitude towards rump-Yugoslavia was not defined by ideology. Another reason for the changing attitude was the fact that official Belgrade was more cooperative with Russian efforts to divide Belgrade and Pale.[39] Russia's diplomacy used all its influence and energy to support the Vance–Owen plan as the main field of cooperation with the West; Russian attempts to grab the initiative in crisis-regulation were also determined by fears of the possibility that President-elect Clinton might remember his election campaign promises to bomb the Serbs. The Kremlin was afraid that such a move might increase the influence of the anti-Yeltsin opposition in parliament, making more difficult the adoption of the new Constitution as the symbol of the final rejection of their communist past and the creation of a legal base for the transformation of Russia.

All events of this phase were subordinated to the domestic power crisis in Russia itself – a crisis exposed during the April 1993 referendum approving Yeltsin's position, and by the fight with the Supreme Soviet in October 1993. Then there was the need to confront the drift towards military action against any one of the conflicting sides (presumably the Serbs). Moscow tried not to allow NATO to play the decisive role in conflict-regulation. For Russian diplomats the mechanism of the North Atlantic Co-operation Council (NACC) was far preferable to NATO as such. In the first half of 1993 there was an additional form of cooperation with the West, acting with the Americans via the newly created institution of two (American and Russian) special representatives, supporting the negotiating mechanism set up by the London conference and trying to coordinate its activities with the UN Security Council.

The statement of Yeltsin at the news conference after meeting George Bush on 3 January 1993 was the first sign of the changing Russian approach to the crises. Yeltsin stated, 'we want to try to draw the line on the armistice in Serbia and in Yugoslavia in general'. He declared that Russia will be 'more active than before'.[40] In the middle of January 1993 Russian diplomacy launched a political offensive trying to put pressure on both Belgrade and the Bosnian Serbs, in the meantime attempting to divide the two parties. Yeltsin's promising phrase began to be deciphered. The Russian Foreign Ministry put forward an initiative called the 'Russian plan' which might be summarised as follows:

(1) Insistence on a political solution, that is, opposition to any ideas intending to resolve conflict by military force (intervention from outside or military victory of the conflicting sides) because in the Russian view this would lead inevitably to the 'Lebanon-isation' of the war; (2) resistance to lifting the embargo in the ex-Yugoslavia area (that is, to prevent any attempt to arm the Bosnian Muslims or to give additional supplies to units of the Bosnian Serbs); (3) attempts to impose sanctions on Croatia in an effort to prevent its active involvement in Bosnia and to stop it from any military action against the Croatian Serbs; (4) active support for the Vance–Owen plan by putting pressure on the Bosnian Serbs via Belgrade or directly trying to force them to acquiesce in its provisions.

Realising the economic weakness of their country, Russian diplomats still tried to play a 'special role' within the framework of the international community. Russian proposals were more concrete than those proclaimed in Clinton's plan ('six steps'). Attention was focused on Bosnia, but Russian diplomats always insisted on taking steps towards seeking a general political solution to the whole of the former Yugoslavia. The main emphasis was on the necessity to accept the Vance–Owen plan by all sides and the implementation of it under UN control. Cooperation with the US representative remained the main field of Russian activity. Diplomats stressed the partnership nature of this enterprise.

Russian diplomacy forced the Bosnian Serbs in a referendum to agree to the Vance–Owen plan. The special statement of the Russian president in March that 'Russia would not protect those who set themselves against the international community', warning of the danger of 'severe retaliation by the international community' against those who 'stake their position on using force' demonstrated that Yeltsin was interested in crisis-regulation on Vance–Owen lines. In the same statement Yeltsin, interested in regulation with full Russian participation, proposed a second London Conference and declared the necessity to 'dot the i's and cross the t's' in the Bosnian drama.[41] Yeltsin demonstrated both to the West and to domestic politicians Russia's role in the conflict. At the same time Russian diplomats

became convinced that the Bosnian Serbs were a more independent factor than had been considered before. Russian diplomacy realised that Milosevic's authority among the Serbs
remained extremely high, but 'he can't give orders to all'.[42]

Further attempts to convince the Serbs to say 'yes' to the
plan failed after the May referendum. Russian diplomacy was
convinced once again of the influence of military extremism
among the Bosnian Serbs and of people's will to fight for their
lands, but at the same time stressed the necessity to accept the
democratic character of this uncomfortable decision.

Active Russian policy allowed Russia to secure her influence in attempts to regulate the conflict. After Andrey Kozyrev's
long trip to Belgrade, Split and Bonn in May, he signed the
Washington accords allowing Russia to go further towards the
institutionalisation of her participation in conflict-regulation.
Kozyrev played a prominent role in facilitating the acceptance
by the West of *de facto* Bosnian partition after the collapse of
the Vance–Owen plan. In June Russia proposed the set of measures called Russian plan 2. At the same time Russian diplomacy
resisted pressure to send her own peace-keeping troops, saying
that Russia was ready to give planes for their transportation to
Bosnia but only after the UN Security Council decision. During the summer Moscow supported the continuation of the
Geneva talks between all three sides of the Bosnian conflict.

The disbanding of the Supreme Soviet in October 1993 made
it possible for Russian diplomacy to act more independently in
international relations without parliamentary control. Nevertheless Kozyrev rejected any possibility of organising military
intervention against the Serbs, promising Russia's veto of that
proposal.

Phase 4 (1994). The period after the December 1993 elections to the new Russian parliament opened phase four in Russian policy towards the crisis in the former Yugoslavia. Serious
electoral reverses for the reformers of 1992 demonstrated the
erosion of both popular and elite support for economic reform.
The election results forced Yeltsin to redouble his efforts to
find a new political base in the state bureaucracy, and to moderate his political and economic course. The implications for
Russian behaviour in international affairs was a mixed course
of cooperation and conflict with the West, including presumably the United States. The Russian authorities openly absorbed

the rhetoric of nationalism. At the same time the creators of Russian diplomacy tried to preserve 'the possibility of cooperation with the West'. They confirmed the idea of 'strategic partnership' with the USA.

Kozyrev made more explicit his political views, that the 'Russian Federation is doomed to be a great power' and therefore 'not a junior, but an equal partner'. He criticised the 'dangerous illusion . . . the almost manic wish to see the USA as the only single leading power in the contemporary world', and the 'fixed idea of American leadership'. At the same time Russia proclaimed her wish for a more independent approach to world matters since 'partnership based on common values and even sympathies does not mean the refusal of the hard, even aggressive policy of defending one's own national interests, competition and disputes from time to time'. Some successes from this point of view had been achieved.[43] Therefore the elements influencing Russian policy at this time were: (1) further affirmation of Russia as a great power through acceptance into the G-7; (2) an agreement with the EU with two symbolic summits per year; (3) inclusion in the Paris 'club' as a creditor. These emerging characteristics contributed to Russian assumptions of great power responsibility for the maintenance of international order and her own sphere of influence where the actions of other great powers should be agreed.

The influence of the rhetoric of the victors at the elections led to more attention being paid to Russian minorities in the former Soviet republics. In his New Year's Appeal to Russians, President Yeltsin promised to defend the Russian population everywhere. More attention to this matter contributed to better understanding with Belgrade. The hesitation of the international community to understand the Russian position on this matter raised more sympathetic feelings to their 'Serbian brothers' and forced observers and policymakers to reconsider the situation in the former Yugoslavia and the previous united approach with the West.

One of the peculiarities of this phase was the active involvement of almost all political forces and leaders across the political spectrum in shaping Russian policy towards Yugoslavia (from the 'hero of the December elections', Vladimir Zhirinovsky[44] in January–February and May, to Yegor Gaidar in September). The Orthodox Patriarch Alexii and Defence Minister Pavel

Grachev also paid much attention to the crisis. The discussions of 'the Yugoslav problem' moved up to second place on the list of deputies' priorities.

The main features of Russian policy towards the Yugo-crisis in this phase were: (1) explicit resistance to a military decision, military actions of any type to require prior authorisation from the UN Security Council, that is, only with Russia's permission; (2) a more independent role for Russia in managing the conflict, partly as a response to the fear of increasing isolation from the West, partly because of the changing political climate after the December elections, partly in affirmation of Russia's status as a great power with her own interests which should be protected, even without consultations with others; (3) attempts to find a Russian 'carrot' for Serbia, and a readiness to develop relations if Belgrade should meet the requirements of the international community; (4) creating and being actively involved in a new mechanism of conflict-regulation – the 'contact group' – meaning a new phase of cooperation with the West on an equal basis.

During this period it seemed that Russia might be ready to confront the international community because of the Serbs.[45] The results of the elections in the new parliament resulted in a hard-line approach to military action by NATO in ex-Yugoslavia. The first action on foreign policy of the newly elected Duma was the Statement on Yugoslavia drafted jointly by three powerful factions (LDPR, communists and 'agrarians'). The unity of the deputies (even members of Gaidar's faction voted for the text) pressured the Russian authorities into a more active stance towards the crisis. It reconciled the government's domestic need to appear responsive to pro-Serbian sentiments. The first step was initiated by Prime Minister Chernomyrdin himself with his criticism of international plans to bomb the Serbs.[46] Further independent actions were carefully prepared. It was also important for the authorities to appear responsive to Duma sentiments, including anti-Western sentiments, yet still retain good relations with the West. Yeltsin needed to avoid any immediate issue that could either damage relations with the West, or lead to domestic political difficulties after attack by the newly elected lower house on the ground of betraying the Serbs by an 'aggressive NATO attack'. It seems that a skilful trick was thought up to blame the West for the lack of will to cooperate with Russia.

Moscow criticised Washington for not keeping the Kremlin informed of the NATO decision to bomb Bosnian Serb positions.[47] Later Kozyrev mentioned that 'NATO's [February] ultimatum was imposed without Russia' and stressed the impossibility and unacceptability of Russia's exclusion from common attempts to regulate the Bosnian problem.[48]

The NATO ultimatum had put Yeltsin under considerable political pressure from ultra-nationalist adversaries at home. During that period Russian diplomats, and President Yeltsin himself, were able to accomplish two important tasks. On the one hand, they managed to add more drama to the crisis by insisting loudly, even petulantly, that Russia would not be left out of any solution to the Yugo-crisis, emphasising to the West the necessity of cooperation. They demonstrated that they could surprise the West.[49] On the other hand, they demonstrated 'firmness' regarding international affairs in response to domestic criticism. 'Our aim is to make sure that the ultimatum is never carried out, that the air strikes never take place', said Deputy Foreign Minister Sergei Lavrov, in the Duma.[50] The third line of activity was the attempt to renew cooperation with Belgrade and Pale. A special presidential representative passed Yeltsin's appeal to Milosevic and Karadžić asking for acceptance of the Russian withdrawal plan. The Russian media mentioned that he coordinated his activity with Russian top military official General Podkolizin. Finally, Russian peace-keeping troops were deployed around Sarajevo after the Serbian acceptance of Moscow's guarantees.

After that Russian diplomacy went on the offensive. It was Russia's turn to gloat. Moscow challenged the West to put pressure on the Muslim-led Bosnian Government, as did Andrei Kozyrev in Athens on the Bosnian Serbs.[51]

There were several results of the Sarajevo manoeuvre. Russia suddenly interposed itself in the standoff to persuade the nationalist Serbs besieging the capital to comply with a NATO ultimatum without losing face. Yeltsin scored a badly needed diplomatic triumph, that really worked for him at home as well as abroad. Russia was able to claim that it was right to exploit the historic Slavonic and Orthodox bonds in the interest of negotiating peace and proved Moscow's constant intentions to decline any attempts to use the military force of the international community against the Serbs.[52] Another Russian success was connected with the lifting of the blockade of the airport at Tuzla.

Washington's diplomatic response – the signing of a Muslim–Croatian confederation – met with great reservations in Russia. Although Siladzic and Granic informed Russian officials of their plans, Kozyrev expected further explanation at a meeting with the US Secretary of State Warren Christopher. During talks with Granic, Churkin tried to propose some sort of confederative agreement between Serbia and Croatia. Granic rejected this decisively. Kozyrev did not formulate his thoughts at all clearly. Churkin also did not clarify the situation, stating that Russia was 'continuing to study' the Washington agreements and their possible legal consequences. Some observers thought that the Washington accord could lead to a destabilisation of the Kosovo problem. The Russian Foreign Ministry took a wait-and-see position, carefully avoiding any comments. Nevertheless, tensions with Washington and NATO during the winter transformed into a renewal of cooperation in the Spring. Russia took a more helpful position in the contact group after the crisis around Gorazde. Moscow was for converting this group into a new London-type conference to try to find a political solution to the crisis. Russia was now more than ever interested in a summit conference on Bosnia (or ex-Yugoslavia).

The ideology of this policy was an attempt to break with the *de facto* practice of great-power patronage of opposing parties to the conflict (Russia–Serbs, the USA–Muslims, Germany–Croats). The aim was to destroy the illusions and hopes of the fighting parties about the disunity of the Great Powers concerned. Russian diplomats saw these hopes as the main reason for the protagonists not to agree with the 'plans' proposed to them.

Russian diplomats succeeded finally in attempts to divide Belgrade from Pale, which had been their aim since Spring 1992. But after two years, the possibilities for Milosevic to influence Karadzic or especially the military commanders of the Bosnian Serbs had reduced significantly. Russian diplomacy may have failed to reduce violence in Bosnia but it managed to return Belgrade to the path of cooperation with the international community.

From now on, Russian diplomacy was more cooperative. Moscow agreed with the possibility of NATO air strikes after consultations in the Security Council according to the adopted resolutions, and, after some hesitation, with the Washington plan for a Muslim–Croatian confederation. But any appeals or US plans for lifting the arms embargo on the Bosnian Muslims were strongly opposed in Moscow. In this respect Russia's steps towards preparing to lift sanctions against rump-Yugoslavia as a reward for Belgrade's cooperation against the Bosnian Serbs have a dual nature. They may be interpreted not only as a Russian 'carrot'[53] but also as a response to the potential unilateral lifting of sanctions by the Clinton administration under strong pressure from Capitol Hill and other pro-Muslim factions.

CONCLUSIONS

In international perspective, by the end of 1994 Russian policy towards the former Yugoslavia helped Moscow leaders to affirm Russia as a great power participating actively in crisis-regulation and stopping the spread of conflict all over Europe. In domestic perspective, it underpinned Yeltsin's policy on the disintegration of the Soviet Union. After the appearance of the Russian Federation as an active independent actor, the constant increase in Russian influence from a position of abstention via participation in the London conference and the institution of special representatives legitimised the involvement of Russia on an equal basis in the resolution of the conflict. Throughout the whole period Moscow was consistent in certain principles of its policy:

(1)   Opposition to a military decision.
(2)   Attempts to separate the various parties; on this ground to lift or ease the UN sanctions against rump-Yugoslavia.
(3)   Search for a mechanism of influence in managing the crisis besides that of the UN (but with the Security Council as the ultimate authority).
(4)   Insistence on the equal responsibility of all participants in the conflict.
(5)   Opposition to any decisive role for NATO. Russia was prepared to allow NATO involvement only under the control of the UN Security Council; any other variant minimised Russian influence.

(6) Attempts to discover a 'system solution' to the crisis in the former Yugoslavia as a whole, including latent and potential crises (Serbian Krajina in Croatia, the Kosovo problem, minority rights as interconnected issues), rather than focusing on particular flashpoints (the allegedly 'sensational' Western approach).

NOTES

1. According to three criteria: the level of cooperation with the West, the level of tension in the Russian Federation, and the involvement of the international community in dealing with the crises.
2. The Soviet Foreign Ministry commented that the decisions of the Croatian and Slovenian parliaments could not be considered as 'ones assisting in the solution of difficult problems in Yugoslavia'. Moscow stressed the importance of preserving Yugoslavia's 'unity and integrity, the inviolability of her borders (including internal ones), the right of nations to decide their own fate, to support legal structures of power trying to preserve the Yugoslav state'. *Vestnik ITAR-TASS*, 26 June 1991. See also the statement of the Soviet Foreign Ministry regarding the necessity to cooperate with the Yugoslav government regarding the preservation of the integrity of the SFRY. *Vestnik MID SSSR*, 31 July 1991, No. 14(96).
3. Interview with high-ranking diplomat of Russian Foreign Ministry, 10 November 1992.
4. See Joint Soviet–American Statement, 30 July 1991, in *Vestnik MID SSSR* Nos. 16–18, p. 16. During his stay in Kiev the American President warned his hosts of the danger of 'suicidal nationalism'. On Bush's 'Chicken speech' see Michael Beschloss and Strobe Talbott, *At the Highest Levels* (Boston: Little, Brown, 1993), p. 414.
5. *Vestnik*, Ministry of Foreign Affairs [hereafter *MID*], No. 18(100), 30 September 1991, p. 34. Later observers wrote that only the results of the failed coup released the Germans from 'horrible expectations' that Moscow would support Serbia. See *Russia Weekly* (in Russian), 6 October 1992, p. 5.
6. *Vestnik MID*, 19 September 1991.
7. Both Balkan leaders accepted goodwill missions of the international community (the USSR, the USA, and the EC). *Vestnik MID SSSR*, No. 21, 15 November 1991, p. 14.
8. The most that they tried to reach was Gorbachev's acceptance to include the RSFSR's representatives into the Soviet delegation in international meetings. See Andrei Kozyrev, 'Most cherez Rubikon' ('The Bridge over the Rubicon'), *Novoye Vremya*, 45 (1990) pp. 26–7; Ruslan Khasbulatov,

'Rossiya: pora peremen' ('Russia: the time of change'), Megapolis-Takom, *Russkaya Enciklopediya*, 1991, pp. 179–81.

9.   Pavel Felgengauer, 'Will Yugoslavia be the new Lebanon?', *Nezavisimaya gazeta*, 2 July 1991; Andrei Vsevolzhskiy, 'Yugoslav Crises: The Special Opinion of Moscow', ibid., 9 August 1991.

10. *Vestnik MID SSSR*, No. 24, 31 December 1991, p. 13.

11. Pavel Felgengauer, 'The defeat of Croatia is inevitable. Only foreign intervention can stop the bloodshed', *Nezavisimaya gazeta*, 18 September 1991.

12. Boris Yeltsin, 'Zapiski Presidenta' (Presidential Notes) *Ogonek*, 1994, pp. 242–3. For example Andrei Kozyrev interrupted his diplomatic tour in the Yugoslav republics to participate in discussions over the 'Crimean problem' in parliament in May 1992.

13. The background for this idea was the meetings of Polish and Czechoslovakian dissidents in the 1970s. See Janusz Bugajski and Maxine Pollack, *East European Fault Lines: Dissent, Opposition, and Social Activism* (Boulder, CO.: Westview Press, 1989), pp. 100–107.

14. See the interview with Yurii Deriabin in *ITAR-TASS* (in Russian), 12 February 1992, Series 'SE'-24.

15. Ibid., lists 24–35.

16. At the time Serbia had suspended its bombing of civilian targets and accepted UN peace-keeping troops in certain areas of Croatia, mainly Krajina.

17. On the other hand, Russia condemned accusations in the local media of Russia being anti-Yugoslav and anti-Serb as totally 'groundless and dangerous'.

18. Yevgenii Matonin, 'Sankcii prinyati: K chemu oni privedut', *Nezavisimaya gazeta*, 3 June 1992; Boris Rodionov, 'Sankcii protiv Yugoslavii nye uchli interesov Rossii', *Izvestia*, 4 June 1992; Andrei Khimenko, 'Zachem rubit' suk, na kotorom sidit na odno stoletiye rossiyskaya diplomatiya na Balkanakh', *Nezavisimaya gazeta*, 9 June 1992.

19. Boris Yeltsin, 'Zapiski Prezidenta' (Presidential Notes), *Ogonek*, 1994, pp. 264 and 255.

20. This assessment was confirmed by the information leaked from diplomatic sources to the ultraconservative weekly *Den'* (The Day). Regarding the publication of the Russian representative's memo to the UN, see Suzanne Crow, 'Russia's Response to the Yugoslav Crisis', *RFE/RL Research Report*, Vol. 1, No. 30, 24 July 1992, p. 32.

21. 'Slavonic committees' were created by intelligentsia in the last century to support the liberation struggles of ethnic Slavs and were assisted by Russian volunteers who came to the Balkans.

22. *Izvestiya*, 30 June 1992.

23. Presidential candidate Bill Clinton argued that air strikes against Serb positions should be used, almost exactly at the same time as Lord Owen was arguing publicly that selective air strikes should be used to tip the balance against the Bosnian Serbs.

24. 'Yugoslavia in flames' (in Russian), Moscow, 1992, p. 235. The Resolution of 26 June was much more pragmatic than others. It had been adopted when competition between the Supreme Soviet and Yeltsin's

administration was at the very beginning. Later discussions were used by the opposition to attack Kozyrev's and Yeltsin's reforms. Earlier discussions and the adopted resolution were much closer to real foreign policy problems than later ones in December 1992 and January and April 1993.

25. On 28 June the UN Security Council declined to consider a military ultimatum against rump-Yugoslavia, preferring to concentrate on economic sanctions as a means of influencing Belgrade. It confirmed the priority of 'humanitarian' over political objectives in Bosnia.

26. These events in the Yugoslav War coincided with Russian diplomatic attempts to persuade Europe to pay more attention to Russian minorities in the Baltic region. Gusarov, responsible for these matters in the Foreign Ministry, warned of the danger of repeating the Yugoslav tragedy in Baltic countries because of 'violation of rights of one nation by another one', *Trud* (in Russian), 30 July 1992, p. 3.

27. See *Diplomaticheskiy vestnik*, No. 17(18), 1992, pp. 40–4 including the statement by Russian Ambassador to the UN Security Council on 12 August 1992.

28. Some sort of mutual cooperation with Washington on the crises was revived as a result of a pre-London meeting between Kozyrev and Acting Secretary of State Lawrence Eagleburger on the eve of the London conference. Wireless File, 25 August 1992, USIA US Embassy Moscow, Russia, p. 4.

29. He insisted on non-recognition of territorial gains by force, and ending of 'ethnic cleansing' as the primary tasks facing the international community. Kozyrev proposed strict international monitoring of the situation and did not rule out the possible use of punitive action against violators. He also insisted that the Bosnian crisis was to be dealt with as a multiethnic, multiconfessional issue. *ITAR-TASS* (in Russian), 28 August 1992; series 'SE', p. 7.

30. At the parliamentary hearing 17 December 1992, Deputy Minister Anatolii Adamishin stated that 'we are working to support those forces, Panic and Cosic presumably, in Yugoslavia who stand for using nonviolent means of crisis resolution'. See 'Yugoslavskiy krizis i Rossiya', pp. 134–5.

31. Statement by Vitalii Churkin at a briefing in the Ministry of Foreign Affairs, 30 October 1992. See, *Diplomaticheskiy vestnik*, Nos. 21–2, 15–30 November 1992, p. 68.

32. Transcript of news conference by Yevgenii Ambartsumov. See 'Yugoslav Crisis and Russia' (in Russian), Moscow, 1993, p. 280.

33. 'Commersant-DAILY' (in Russian), 12 December 1992.

34. The Russian Foreign Minister stressed that despite efforts of some deputies of the Supreme Soviet to convert existing disagreements into ideological differences, Russia is emphasising ideas of partnership, not confrontation. See the interview with Andrei Kozyrev, 'Russia is Main Priority for the USA', in *Moscow News* (in Russian), 7 March 1993.

35. Although the observers mentioned that Yeltsin had shown few signs of wanting to change his course, he had proved in economic policy that he was capable of trimming. It should not be taken for granted that

the current 'Western' consensus will remain for long. See 'Westward no?', *The Economist*, 4 July 1992.

36.   The shift was also evident among ruling elites where the liberal internationalist ideology gave way to *realpolitik*.

37.   See J. Adams, 'Legislature asserts its role in Russian Foreign Policy', *RFE/RL Research Report*, Vol. 2, No. 4, 22 January 1993.

38.   The most prominent of Yeltsin's criticisms was made just prior to his departure for India on 22 January. See *Commersant-DAILY*, 27 January 1993.

39.   At the hearings in the Supreme Soviet on 18 February 1993, Kozyrev mentioned fears shared by Russia and the West that Milosevic intended 'war'. According to Kozyrev these assumptions proved wrong since Milosevic used his electoral mandate to support the Vance–Owen Plan. He expressed his hope that these feelings would be vindicated. See 'Yugoslav Crisis and Russia', op. cit., pp. 171–2.

40.   *Diplomatichesky vestnik* (in Russian), Nos. 1–2, 1993, p. 28.

41.   Yeltsin also stressed the importance of unity among the five permanent members of the Security Council and other international actors in managing the crisis, and reminded them of previous Russian initiatives towards the Bosnia crisis. See *Vestnik ITAR-TASS*, 10 March 1993.

42.   See interview with Vitaliy Churkin in *Moscow News* (in Russian), 21 March 1993.

43.   In this phase Russia managed to realise some important international objectives: the G-7 meeting in Naples was partly converted into a 'political G-8'; the Accord on cooperation with the EC was signed (after a lengthy delay); Russia was included in the Paris club of creditors; the efforts of the CIS to receive observer-status in the UN met with international support; Russia's influence in Eastern Europe was confirmed by postponing East European entry into NATO; and finally, Moscow's efforts to unite the CIS through economic cooperation finally met with success.

44.   The active attitude in support of a great community uniting all Orthodox believers (all Slavs from Knin to Vladivostok) became one of Zhirinovsky's leading ideas. See Surge Plekhanov 'Zhirinovsky: What is he?', *Eurasia-Nord*, 1994, p. 161.

45.   The Yugo-crisis may be viewed as one of several attempts by Yeltsin to distance himself from previous attitudes towards the West.

46.   Chernomyrdin's interest may be explained by his intentions to work out a foreign policy programme for his prospective presidential election campaign. See Maxim Yusin, 'Victor Chernomyrdin corrects Andrei Kozyrev's position', *Izvestiya*, 3 February 1994.

47.   See Vasilii Kononenko, 'Clinton Could Make a Phone Call to Yeltsin if He Really Wanted To', *Izvestiya*, 12 February 1994. The commentator pointed out that Anthony Lake had managed to keep in regular contact with the Russian Foreign Affairs Ministry.

48.   See Andrei Kozyrev, 'Russia and the USA: The Partnership is not Premature, it is Overdue', *Izvestiya*, 11 March 1994.

49.   Some evidence exists that this Russian act was not expected by the

West. White House officials said that they first learned of the Russian offer from reports on CNN.

50. Celestine Bohlen, 'Russia's Balkan Card', *The New York Times*, 18 February 1994.

51. Kozyrev, who was in Athens for talks, said 'The Bosnian Serbs have agreed to withdraw all heavy artillery due to the appeals of President Yeltsin and promises of Russian peace-keeping troops in the area. We, therefore, expect our Western partners to encourage the other side to withdraw their weapons. It is time for them to act rather than talk about ultimatums', Celestine Bohlen, ibid.

52. At the same time the Russian media pretended to label this move as support for NATO so as not to lose face in case of military failure. Konstantin Egert, 'Russia saved not only Sarajevo, but the prestige of NATO', *Izvestiya*, 26 February 1994.

53. Among other 'carrots' was the mission to Belgrade of Defence Ministry Pavel Grachev with a special message to Bosnian Serbs from Yeltsin. During his meeting with Bosnian Serb leaders at the Russian Embassy in Belgrade, Grachev tried to assure General Mladic and Karadzic that the Bosnian Serbs have the right to create their own state within a future confederation. See Andrei Baturin, 'Did Bosnian Serbs Say "Yes" to Pavel Grachev?', *Izvestiya*, 28 July 1994.

3 German Perspectives
Marie-Janine Calic

The German role in the handling of the Yugoslav crisis has been harshly criticised. While moderate observers saw the newly united Germany as not yet capable of responding adequately to the security challenges of the post-Cold War era, more radical voices accused Germany of trying to dominate Europe. The thesis of this chapter is that the German approach to the Yugoslav crisis was influenced by:

(1) The consequences of the dramatically shifting power structure after the collapse of the Eastern bloc.
(2) Historical experiences and cultural ties.
(3) Constitutional constraints and the debate on the legitimacy of future out-of-area deployments of the Bundeswehr.
(4) The fact that vital German interests were not at stake in the Balkans.

Its conclusion is that, given the particular historical and constitutional conditions prevailing, German policy has been less assertive than many suppose.

1. GERMANY IN A NEW ERA

For better or worse, at the end of 1991 Germany faced a new era. Following the collapse of the political system in the GDR in late 1989, unification of the two German states quickly took shape. As a first step, on 1 July 1990 the Monetary, Economic and Social Union took effect. In accordance with the Unification Treaty the division of Germany formally ended on the night of 2/3 October 1990. With the so-called Two plus Four Treaty, negotiated by the governments of the two German states, together with the United States, France, Britain and the Soviet Union, the Federal Republic gained full sovereignty. The treaty was signed on 12 September 1990 in Moscow.

When by the end of 1990 the Yugoslav crisis had accelerated,

German public opinion was completely preoccupied by internal problems. Reconstructing the East German economy burdened the national budget with increasing costs. Moreover, it was not clear whether it would be possible to overcome the psychological gap between West Germans and East Germans. Compared with the radical changes of the political landscape in East Central Europe, the achievements of unity and full sovereignty, the dissolution of multiethnic Yugoslavia and its consequences seemed to be of minor importance.

Nevertheless, the revolutionary changes in the political order of Europe opened a wider debate on the future of German foreign policy. On the one hand, the break-up of the Warsaw Pact has led to a fundamental improvement in Germany's strategic situation, as the two superpowers no longer faced each other on German soil. On the other hand, new challenges emerged. The East–West conflict has been replaced by a multitude of dynamic developments and complex risks, such as the consequences of national minority problems and border disputes, ethnic antagonism and civil war, requiring new instruments for conflict prevention and crisis management.

Therefore, the issues of continuity and change, of values and interests, and, last but not least, the question of international responsibility were put on the German agenda.[1] By virtue of its political and economic strength, leading politicians in Germany expected their country to play a key role in the new Europe. But, due to recent German history, redefining Germany's international position has been a sensitive issue. In view of widespread European suspicions about Germany's secret wish for hegemony, many Germans felt uncomfortable with the new situation.

Apart from unification there were four major events driving Germany's foreign policy debate.[2] The first was the Gulf War, raising the question of military engagement beyond that of defence of the country. As the German Bundeswehr, constitutionally, was not allowed to take action out of the NATO defence area, Germany's role was limited to financial contributions. This touched the sensitive issue of national prestige and raised the question of legitimate use of German armed forces.

The second series of events was the putsch of Moscow and

the break-up of the Soviet Union, raising deep concern over the future stability of Eastern Europe. The containment of the consequences of the dissolution process absorbed a major part of German diplomatic forces. Preoccupied by the aftermath of these events, nobody seriously expected that one of the biggest diplomatic crises after 1945 would arise out of the Balkan turmoil.

The third major development was the intensification of European integration by expanding the European Community (EC) with a Common Foreign and Security Policy and the creation of a new cooperative security order in the framework of the CSCE. After the end of the Cold War the German expectation for keeping peace in Europe was through the strengthening of mutual confidence and stability. Most scholars and officials agreed that Germany's new foreign policy must be embedded in the network of regional and international institutions. In 1991, however, common foreign and security policies remained far off on the horizon. On the contrary, the prospects of the European monetary union, envisaged in the Maastricht Treaty of December 1991, raised the fear that Germany had given away its financial stability, and had gained little more than a vague possibility of closer political cooperation.

The fourth event driving the German foreign policy debate was the dissolution of Yugoslavia and its consequences. When by the end of June 1991 the multiethnic state finally broke up, many Germans felt disappointed in view of the confused and ineffective attempts of the EC to handle the crisis. German public opinion has been bewildered by the half-hearted response to the human tragedy unfolding in the former Yugoslavia. By the Autumn of 1991, the failure of the EC to bring about a peace arrangement revealed disagreement over whether or not to recognise the former Yugoslav republics Croatia and Slovenia. Some analysts go so far as to claim that the German approach to the break-up of Yugoslavia was influenced by the Maastricht negotiations. 'Kohl's Euro-policy had already met with strong opposition in the German media in late 1991, when the conflict over the EC's Yugoslav policy was coming to a head and Bonn jumped the gun on diplomatic recognition of Slovenia and Croatia. In many ways, recognition was a direct result of Kohl's surrender at Maastricht.'[3] Anyway, the Yugoslav crisis promised to be a first test case for the newly united Germany.

2. THE BURDENS OF HISTORY

Most emphasis has been laid on the assumption that, for historical reasons, Germany had a special interest in handling the Yugoslav crisis. The return of historical and cultural affinities and aversions gave rise to a lot of speculation but rather little documentation.[4] There is no doubt that to a considerable extent the German view of the Yugoslav conflicts has been influenced by cultural ties as, for centuries, the territory of Slovenia and Croatia formed part of Austria-Hungary. But not many Germans actually know that during the nineteenth century Serbia had been an area of German interference as well. Intellectuals in Germany, as elsewhere, looked with great interest and enthusiasm upon the Serbian nation. Among their number were Johann Wolfgang von Goethe, Jacob Grimm and Leopold von Ranke, the last of whom in 1829 dedicated one of his main works to the Serbian revolution. The situation changed somewhat when during the First World War Germany allied with Austria-Hungary against Serbia. Following the assassination of the Austro-Hungarian Arch-Duke Franz Ferdinand in 1914 Serbia was perceived as one of Germany's main adversaries.

When in 1991 the Serbian–Croatian war broke out, old historical and cultural stereotypes reappeared. While the Serbs were viewed by all as crude and backward people, the Slovenes' and Croats' image as small nations fighting for their independence roused wide sympathy. Such emotions were heightened by the presence of a sizeable Croat community and the close ties many Germans feel with a country familiar from holidays. Many media reports and commentaries were characterised by simplifications, such as the 'good' Croats and the 'evil' Serbs. Only after months of war, German public opinion became more differentiated. The euphoria of 1991 gave way to despair when at the end of 1992 the Croat–Muslim fighting started and when Franjo Tudjman and Slobodan Milosevic, the presidents of Croatia and Serbia, expressed their wish to carve up Bosnia.

The strong German support for Slovenian and Croatian independence has created suspicions that historical alliances have somehow survived and that the newly united Germany was seeking hegemony over the old Yugoslavia. Bonn was accused of trying to re-establish a sphere of influence in South-eastern

Europe. This referred to Germany's special economic interest in South-eastern Europe since the nineteenth century. For nearly a century, German political economists, starting with Friedrich List, had been arguing that Germany needed a *Großraum*, a 'living space', in order to achieve economic and military security. This would be essentially an area adjacent to Germany with surplus agricultural products and raw materials which could serve as an adjunct to German industry.[5] Thus, the Balkans played a key role in its concept of *Mitteleuropa* which laid the foundations of the economic penetration of the area.[6] During the 1890s the German government tried to widen Germany's economic influence in the Balkans. As a result, British and French economic dominance in South-eastern Europe had been replaced by the growing commerce of all the Balkan states with Germany.

During the interwar period Germany did not relinquish its pre-eminent position. Hitler's special interest in the Balkan economies dated from 1935 when the need for rearmament and the wish for agricultural self-sufficiency dictated the stimulation of trade with the area. Exchange controls and clearing agreements helped to increase German trade with South-eastern Europe. As early as 1936, Yugoslav exports to Nazi Germany passed 80 per cent of the total. An appreciable amount of non-ferrous ores, initially bauxite and chrome, as well as most Yugoslavian wheat and pig exports were sent to the Reich.[7]

Apart from economic cooperation there was another factor influencing earlier Yugoslav–German relations. Due to the colonisation policy during the Habsburg rule, the South Slavic areas inherited a considerable German minority.[8] After further emigration of Germans to the Banat and Backa, to Croatia, Slavonia and Bosnia, on the eve of the First World War, about half a million Germans were scattered across the South Slavic area. According to the 1931 census there were 499 969 Germans living in the territory of the Yugoslav Kingdom. Of these, some 300 000 were in Vojvodina, 100 000 in Croatia and Slavonia, 40 000 in Slovenia, and 16 000 in Bosnia and Dalmatia.[9]

During the interwar period Germany had a strong interest in the fate of the minorities living in the successor states. Organisations which wanted to serve the interest of the Germans abroad, such as the *Verein für das Deutschtum im Ausland* (VDA) and the *Deutsche Auslandsinstitut* (DAI), enjoyed the moral and financial support of the German government who had the revision of peace treaties in mind. In Yugoslavia, therefore, these so-called *Volksdeutsche* by and large were seen as the Fifth Column of Nazi Germany.[10]

In 1941, Germany and Italy divided up the Yugoslav state. Serbia and the Banat were placed directly under German military occupation. In Croatia and most of Bosnia-Herzegovina Hitler and Mussolini established the so-called Independent State of Croatia under the rule of the fascist Ustasha movement, in fact a brutal occupation regime. During the Second World War many ethnic Germans served in the *Waffen SS*, which operated in the Balkans against the partisans. Its activities made the non-German population in Yugoslavia hostile to Germans in general and profoundly influenced the perceptions on both sides. After the Second World War, generalisations survived according to which all ethnic Germans were fanatical supporters of Hitler, promoters of Nazism, and during the war, a fifth column of the advancing German armies. The expulsion of the several hundreds of thousands of *Volksdeutsche* were justified by these accusations.[11]

Nevertheless, the Yugoslav–German relations after the Second World War can be described by and large as 'close and constructive'.[12] Yugoslavia was among the first countries to open diplomatic relations with the Federal Republic. Germany became Yugoslavia's most important trading partner again. In 1990 the Federal Republic supplied 18 per cent of Yugoslavia's total imports and absorbed 16 per cent of its exports.[13] Every year more than two million West Germans spent their holidays in Yugoslavia, while a community of about 700 000 *Gastarbeiter* from Yugoslavia were living in Germany.[14]

Despite manifold historical ties and geographical proximity the overwhelming majority of Germans knew little about Yugoslavia and her problems. Politics and the media approached the Yugoslav crisis with an appalling naivety. As in the United States, scholars, diplomats and politicians 'could not understand why the South Slavic leaders did not sit down at a table, talk through their problems, compromise here and there, reach a consensus, and then go about the task of becoming loyal citizens of a new nation and state. They did not comprehend the complexities of the situation or the intensity of feelings connected with them.'[15]

The issue was further complicated by the misunderstanding

of the nature of the conflicts. Many observers simply under-estimated the dimensions and effects of the war. Most of them interpreted the case in genuine ethnic terms, while other sources of conflict, such as the distribution of economic resources, or political and military power among nations and republics, were completely neglected.

Above all, German public opinion was attracted by the Slovenes' and Croats' striving for independence which was an expression of its own ideal of self-determination. Historically, the Germans conceived of the nation primarily as a community determined by descent, language and culture. Thus, they interpreted the right to self-determination differently from the Americans or the French, for example, who interpret national-ism from a political rather than an ethnic standpoint. According to their conception of state, a nation is based on civic values, tra-ditions and institutions. Moreover, the Germans were not famil-iar with the problems of ethno-national or regional movements within their country, thus there was a lack of sensitivity towards an extensive interpretation of the right to self-determination there.

Consequently, German debate about what to do in the for-mer Yugoslavia was a highly emotional one. Due to the crimes committed by Hitler the question of how to deal with aggres-sors has been a sensitive topic. When the first horrible pictures from the Yugoslav battlefields were published, many Germans believed that inherited guilt from the Nazi era obliged the inter-national community to stop the human tragedy by means of force. As elsewhere, many intellectuals and politicians in Ger-many passionately called for military intervention. But, did the Nazi past indeed oblige the military forces of the new Germany to prevent aggressive conquest and mass expulsion in the for-mer Yugoslavia or did it, on the contrary, force the country to refrain from any military engagement in the area? Obviously, history was not able to give an appropriate answer to the ques-tion of what should be the proper response to the Yugoslav war.

3.   THE QUESTION OF RECOGNITION

Until mid-1991 the German government stayed in line with the EC which was concentrating on trying to promote a united

Yugoslavia. Despite the rapid fragmentation of the Yugoslav Federation the Germans agreed that a solution had to be found on
the basis of the following principles: a large degree of independence for the republics, the preservation of a common Yugoslav
institutional framework and far-reaching rights for the ethnic
minorities.

After the outbreak of the hostilities between the Yugoslav Federal Army and the republics striving for independence, German
Foreign Minister Hans-Dietrich Genscher came under strong
pressure. Leading Social Democrats, such as party leader Björn
Engholm and foreign policy spokesman Norbert Gansel, demanded recognition of Croatia and Slovenia, and applied for
a special meeting of the Bundestag. Strongly supported by the
German mass media, more and more Christian Democrats,
such as foreign policy spokesman Karl Lamers, also challenged
Genscher, claiming to fulfil the right to self-determination of
the Yugoslav nations.[16]

As early as July 1991, consensus appeared to be emerging in
Bonn on changing Germany's foreign policy towards Yugoslavia. Genscher declared that if the Yugoslav People's Army (YPA)
continued to disturb the peace efforts, recognition of Slovenia
and Croatia could become inevitable.[17] Thus, he referred to a
memorandum on the country's conduct in the conflict worked
out in May 1991 in which officials of the German Foreign Ministry recommended support for Croatia and Slovenia as a democratic and market-orientated bridge between the EC and the
Balkans.[18]

In the following months, German diplomats repeatedly maintained that Serbia was using the negotiations as a diplomatic
shield to continue the war and tried to convince their European
partners to recognise the breakaway republics as independent
states. Contrary to what some observers claimed, Bonn had little
interest in handling the Yugoslav crisis within any other international framework than the EC. At the meeting of the EC Foreign Ministers on 6 October 1991 it was agreed that 'a political
solution should be sought in the perspective of recognition of
the independence of those republics wishing it, at the end of
a negotiating process conducted in good faith and involving
all parties'.[19]

However, there were different opinions about the handling
of the war of dissolution and the question of recognition. While

most of the Europeans shared the opinion that Yugoslavia could be maintained, only the Germans argued at this time that the federal state had already disintegrated into individual components. Despite rather strong opposition within the EC, Bonn believed that the internationalisation of the Yugoslav crisis, ensuing from recognition, would deter the Yugoslav army from expanding the conflict. Furthermore, they estimated that the international community could exert effective pressure to end the hostilities. Unfortunately, none of these hopes was realised.

Many EC members feared that the decision to recognise the republics striving for independence would lead to an escalation and widening of the conflict. In a leading article *The Times* wrote, 'the most probable result would be to intensify the fighting in Croatia and spread the war'.[20] Contrary to leading politicians and journalists abroad, only a few German diplomats and experts warned against early recognition of the breakaway republics with regard to Bosnia and Macedonia. Disregarding the advice of a strong anti-recognition coalition including the UN Secretary-General, Javier Perez de Cuellar, George Bush, and the negotiators of the international community, Cyrus Vance and Lord Carrington, in early December 1991 the German government announced its willingness to recognise Slovenia and Croatia unilaterally by Christmas. Under strong German pressure, the EC Foreign Ministers decided on 16 December that they would 'implement' recognition of those Yugoslav republics that requested it on 15 January, provided they respected democracy and minority rights and supported UN and EC peace efforts.[21] Applications were to be sent to the EC Arbitration Committee headed by the French constitutional expert Robert Badinter, who was expected to deliver his final report in January 1992. Nevertheless, Germany recognised the independence of Croatia and Slovenia on 23 December, three weeks before the date agreed by the EC, and promised to open diplomatic relations.

The German urge to recognise Slovenia and Croatia has been harshly criticised. Many have pointed a finger at Bonn for forcing the EC into early recognition.[22] The EC mediator Henry Wynaendts, the US Secretary of State Warren Christopher and the French Foreign Minister Roland Dumas all held Genscher responsible for the widening warfare in the Balkans.[23] Did not recognition deprive the EC negotiators of the leverage to find an overall political solution?

German officials and the media reacted to the international criticism by emphasising that all EC member states in fact agreed to recognition, thus sharing responsibility for the political consequences. Recognition was designed to strengthen democracy and resistance against the Serb aggression, the German ambassador to the United States wrote.[24] However, the internationalisation of the crisis was not able to prevent the war from spreading. When Croatia was recognised as a sovereign state, the Serbs had already achieved their territorial objectives in Krajina and East Slavonia. Large parts of Croatia were in Serb hands. In April 1992, EC countries and the United States also recognised Bosnia and Herzegovina. This was followed shortly thereafter by an escalation of the fighting, since the Serbs resisted any separation from their Yugoslav homeland.

It was highly contradictory to recognise the dissolution of the multinational Yugoslavia while trying to hold Bosnia together. The long-term consequences of recognition were hardly thought through. Why should not Serbs and Albanians have the right to national unity and self-determination, if this was granted the Croats? Moreover, the credibility of the German approach depended ultimately on the ability and willingness of the international community to use military force. Yet none of them, least of all Germany, was prepared to protect the new independent states by military means. Not surprisingly, the internationalisation of the Yugoslav crisis could not prevent violence unless major actors were prepared to guarantee territorial integrity by force.

Regarding the undeniable dissolution of the multiethnic state, the crucial question was not whether the republics would achieve independence, but when and under what conditions. Bosnia's way to independence in particular was overshadowed by some severe structural problems. During 1991 the ruling parties became deadlocked over issues related to Bosnian sovereignty and the future constitutional structure of the multiethnic republic. The fruitless debate on the establishment of the republic created a persisting constitutional and legal vacuum, and provoked the total disintegration of Bosnia's state structures well before international recognition. There was very little hope that the sovereignty of the multiethnic republic could be maintained.[25] The complexity of the situation in the former Yugoslavia was more than German diplomats and other major actors could comprehend.

Some observers argued that Germany had no consistent Balkan policy whatsoever, but relied purely on moral considerations. 'Evidently, by recognising Croatia and Slovenia, German foreign policy was not assuming more responsibility for the Balkans. It simply used this highly symbolic action to escape further commitments in the peace-keeping effort. The apparant German ambition merely disguised the actual paralysis of its foreign policy.'[26] The question of recognition was embedded in the broader discussion of the legitimate use of force in international politics.

4.   THE GERMAN DEBATE ON MILITARY INTERVENTION

The recognition debate took place in view of the fact that Germany would not be able to participate in any military operation out of the North Atlantic Treaty area. Due to recent German history, under the German constitution, military forces are supposed to act under only two circumstances: self-defence of German territory and participation in allied missions within NATO territory. Article 87a of the Basic Law says: 'Apart from defence, the armed forces may only be used to the extent explicitly permitted by this constitution.' Article 24 authorises the Federal Republic to enter a mutual collective security system. In doing so it will consent to such limitations upon its rights of sovereignty as will bring about and secure a peaceful and lasting order in Europe and the world.

Regardless of the constitutional constraints in Germany, as well as in other Western countries, many intellectuals and politicians passionately called for military intervention in Croatia and in Bosnia-Herzegovina, or at least the lifting of the arms embargo in favour of the Muslims. This so-called bellicose wing came from various political parties as well as from the peace movement. Thus, opposition to the Government's policy cut across political lines. In view of the terrible violations of human rights in the former Yugoslavia, however, the possibility of military solutions was also intensively debated.

Since the Gulf War a tortuous controversy within Germany

focused on the question of whether the German Basic Law as such prohibited out-of-area deployments of the Bundeswehr.[27] Whilst some politicians and constitutional experts argued that the constitution authorised the employment of the Bundeswehr only in the case of Germany or one of its NATO partners being attacked, others believed that the use of force 'out of area' had already been permitted, provided it occurred within the framework of the United Nations.[28]

Both governing parties, the Christian Democrats and the Liberals, agreed that Germany must participate in peace-keeping as well as peace-enforcement actions mandated by the UN. The government argued that non-participation would compromise Germany's reliability as a partner in the Atlantic Alliance and that the Federal Republic had to fulfil its duties as a 'world citizen'.[29] Leading politicians considered that Germany could no longer enjoy 'the luxury of being an economic giant but a political dwarf.' In order to win a rotating seat on the UN Security Council and a permanent seat thereafter, Germany should be prepared to share the international burden of crisis management, including the contribution of Bundeswehr soldiers to UN peace-keeping forces. Last but not least, there was strong criticism within the Christian Democrats against the perceived 'do-nothing-policy' of the government towards the conflicts in the former Yugoslavia.

With the exception of the PDS (the successor to the former Communist party in the GDR), the main opposition parties, the Social Democrats as well as the Greens, could find no consensus. Whilst the party conventions of the Greens clearly rejected any deployment of German soldiers abroad, some leading politicians called for humanitarian intervention to stop the bloodshed in Bosnia. But the feminists and the so-called 'realist' wing met the decisive opposition of the clear-cut anti-militaristic forces within the party. The majority of the Greens seemed to prefer strictly non-violent means of foreign policy.

The debate within the Social Democrats was even more controversial. When in 1991 the former party leader Björn Engholm pleaded for German participation in blue helmet missions, he encountered opposition from both sides. Some, such as Caucus leader Hans-Ulrich Klose, and the foreign policy experts Norbert Gansel and Karsten Voigt, recommended authorisation for all deployments within the framework of the UN. Others, chiefly the pacifists and the left wing, rejected the use of military force in general.[30] The SPD was also split over the question of whether Germany should participate in the NATO activities in order to protect the eventual withdrawal of the UN peace-keeping forces. Party leader Rudolf Scharping maintained that Germany must be ready to live up to its international obligations. But politicians of the party's left wing, such as the MP Heidemarie Wieczorek-Zeul and the Prime Minister of Saarland, Oskar Lafontaine, clung to the distinction between permissible UN peace-keeping activities and impermissible NATO-only peace-enforcement operations.

Notwithstanding vehement criticism of European policy in Yugoslavia, the majority of Germans seemed to prefer non-military solutions. Opinion polls continued to show a public unwilling to commit ground forces. In late summer of 1992, 39 per cent of Germans agreed that the Bundeswehr should not participate in military missions 'out of area', and 44 per cent supported unarmed peace-keeping operations under the umbrella of the UN. Only 14 per cent thought it would be appropriate to include German Bundeswehr in any peace-enforcement activities.[31] Despite a trend of growing support for different kinds of UN deployments by the Bundeswehr, a great part of the German public remained reluctant to accept the use of military force for other than defence matters. In December 1994, 53 per cent of those polled opposed the deployment of Bundeswehr in Bosnia, but at the same time supported the UN peace-keeping operations. More than 50 per cent agreed that the blue helmets should be entitled to use military force in order to secure the transport of humanitarian goods.[32]

Regardless of the ongoing debate about whether the Bundeswehr was or was not allowed to operate outside the NATO area, the Ministry of Defence began its planning for future German participation in global missions. In addition to making a contribution to the collective defence of Alliance territory, both the Defence Guidance of November 1992 and the *Bundeswehrplan* 1994 emphasised the tasks of crisis management and conflict prevention. For this purpose, the White Paper pointed out that Germany needed standing, rapidly available and mobile forces. Therefore, the main defence forces (MDF) were to be complemented by reaction forces (RF), that is contingents that can be employed for conflict prevention and crisis management within the Alliance framework and as a contribution to international peace missions. From October 1993 onwards two German battalions were trained for UN missions.[33] At the same time, the government gradually expanded Germany's out-of-area presence. In the aftermath of the Gulf War in 1991 the Bundeswehr was active in providing personnel and material support to UN missions. The first German soldiers ever to assist in a UN peace-keeping operation were the members of a medical unit sent to Cambodia in Spring 1992. In 1993, 1700 German soldiers participated in the UNOSOM II mission in Somalia.

In the Balkans, German soldiers were to participate in four international missions. Under the umbrella of the UN the German Air Force has been participating in the international Zagreb–Sarajevo airlift since 3 July 1992 and since 28 March 1993 in the airdrop of supplies over Eastern Bosnia. Since 18 July 1992 the German Navy has been supporting the NATO and WEU measures conducted to monitor the embargo on the former Yugoslavia in the Adriatic. Last but not least, in October 1992 German military personnel became part of NATO's AWACS radar-aircraft crews patrolling Bosnian airspace.[34]

In April 1993 the Free Democrats and the Social Democrats put this matter before the Federal Constitutional Court in Karlsruhe. They argued that the government had illegally provided troops for the UN operation in Somalia and for NATO's enforcement of UN sanctions against Serbia and Montenegro, as well as for the patrolling of the airspace over Bosnia. Germany's highest judges had to decide whether German soldiers can be put into action outside the NATO defence area in UN peace operations. In two provisional judgments, in April and June 1993, the German Constitutional Court refused to suspend the AWACS mission and the Bundeswehr's involvement in Somalia. On 12 July 1994, it ruled that Germany could take part in military operations beyond the country's borders without having to modify its constitution.[35] The judges agreed that the constitutional provisions authorising German participation in security organisations like NATO, the WEU, and the UN also meant that the Federal Republic could take part in their operations abroad. 'Peace forces and their task of securing peace are part of the United Nations' system of collective security as it has developed through the practical application of the UN charter, which the Federal Republic of Germany joined in 1973', the judges ruled.[36] But at the same time they required that any mission of this type had to be authorised by a simple majority of the German parliament, as the Constitution obliges the Federal Government to seek enabling agreement by the German Bundestag, as a rule in advance, before committing the armed forces to action. By going ahead in Somalia and in the former Yugoslavia in 1992 and 1993 the coalition had violated Germany's Basic Law, the judges concluded.[37]

In spite of the fact that the German brigade in Somalia had already pulled out in February 1994, the government stated it would 'promptly' seek explicit parliamentary approval of German participation in the continuing operations. At a special meeting on 22 July, the Bundestag, with 424 in favour, 48 against, and with 16 abstentions, approved of the participation by German soldiers in current missions.

Immediately after the ruling of the Constitutional Court, Foreign Minister Klaus Kinkel cautioned 'against overestimating our importance . . . We have done well with our policy of restraint. In the future, we will still be saying "no" more often than "yes".'[38] Kinkel made clear that German participation in international peace activities will depend on certain conditions: any mission must be legitimised by international law, the risk must be calculable, any military operation must help to find a political solution.[39] Furthermore, he stressed that the ruling 'will not lead to the militarisation of Germany's foreign policy'.[40] Germany would never pursue an interventionist policy.

In December 1994 the request from NATO for German Tornado planes to be deployed in Bosnia reopened deep wounds over Germany's new role in Europe. NATO asked the German government to send Tornado fighter-bombers to help protect UN peace-keepers. The Tornadoes would be part of the air armada which was patrolling the skies of Bosnia to enforce the no-fly zone and could be called on to oversee a UN pull-out under fire. This would have been the first deployment of German fighting forces abroad since the end of the Second World War. Being aware of the sensitivity of the issue the government delayed taking a decision. After the October elections it was by no means certain that the German parliament would approve such a deployment. Finally, it was noted that there was 'no formal or official demand' from NATO, and that the government therefore saw 'no need to take a decision.'[41] But on 20 December 1994 the government declared it would be ready to provide logistical assistance and combat air cover, but not ground troops, in the event of a withdrawal of UN peace-keeping forces from Bosnia.

In the face of NATO's request Foreign Minister Klaus Kinkel expressed reluctance. For historical reasons, the domestic taboos about participation in military action abroad remained strong. Hitler's cutting up of Yugoslavia in 1941 and the four-year occupation by the German Wehrmacht were not yet forgotten. Serbs had expressed suspicion that Germany's real aim is a 'fourth Reich' in the Balkans. Therefore, the German government was thoroughly convinced that the presence of German soldiers in the former Yugoslavia would intensify the conflict. Kinkel said it was necessary to think 'very seriously' about the question of whether the former Yugoslavia is the 'place where we must make a stronger commitment following the decision of the constitutional court'.[42] 'German soldiers would be part of the problem, not part of the solution', the German defence minister, Volker Rühe, added. Only the Christian Democrat parliamentary leader, Wolfgang Schäuble, mentioned the possibility of Bundeswehr participation in any UN implementation of a truce in the former Yugoslavia.[43]

Moreover, the majority of German military experts believed that ends and means of troop deployments were out of all proportion, that the political and military risks were incalculable and that the chance of a political success was very small.[44] Nobody knew on what political and constitutional grounds Serbs, Croats and Muslims could live together. A second argument concerned the extent, duration and thus the costs of any military engagement. Experts thought an army of from 100 000 up to 500 000 soldiers to be necessary in order to stabilise the region on a long-term basis. There was little inclination to participate in such a costly operation. Furthermore, due to the geography of Yugoslavia and the guerrilla activity of the warlords a military intervention would undoubtedly be of considerable danger to the ground forces. During the Second World War the German Wehrmacht learned about the methods of the partisans.[45] As far as this was concerned, German arguments hardly differed from those of other European countries.[46]

Nevertheless, the German defence minister emphasised that

the trend towards Germany's greater military involvement will continue: 'We know that military missions are expected of us – and that we will have to respond to these expectations.'[47] Thus, the debate on how the international community should react to the Balkan war proved to be a catalyst empowering Germany to participate in international blue helmet missions and peace-enforcement operations, even though a deployment in the former Yugoslavia itself was out of the question.

5. TOWARDS CONTAINMENT POLICY

As an alternative to military solutions the German government, among others, recommended the imposition of diplomatic, political and economic sanctions against Serbia and Montenegro.[48] But it was not until the outbreak of the war in Bosnia-Herzegovina, which had been recognised as an independent state in April 1992, that the Security Council through its resolution 757 paved the way for an extensive trade embargo. In fact, it was soon proved to be true that the UN embargo of 30 May 1992 did not basically change the position of the Serbs. Although the sanctions have caused serious damage to Serbia and Montenegro, they have not achieved their political and military intention. Neither the cessation of the war nor a fundamental political change inside Serbia has been brought about. As one of the few remaining options aimed at stopping the war the German government demanded a total isolation of Belgrade in February 1993.

German policy towards Yugoslavia developed essentially out of two premises: first, it was clear that neither Germany nor any other country would become militarily engaged in the war, thus eliminating all violent alternatives; secondly, it was equally clear that economic sanctions would need a long preliminary phase in order to have any effect at all. Thus, Bonn and other EC countries took the course of a policy of containment. This policy of damage limitation seemed to serve best Germany's national interest and had several goals. What German interests, if any, were at stake in ex-Yugoslavia?[49]

First of all, the war in the former Yugoslavia jeopardised the rule of law, human rights and the restructuring of the political order towards democracy in Eastern Europe. Any direct violation of these fundamental principles and goals posed a direct threat to Germany's interest in maintaining stability and order in Europe. The unprecedented cruelty of the war undermined all rules of conduct that the European states had elaborated to ensure peace and security on the continent.[50] A second interest developed out of the geopolitically central location of the Federal Republic and its relative proximity to the war-torn regions. Since the outbreak of the hostilities a huge refugee wave was moving away from the violence into neighbouring countries, principally Germany. In only a few months, some 324 000 Yugoslavs had come to the Federal Republic, imposing political and economic strains. Following the so-called asylum debate, a major issue in German politics since the 1980s, politicians tried to stop the influx of refugees as quickly as possible. Many Germans seemed convinced that further immigration had to be prevented.

Furthermore, the long-term stability of the region was at stake, in many respects. As a result of the widening warfare in Bosnia, other neighbouring countries such as Albania, Greece and Bulgaria, and Turkey itself, might be drawn in, thus causing a full-scale Balkan war. This was another important factor to be considered in preventing the spread of war to other regions, first of all to Kosovo and Macedonia. On the other hand, the national and religious consciousness of the Muslims has increasingly become important following the ethnic cleansing activities of the Serbs. There was the attendant risk of fundamentalism and terrorism arising out of the desperate displaced populations. Last but not least, the events in the former Yugoslavia set a precedent. The expulsion of many hundreds of thousands of people and the redrawing of borders by force could serve as a bad example for other hot-spots in Eastern Europe. Preventing the regional proliferation of belligerent action was viewed as a prime diplomatic goal.

A damage limitation exercise became more urgent as the war went on and public outrage soared. There was a strong feeling that the shameful ineffectiveness of the international community threatened the prestige and credibility of Western security institutions. Divergences between European governments over how to handle the Yugoslav crisis provoked severe tensions within the alliance. Mutual recriminations over omissions and commissions undermined the existing security structures.

In this way, the Yugoslav war deeply affected the identity and coherence of the West.

And yet, despite these major challenges at the international level, the Yugoslav war was primarily defined as a humanitarian problem, rather than as a danger to security. In May 1992 the UN Security Council declared in its resolution 752 the urgent necessity of supporting the people in Bosnia. The German Foreign Minister repeatedly emphasised the German humanitarian commitment.[51] In 1993 the Federal Republic contributed DM 34 million to the airlift to Sarajevo, DM 16 million to the German share of transport assistance, and DM 65 million to finance the embargo surveillance.[52] As of October 1994, Bonn had disbursed DM 725 million for humanitarian purposes in the former Yugoslavia.

Primarily humanitarian motives led Bonn to play a more active part in the course of 1993. On the approach of the second winter of war, a joint Franco-German peace initiative was launched. Experts had predicted that during the winter vast numbers of civilians would die through starvation and lack of medical supplies. In a letter sent on 8 November 1993 to their colleagues, the two Foreign Ministers, Alain Juppé and Klaus Kinkel, suggested a stage-by-stage approach to bring about a peace arrangement, consisting of an agreement on a territorial solution in Bosnia, and a *modus vivendi* in Krajina; immediately afterwards, two conferences would be held during which questions of implementation and other remaining problems would be discussed. The proposal envisaged gradual suspension of sanctions against Serbia and Montenegro and promised strong economic support to Croatia and Bosnia.[53]

The proposal proceeded from the fact that the Serbs had already achieved most of their war aims. The peace plan envisaged the creation of a Serbian–Muslim–Croatian confederation and was in line with the Croatian and Serbian demands to carve up Bosnia. Following a transitional period the future Bosnian constituent states were enabled to opt for unification with the neighbouring republics. In order to achieve a gradual relaxation of sanctions the Serbs were expected to accept and effectively implement this plan. Thus, contrary to earlier declarations, the German government for the first time indicated that it would be possible for the Serbs to regain access to the international financial and other markets. Foreign Minister

Klaus Kinkel continued to maintain that 'aggression must not be allowed to succeed in Bosnia'. Evidently warlike activities should be terminated even at the expense of an unjust peace settlement.

In view of strong pressure from public opinion, both in the US and Germany after the collapse of the Geneva peace talks in February 1993, the German government began a campaign to lift the international arms embargo on Bosnia and Herzegovina. Together with the Americans the German government argued that the Muslims should be given weapons to defend themselves. Even though Kohl and Kinkel had always been close to the American view, they made clear that Germany would not drop out of the European convoy on the embargo issue. Washington appeared to be shifting its policy towards arming the Muslim forces, but the Federal Republic would not support a selective lifting of the arms embargo.

After the international recognition of the former Yugoslav republics, Germany played a far more modest role than at the outset of the war. For many months, German diplomacy stayed in the background but at the same time Bonn actively supported all efforts by the international community to end the war. In the framework of the international peace efforts German diplomats helped to negotiate an agreement to set up a Croat–Muslim Federation loosely linked to Croatia in March 1994. Germany became a member of the International Contact Group and participated in guiding the peace talks between the belligerent parties thereafter. In order to reconcile the enemies, the former Mayor of the city of Bremen, Hans Koschnick, was sent as EU administrator to Mostar.

CONCLUSION

The outbreak of the Yugoslav crisis coincided with the beginning of a new era for Germany. Preoccupied by internal problems and confused about the country's future international role, German Balkan policy suffered from fundamental errors and omissions. Policy towards the former Yugoslavia was characterised by misperceptions and faulty analyses of the long-term challenges, and by a lack of adequate policy concepts. Germany, however, had this in common with many other major actors.

The German view on the Yugoslav war was overshadowed by the historical experience of the Nazi past. Many Germans believed that inherited guilt obliged the Federal Republic to assume responsibility for the people in the former Yugoslavia. But, due to historical reasons, the Basic Law did not allow the participation of the Bundeswehr in any military operation out of the North Atlantic Treaty area. Thus, the internationalisation of the crisis through recognition of the former Yugoslav republics as independent states was seen by many in Germany as the only way to contain the war. But, obviously, the weakness of the German approach was that the Federal Republic was not prepared to back up its policy by force. A major problem of the German approach to the conflicts in the former Yugoslavia, therefore, consisted in creating a new political order in the Balkans that no one was willing or able to protect.

Nevertheless, the case of Yugoslavia opened a wider debate on the legitimate use of force in international relations. Thus, Germany's policy towards the former Yugoslavia was embedded in a reconsideration of the country's international role in general. Despite the reluctance to send ground forces to the Balkan battlefields the cruelty of the Yugoslav wars and the question of how to respond to them proved to be a catalyst in legitimising out-of-area deployments of the Bundeswehr. But even after the ruling of the German Constitutional Court allowing the Federal Republic to take part in military operations beyond the country's borders, Germany abstained from military involvement in Bosnia. The events in the former Yugoslavia were not regarded as a major concern in German foreign policy. Despite the Court ruling, Germany's policy towards the former Yugoslavia adheres to the basic lines followed since 1992.

NOTES

1.   A. Zunker (ed.), *Weltordnung oder Chaos?* (Baden-Baden: Nomos, 1993); K. Kaiser and H. W. Maull (eds), *Deutschlands neue Außenpolitik*, vol. I (Munich: Oldenburg, 1994); W. Heydrich *et al.* (eds), *Sicherheitspolitik Deutschlands: Neue Konstellationen, Risiken, Instrumente* (Baden-Baden: Nomos, 1992).

2. M. H. A. van Heuven, 'Testing the New Germany: The Case of Yugoslavia', *German Politics and Society*, XXIX (1993), pp. 52–63.
3. W. Krieger, 'Toward a Gaullist Germany? Some Lessons from the Yugoslav Crisis', *World Policy Journal* (Spring 1994), pp. 26–38.
4. E. Rondholz, 'Deutsche Erblasten im jugoslawischen Bürgerkrieg', *Blätter für deutsche und internationale Politik*, XXXVII (1992), pp. 829– 838; M. Korinman, 'L'Autriche, l'Allemagne et les Slaves du Sud', *Hérodote* 63 (1991), pp. 52–65; Y. Lacoste, 'La question serbe et la question allemande', *Hérodote* 67 (1992), pp. 3–48.
5. E. A. Radice, 'The German Economic Programme in Eastern Europe', in M. C. Kaser (ed.), *The Economic History of Eastern Europe*, vol. II (Oxford: Clarendon Press, 1986), pp. 299–308.
6. H. C. Meyer, *Mitteleuropa in German Thought and Action 1815–1945* (The Hague, 1955).
7. J. R. Lampe and M. R. Jackson, *Balkan Economic History, 1550–1950* (Bloomington: Indiana University Press, 1982), p. 468.
8. H.-U. Wehler, *Nationalitätenpolitik in Jugoslawien. Die deutsche Minderheit 1918–1978* (Göttingen, 1980).
9. *Definitivni rezultati popisa stanovnistva od 31. marta 1931 godine* (Beograd 1938).
10. D. Biber, *Nacizem in Nemci v Jugoslaviji 1933–1941* (Ljubljana, 1966); P. Bagnell, *The Influence of National Socialism on the German Minority in Yugoslavia* (Ann Arbor, 1977); A. Komjathy and R. Stockwell, *German Minorities and the Third Reich* (New York, 1980).
11. *Das Schicksal der Deutschen in Jugoslawien. Dokumentation der Vertreibung der Deutschen aus Ost-Mitteleuropa*, vol. V, 2nd ed. (Munich: DTV, 1984).
12. H. Sundhaussen, 'Jugoslawisch-deutsche Beziehungen zwischen Normalisierung, Bruch und erneuter Normalisierung', in O. N. Haberl and H. Hecker (eds), *Unfertige Nachbarschaften* (Essen: Reimar Hobbing, 1989), pp. 133–51.
13. *Statisticki godisnjak Jugoslavije* (Belgrade, 1991), p. 318.
14. B. Pavlica, *Jugoslavija i SR Nemacka 1951–1984* (Smederovo, 1989), p. 152.
15. Ch. Jelavich, 'American Perceptions of the South Slavs, 1875–1941', *Rad 405 JAZU*, vol. XXII (Zagreb: Jugoslavenska Akademija Znanosti i Umjetnosti, 1984), p. 203.
16. H.-J. Axt, 'Hat Genscher Jugoslawien entzweit? Mythen und Fakten zur Außenpolitik des vereinten Deutschlands', *Europa-Archiv*, XLVIII 12 (1993), pp. 351–60.
17. *Süddeutsche Zeitung*, 8 July 1991.
18. M. Thumann, 'Between Ambition and Paralysis: Germany's Balkan Policy, 1991–1994' in *The Balkans and CFSP. The Views of Greece and Germany* (Brussels: Centre for European Policy Studies, 1994), p. 25.
19. M. Libal, 'Grundfragen der Jugoslawienkrise aus deutscher Sicht', in G. Wagenlehner (ed.), *Konflikte, Konfliktlösung und Friedenssicherung in Südosteuropa* (Munich, 1994), pp. 234–8.
20. *The Times*, 11 December 1991.
21. 'Guidelines on the Recognition of New States in Eastern Europe and in the Soviet Union, adopted by the Council of the European Community

on 17 December 1991', in H.-J. Heintze, *Selbstbestimmungsrecht und Minderheitenrecht im Völkerrecht. Herausforderungen an den globalen und regionalen Menschenrechtsschutz* (Baden-Baden, 1994), p. 231ff.

22. J. Newhouse, 'Bonn, der Westen und die Auflösung Jugoslawiens. Das Versagen der Diplomatie – Chronik eines Skandals', *Blätter für deutsche und internationale Politik*, XXXVII (1992), pp. 1190–205; A. Mühlen, 'Die deutsche Rolle bei der Anerkennung der jugoslawischen Sezessionsstaaten', *Liberal*, XXXIV (1992), pp. 49–55; A. Heinrich, 'Neue deutsche Außenpolitik. Selbstversuche zwischen Zagreb und Brüssel', *Blätter für deutsche und internationale Politik*, XXXVI (1992), pp. 1446–58.

23. H. Wynaendts, *L'engrenage. Chroniques yougoslaves, juillet 1991–août 1992* (Paris, 1993).

24. *The Washington Post*, 28 June 1993.

25. M.-J. Calic, *Der Krieg in Bosnien-Hercegovina. Ursachen Konfliktstrukturen, internationale Lösungsversuche* (Frankfurt: Suhrkamp, 1995).

26. Thumann, op. cit., p. 29.

27. B. K. W. Bähr, 'Verfassungsmäßigkeit des Einsatzes der Bundeswehr im Rahmen der Vereinten Nationen', *Zeitschrift für Rechtspolitik*, XXVII (1994), pp. 97–103; J. H. Schwarz and A. Steinkamm (eds), *Rechtliche und politische Probleme des Einsatzes der Bundeswehr 'out of area'* (Baden-Baden: Nomos, 1993).

28. O. Diehl, 'UN-Einsätze der Bundeswehr. Außenpolitische Handlungszwänge und innenpolitischer Konsensbedarf', *Europa-Archiv*, XLVIII (1993), pp. 219–27.

29. H. Müller, 'Military Intervention for European Security: The German Debate', in L. Freedman (ed.), *Military Intervention in European Conflicts* (Oxford: Blackwell, 1994), pp. 125–41.

30. Ibid., p. 134.

31. Ibid., p. 140.

32. *Süddeutsche Zeitung*, 17/18 December 1994.

33. *Informationen zur Sicherheitspolitik. Die Bundeswehr der Zukunft – Bundeswehrplan '94* (Bonn: Federal Ministry of Defence, 1993), p. 5.

34. *White Paper on the Security of the Federal Republic of Germany and the Situation and Future of the Bundeswehr* (Bonn: Federal Ministry of Defence, 1994), p. 66.

35. *Stichworte zur Sicherheitspolitik*, VIII (1994), pp. 17–34.

36. Ibid., p. 25.

37. Ibid., p. 34.

38. *Bulletin*, 22 April 1994, p. 311.

39. *Bulletin*, 26 July 1994, p. 663.

40. 'Erklärung der Bundesregierung. Konsequenzen aus dem Urteil des Bundesverfassungsgerichts', *Bulletin*, 26 July 1994, p. 658.

41. *Süddeutsche Zeitung*, 8 December 1994.

42. *Atlantic News*, 3 December 1994.

43. *Neue Zürcher Zeitung*, 20 April 1994.

44. H. M. Mey, 'Germany, NATO, and the War in the Former Yugoslavia', *Comparative Strategy*, XII (1993), pp. 239–45.

45. J. Hippler, 'Irreguläre Kriegführung und die Schwierigkeiten externer

Intervention', in V. Matthies (ed.), *Frieden durch Einmischung?* (Bonn, 1993), pp. 139–54; M. F. Cancian, 'The Wehrmacht in Yugoslavia: Lessons of the Past?', *Parameters* 23 (1993), pp. 75–84; *German Antiguerilla Operations in the Balkans (1941–1944)* (Washington, DC, 1989).

46. P. M. Cronin, 'Perspectives on Policy and Strategy', *Strategic Review*, XX (1992), pp. 65–9.
47. *The Independent*, 8 December 1994.
48. *Süddeutsche Zeitung*, 29 July 1992.
49. L. Rühl, 'Einige Kriterien nationaler Interessenbestimmung', in W. Heydrich, *Sicherheitspolitik Deutschlands*, pp. 741–59; M. Stürmer, 'Deutsche Interessen', in Kaiser and Maull, op. cit., pp. 39–61; D. Senghaas, 'Was sind der Deutschen Interessen?', *Blätter für deutsche und internationale Politik*, XXXVIII (1993), pp. 673–87.
50. U. Nerlich, 'Balkan Security in the European Post-Cold War Environment: Challenges and Policy Choices for the West', in F. St. Larrabee (ed.), *The Volatile Powder Keg: Balkan Security after the Cold War* (Washington, DC: Rand, 1994), pp. 275–92.
51. Auswärtiges Amt/Arbeitsstab Humanitäre Hilfe, *Die humanitäre Hilfe der Bundesrepublik Deutschland für die Opfer des Konflikts im ehemaligen Jugoslawien* (Bonn, 10 November 1993).
52. *Frankfurter Allgemeine*, 30 July 1994.
53. *Atlantic News*, 24 November 1993.

4 French Perspectives

Olivier Lepick

> From Richelieu to General De Gaulle, the historic mission of France has always been to refuse the construction of any barrier or wall in the heart of the European continent.
>
> Alain Juppé[1]

Given the helpless international context as regards the tragic situation in the former Yugoslavia, France has taken a singular stand. Paris will not be accused of inactivity or indifference, as the French *Casques Bleus* are on the front line and 22 of them have already been killed in action (at the time of writing). Paris was the active instigator of humanitarian aid; and President François Mitterrand made a foray into Sarajevo in June 1992 and opened up the way to this aid in the besieged Bosnian capital. His active policy enabled him to draw attention to other less committed, European partners. Nevertheless, France's attitude is not without ambiguity and ambivalence. As a man of his own generation, shaped by history, Mitterrand did not easily accept the break-up of the Yugoslavian Federation in June 1991, fearing above all a spread of instability to the eastern region of Europe, thus creating a dangerous precedent. It took him a whole year, until the European Summit in Lisbon in June 1992, to recognise the unmistakable responsibility of Serbia for the conflict, even though no Western country has come out of the crisis unscathed. Finally, having emphasised the humanitarian dimension, Paris put off all political decisions for a considerable time until the worsening situation in Bosnia compelled action of some sort.

Undoubtedly the Yugoslav crisis indicates the depth of the challenge that French foreign policymakers had to face in the post-Cold War era. In fact, beyond Balkan implications and consequences, the crisis in former Yugoslavia has affected and even modified many of France's long established diplomatic relations or guidelines such as relations with the reunified Germany, European collective security concerns (NATO, WEU), and the role of the European Union in the security of the continent.

Throughout the crisis, French objectives, based both on historical and legal perspectives, have remained constant: first and foremost, to put an end to the violence, to find a solution equitable for all ethnic groups based on the rule of international law; secondly, to assert a French concern in the peace process; and thirdly, to prevent the conflict from spreading to other regions of the Balkans by establishing a *cordon sanitaire*. Since the outbreak of the crisis in 1991, however, French foreign policy has passed through two major phases. In the first phase, Paris tried to promote its objectives through international organisations such as the EC and then the UN, hoping to reach a 'legal' solution to the crisis.[2] In the second phase, slowly realising that this approach seemed to be hopeless, Paris favoured an opportunistic coalition with its traditional partners in order to end the violence in the region, an orientation leading to the creation of the so-called 'Contact Group' of five countries: France, Great Britain, Germany, Russia and the United States.

BITTER HOPES: FROM EC TO UN

In the initial stage, the French Government followed an active national policy in coordination with the European Community. One should keep in mind that, when the crisis broke out, the Maastricht summit was due to take place at the end of the year. This was a crucial issue for the French Government. President Mitterrand and Elisabeth Guigou, the minister in charge of European affairs, who strongly supported the ambition to achieve monetary union and a common foreign and security policy (CFSP), saw the Yugoslav crisis as a test for the CFSP and an opportunity to demonstrate that the European Community was indeed able to hold a common line. A general consensus rapidly emerged among EC members that Yugoslavia should remain united, and that this issue should be dealt with by the Europeans – and therefore that the United States should not be involved in the crisis management process. This was exactly the political logic that the French diplomatic services adopted. In fact, Paris supported a unified Yugoslavia for several reasons. Most importantly, France feared that the implosion of the Yugoslav Federation could threaten Mikhail Gorbachev's reform policy in the Soviet Union and could also provoke the rise of ethnic and national conflict in the Eastern part of Europe. In this perspective, the French Government considered territorial integrity as important as self-determination and promoted the idea that a unified Yugoslavia would be an island of stability in this volatile region. Finally, French diplomats worried that a *Mitteleuropa* under German influence could emerge from Croatian and Slovenian independence.[3] Germany's focus of attention shifting east could undermine the Franco-German will and dynamism to deepen the European construction as it was expressed in the Maastricht Treaty.

France's activism to promote the Yugoslav Federation's unity was coupled with the clear intention not to blame Serbia exclusively for the outbreak of the civil war. To a large extent, France's position can be understood through the historical Franco-Serbian friendship built, as François Mitterrand declared in May 1991 while welcoming Prime Minister Ante Markovic, since 'the Napoleonïc era and reinforced by the two world wars'.[4] But it also signifies a deliberate attempt to act as an intermediary between Serbia and the international community. This approach was quite similar to the one France adopted towards Iraq at the beginning of the Gulf crisis. If successful, this attempt could be positive in many ways: first, Serbia would be grateful to France for having defended her cause; France would also have confirmed its influence in the region without displeasing its traditional allies (Serbia and Greece); and finally the French Government would have then played a central role in the peace process. This is one of the reasons why France maintained its rather neutral attitude until June 1992.

When Slovenia and Croatia declared their independence in June 1991 despite EC pressure, François Mitterrand and Roland Dumas, the minister of foreign affairs, voiced their disagreement, arguing that immediate recognition would increase tensions and violence. Throughout the autumn, as the crisis deepened following the signing of the Brioni Accords in July 1991, a dispute emerged between France and Germany over the issue of recognition.[5] The French Government maintained that independence should be decided at the EC level and only after issues such as refugees, borders and human rights had been settled. By the end of November, the German Government expressed its intention to recognise Slovenia and Croatia before Christmas. Through UN Resolution 724 (authorising the dispatch of a small group of military observers), strongly supported by France, Roland Dumas desperately tried to gain time in order to salvage the EC's emerging common foreign policy. On 16 December, Hans Dietrich Genscher announced that Germany would recognise Slovenia and Croatia, obliging France to accept a compromise over recognition. It was decided that any Yugoslav Republic fulfilling certain conditions would be recognised by the EC as a whole on 15 January 1992. But Germany recognised unilaterally Croatia and Slovenia on 23 December. The French Government considered this recognition not only a serious mistake but also a betrayal of the CFSP's aims. Some French officials expressed great concern and some real anger, raising '*le retour de la question allemande*'.[6] The episode generated a latent crisis in Franco-German relations.[7] However, presented with a *fait accompli* and knowing that it had little if any chance of preventing EC recognition of the two republics, France bitterly accepted the 15 January deadline. Afterwards, on numerous occasions, François Mitterrand stated his belief that 'this recognition without preliminary agreements had been a serious mistake'[8] and Roland Dumas declared that 'Germany was holding a crushing responsibility in the speeding up of the crisis'.[9]

Accepting the failure of the EC's attempt to establish peace in the former Yugoslavia and despite initial resistance by EC members, the French Government decided to place its hope in the United Nations.[10] As president of the UN Security Council, France supported a UN resolution to impose a ceasefire and to create a European interposition force in Yugoslavia. On 25 September 1991, UN Resolution 713 gave France only partial satisfaction. In fact, this new approach can be explained through two arguments. France's privileged position in the Security Council enabled French diplomacy to maintain an influential and even a leading role on this issue. Secondly, French officials believed that, for historical and political reasons, a neutral UN force was more appropriate in former Yugoslavia. Anyway, France realised that the WEU was not capable of sending a peace-keeping force to the region. Therefore, France voted in favour of UN Resolution 743 (21 February 1992) which created a UN peacekeeping force, and agreed to send a substantial contingent to Croatia.

In April 1992, as fighting broke out in Bosnia, the EC decided to recognise Bosnia's independence. France supported the process, arguing that extremists in Bosnia represented a small minority and that peace demonstrations in Serbia may call for moderation. But the continuing fighting proved French analysis to be wrong. By the beginning of June, the bombing and besieging of Sarajevo by the Bosnian Serbs had a tremendous impact on French public opinion. Many French intellectuals, voicing a general belief, called for immediate action to protect the inhabitants of Sarajevo. On 8 June, the UN Security Council (UN Resolution 758) authorised the dispatch of 1000 peace-keepers to protect the airport on condition that a ceasefire could be maintained. France immediately agreed to send troops while many other countries (Great Britain, Germany, United States) refused to do so.

At last, during the Lisbon Conference on 26 June, François Mitterrand decided to blame Serbia for being 'the aggressor'. This sudden inflection of French policy was a consequence of numerous factors. Firstly, the continuing fighting in Bosnia had made the longstanding French policy of blaming all the factions equally untenable. The French Government also worried that domestic public opinion, scandalised that repeated atrocities by the Serbs produced no real action from the EC, might have voted 'no' in the forthcoming Maastricht Treaty referendum. In this perspective, at the CSCE meeting in Helsinki, France supported WEU proposals to send some warships to the Adriatic to monitor the UN embargo against Serbia.

All of these factors, combined with EC and UN apathy, led François Mitterrand to make his surprising trip to Sarajevo on 28 June.[11] Though this initiative was an immediate success that enabled UN forces to take control of the airport, France was accused by Britain of threatening EC unity through this national initiative. This episode spurred renewed activism on the part of France, willing to capitalise on a diplomatic breakthrough in its humanitarian success. At the G-7 meeting in Munich, President Mitterrand called for a broader international conference under UN auspices. On that occasion, the French President reiterated that in his opinion a solution could only be found by enforcing international law through the United Nations.[12]

A MORE PRAGMATIC POLICY

By Spring 1992, progressive US involvement in the crisis raised the debate over the use of force. Like Great Britain, France was not against some use of force, but on the condition that peace-keepers on the ground would not be endangered. French for-eign policy was balanced delicately between support for the US sufficient to assure American involvement and resistance to military intervention.[13] This proved to be a hard line to follow. Roland Dumas and François Mitterrand's opinion on military intervention was that 'a military escalation was a dead end'.[14] Throughout the Autumn of 1992, Serbian atrocities and strong criticism from the political opposition in France about the pro-Serb French policy forced the Government to agree to the use of limited force. France voted in favour of UN Security Council Resolution 776 allowing peace-keeping troops to use force if they were attacked. In addition, France proposed a 'no-fly zone' over Bosnia to protect UN ground forces. Despite divergences over the conditions of the 'no-fly zone' enforce-ment, the adoption of UN Resolution 781 showed growing convergence between the French and American Governments concerning the former Yugoslavia.

Tacitly approving US policy, France agreed by the end of the year to increase pressure on the Serbs. The lack of progress in the international conference, repeated war crimes, and fear that the conflict might spill over to Kosovo (with unpredictable consequences for the entire region's stability) led the French to adopt a tougher position. This evolution was stressed by the Chief of Staff, Jacques Lanxade, who declared that the choice lay between using force or withdrawing[15] – a view shared by many French officers. On that occasion, France criticised the US decision not to participate in the peace-keeping operations on the ground.

The Bosnian Serbs' refusal to accept the Vance–Owen plan – a plan that France had firmly supported – ended Mitterrand's policy of balance. In France, this was understood as a bitter failure, and the French immediately took the tough US line towards the Bosnian Serbs. France voted on 31 March 1993 in favour of Resolution 816 mandating the enforcement of the 'no-fly zone'. Recognising that NATO was the only viable organisation to enforce the zone, France failed in its attempt to promote the WEU as a major actor in the crisis.

The change of majority after the March 1993 legislative election did not affect French policy. Balladur and the new foreign minister Alain Juppé immediately reiterated their opposition to the air strikes favoured by the US administration. After the Bosnian Serbs rejected the Vance–Owen plan, France realised that dialogue seemed to produce no effect on the crisis. A feeling of discouragement intensified among French diplomats who had been supporting negotiations for so long. A French diplomat stated that 'France was wasting its time in Bosnia and that those people only want to fight, therefore there is no immediate solution'.[16] Although denying that it had given up the Vance–Owen plan France proposed the creation of six UN-protected Muslim safe areas. By June, the Western nations, including France, had implicitly abandoned the Vance–Owen plan and accepted the division of Bosnia. Although French diplomacy initially showed some reluctance because the use of force could endanger both peace talks and the blue helmets on the ground, the military situation in Bosnia and pressure from the Clinton administration convinced Paris to support potential air strikes. This change in France's policy was based both on the recognition that immobilism might endanger the French role in the peace process, and that French public opinion asked for immediate action, realising that Sarajevo and the Muslim population were in great danger.

French discouragement with the continued lack of progress with the Owen–Stoltenberg plan came to a peak in January 1994. After bitter declarations by Alain Juppé ('One cannot indefinitely send hundreds of millions of francs, leave thousands of men on the ground, if the belligerents refuse all political solution'),[17] the French Government called for greater US involvement and the use of force. France's demand for action was motivated by a combination of criticisms both from French officers and politicians regarding the effect of humanitarian aid on the conflict and sharp criticism toward incompetent UN command structures. Moreover, at this stage of the crisis, the French Government considered that US participation in peace enforcement was essential in order to give negotiations a chance. It was not until another bloody episode (a mortar shell killing 70 people in a Sarajevo market) which inflamed French public opinion, that Paris was able to convince the United States that, at this stage of the crisis, NATO needed to involve itself in the peace-keeping process.[18] By so doing, the French Government ironically initiated US involvement in the crisis.[19]

Throughout the winter of 1994–95, France strongly expressed its resolute opposition to the lifting of the arms embargo on Bosnia.[20] Juppé explained that the French Government believed that lifting the embargo would lead to the immediate renewal of the war and the defeat of the Muslims of Bosnia,[21] which was against the logic French diplomacy had followed throughout the crisis. 'Lifting the arms embargo', he claimed, 'is the solution of despair'.[22] That would only create a blood-bath and prolong the fighting. Indeed in November 1994, Juppé offered a forthright condemnation of expressed American intentions to lift the arms embargo.[23] Paris thought that this decision had simultaneously undermined Western solidarity and led to the most terrible strategic mistake of the Bosnian armed forces so far: a desperate attack from the Muslim enclave of Bihac that finally resulted in a crushing defeat. The French blamed the Americans for encouraging Muslim forces to begin a new offensive and therefore held the Clinton administration responsible for the latest Serbian conquest. After the crisis, a joint statement by Mitterrand and Balladur pointed out that 'the tragic events in Bihac show that any encouragement given to the reconquest of territory by force – and notably the prospect of lifting the arms embargo – is vain and dangerous'.[24] Despite this outward unanimity, however, the Bihac episode revealed acute tensions within the French government. When the Serbs increased their military pressure on Bihac, Mitterrand firmly opposed Juppé's proposals for a resolute ultimatum on the aggressor.

CHANGING THE COURSE OF FATE

At this stage of the crisis, France's perception of the situation was uncertain. On the one hand, Paris considered that substantial improvements had been obtained over one year: indeed, the European Union plan established the basis of a political solution in the region; the NATO ultimatum limited the intensity of the war in Bosnia; the Washington agreements created a Croatian–Muslim federation; the 'contact group' facilitated some coordination of European, American and Russian efforts to solve the crisis; and finally Belgrade's new attitude led to the complete isolation of the Bosnian Serbs. On the other hand, the stubbornness of the Bosnian Serb Government threatened these achievements. Facing this situation, France was concerned to avoid two large political reefs: a 'day-by-day' policy, and the temptation to withdraw.[25]

French policy can be understood through four major concerns: first, even if France does not want to get any further involved militarily in the conflict, Paris intends to hold a tough line and henceforth wants UN or NATO decisions to be strictly respected. Secondly, France wants war criminals, whatever their nationality, to be judged by an international court. Alain Juppé has claimed that this issue was a moral and political necessity in order to settle a durable peace in the region.[26] Thirdly, France clearly supports a negotiated peace in Bosnia and still believes that process to be achievable. Finally, French diplomacy will promote reconciliation between Croatia and Serbia through a multiple stage plan, beginning with a ceasefire and mutual recognition and ending with the settlement of the Serb minority's status in Croatia. In the long term, according to Juppé, the EU should solemnly declare that these countries (Serbia, Croatia, Bosnia and Macedonia) are bound to join the Union.[27]

Throughout the crisis, France has always followed a courageous, though sometimes awkward, activism and surely cannot be accused of indifference. Very few other countries, if any, can pride themselves on having contributed so broadly to the conflict resolution process. Nevertheless, the French position was not without its contradictions and these contradictions reveal the uneasiness characterising French foreign policy since the end of the Cold War. Claiming to promote the EU's common foreign policy but often favouring national goals, France bears a substantial share of the responsibility for the failure of the CFSP over the Yugoslav conflict. The ongoing crisis has also imperceptibly modified the French perception of the US role in the security of the continent. This modification can be clearly seen through the recent softening of France's attitude towards NATO. For the first time since De Gaulle pulled France's armed forces out of the integrated command structure in 1966, the Defence Minister François Léotard attended a ministerial meeting of the alliance in September 1994.[28] This does not mean that Paris has dropped the idea of building an independent European defence structure. France is still far short of full reintegration in NATO or of abandoning its independence in deciding how its armed forces should be used. In fact, the shift reflects the strategic realities of the post-Cold War era, in which France feels the need to be more closely involved in NATO fearing that the United States could become less and less involved in Europe.[29]

NOTES

1. A. Juppé, 'Ex-Yougoslavie: Une volonté de paix', *Le Figaro*, 17 October 1994.
2. One should read the following brilliant article: P. C. Wood, 'France and the Post Cold War Order: The Case of Yugoslavia', *European Security*, **3**, 1 (1994) pp. 129–52.
3. R. Scharping, 'La coopération franco-allemande face aux nouveaux défis', *Politique Etrangère*, **2** (1994), pp. 537–43.
4. *La Politique Etrangère de la France*, Textes et documents, May 1991, p. 19.
5. C. Guicherd, 'L'heure de l'Europe: premières leçons du conflit Yougoslave', *Les Cahiers du CREST*, **10** (March 1993), pp. 16–17.
6. The return of the German question.
7. H. Starck, 'France–Allemagne: entente et mésententes', *Politique Etrangère*, Winter (1993–94), pp. 989–1001 and H. Starck, 'Dissonances franco-allemandes sur fond de guerre serbo-croate', *Politique Etrangère*, Summer (1992), pp. 339–47.
8. *La Politique Etrangère de la France*, Textes et documents, February 1993, p. 92.
9. P. M. De La Gorce, 'Les divergences franco-allemandes mises à nu', *Le Monde Diplomatique*, September 1993, pp. 10–11.
10. J-M. Coicaud, 'L'ONU et l'ex-Yougoslavie: actions et auteurs', *Le Trimestre du Monde*, **4** (1993), pp. 110–11.
11. *La Politique Etrangère de la France*, Textes et documents, June 1992, pp. 197–8.
12. *La Politique Etrangère de la France*, Textes et documents, July 1992, pp. 19–20.
13. Wood, op. cit., p. 141.
14. *La Politique Etrangère de la France*, Textes et documents, August 1992, pp. 122.
15. P. Haski, 'France, un soupçon de serbophilie', *Libération*, 12 March 1993.
16. Ibid.

17. *La Politique Etrangère de la France*, Textes et documents, January 1994, p. 70.

18. 'Textes des déclarations de M. Juppé et M. Léotard du 6 février 1994', *Le Monde*, 6 February 1994.

19. P-M. De La Gorce, 'La crise Yougoslave prise en main par Washington', *Le Monde Diplomatique*, April 1994, p. 11.

20. A. Joxe, 'Ajouter des armes à la guerre', *Libération*, 26 May 1994.

21. A. Juppé, 'Diplomatie Française: un deuxième souffle', *Politique Internationale*, Autumn 1993, pp. 17–18.

22. *La Politique Etrangère de la France*, Textes et documents, May 1994, p. 6.

23. C. Tréan, 'Les dirigeants français divisés sur la position à adopter', *Le Monde*, 29 November 1994.

24. Quoted by R. Stevenson, 'Allied Split on Bosnia Turns Into Public Feud', *International Herald Tribune*, 29 November 1994, p. 2.

25. A. Juppé, 'Ex-Yougoslavie', op. cit.

26. Ibid.

27. Ibid.

28. J. Fitchett, 'France to Resume Seat at NATO Military Talks', *International Herald Tribune*, 3 September 1994.

29. P. Lemaître, 'La redistribution des rôles au sein de l'OTAN entre américains et européens se fait attendre', *Le Monde*, 29 September 1994.

5 British Perspectives
James Gow

Britain played a central role in the international handling of the war of dissolution in Yugoslavia. That role was harshly criticised at different times, from different quarters. Allegations were levelled that British policy was pro-Serbian, that it was a policy of appeasement and a policy of indifference. And yet, whilst British policy was less than glorious, and in the end, a failure, it shared those qualities with other major actors in the international community, as is clearly indicated by other chapters in the present volume. The UK may have stood accused because it played a more significant role in the diplomatic treatment of the crisis than most other states – a role which included the supply of a small secretariat to the European Community (EC) for the duration of the conferences on Yugoslavia, active diplomacy in the United Nations (UN), and the sending of the second largest contingent of troops to operate with UNPROFOR, the UN peace-keeping force in the former Yugoslavia. This reflected its strong commitment to ending the war and its engagement as a major actor on the international stage, as well as its analysis of the various aspects of the situation, within and without the former Yugoslavia.

Whilst the UK's understanding of intra-Yugoslav questions may have been sometimes warped by a tendency to see the past as the present, the judgement of issues at the international level was generally consistent with circumstances. This chapter is an attempt to demonstrate that, given the particular conditions prevailing and the government's understanding of them, British policy, whilst sometimes influenced by extraneous considerations and misperceptions, may have been less misguided and bankrupt than many suppose.[1] The central inadequacy of the British is that shared by almost every other country of significance: political nervousness about the use of force.[2]

THE ISSUE: OBJECTIVES OR OBJECTIONS?

British policy on Bosnia and the Balkans provoked criticism and complaint from many quarters. In the summer of 1993, Prime Minister John Major was forced uncomfortably to depart from his prepared text during an official visit to Malaysia after Malaysian Prime Minister Mahatir had delivered an open and direct attack on British policy towards Bosnia.[3] In mid-October, the US President Bill Clinton, whilst rounding on his European allies in an interview for the *Washington Post*, picked out the British especially for their resistance to his preferred option for Bosnia – a partial lifting of the UN-imposed arms embargo on the territories of the former Yugoslav state. As early as December 1992, Bosnian President Alija Izetbegović asserted that the British were 'the biggest brake on any progress' towards solving his country's war, an accusation which many observers echoed as they assessed the UK's policy as being 'bankrupt'.[4]

Increasing charges of British leadership of an 'appeasement movement' and, consequently, of complicity in genocide stung the UK foreign policy establishment.[5] By the first week in September 1993, Britain had clearly become 'the villain of the piece over Western policy on Bosnia'.[6] Allegations by senior figures in the US, Germany, several Muslim countries and, of course, the Bosnian leadership that the UK was running a policy of appeasement were testily rebutted by UK Foreign Secretary Douglas Hurd: 'These are words which are tossed about.'[7] Within two days of this, the Foreign Secretary assailed British press criticism of UK policy towards Bosnia.[8]

While some took the British position to be pro-Serbian,[9] the real question about UK policy focused not on its objectives, but on its objections to the ideas of others. The central issue always related to the use of force, whether the question was lifting the arms embargo with regard to the forces of the Bosnian Presidency, or external armed intervention, aerial or terrestrial. The UK was always at the heart of the debate and played a pivotal role in determining their outcomes. While the UK position on the use of force issue was predominantly determined by international and regional practicalities, it was also, at least initially, influenced by its perception of the nature of the intra-Yugoslav conflict.

UK UNDERSTANDING OF THE CRISIS AND OBJECTIVES

To some extent, the UK assessment of the war in Yugoslavia initially saw it through historical glasses. There were two
dimensions to this. The first concerned the history of the British debate on intervention in the Balkans in the 1870s. 'The
eastern Question' on armed intervention to prevent the Turks
butchering Bulgarians saw William, Lord Gladstone, leader
of the opposition, arguing strongly for intervention and the
Conservative Prime Minister Benjamin Disraeli resisting. The
conventional wisdom handed down to students of British foreign policy is that history proved Disraeli's 'hands off' policy
right. In some indefinable and unquantifiable way, this conception seems to have guided senior politicians.[10]

There was, however, one big difference from the Gladstone–
Disraeli debates: in the 1990s, there was virtually no opposition
criticism of government policy. This reflected the desperate
wishes of an opposition devastated for over a decade by its security policy position as well as a similar anti-Gladstonian caution.
The similarity of view extended into the second historical perspective. This was on the nature of the Yugoslav conflict itself,
which was understood less in terms of the modern dynamics of
disintegration and more in terms of historic animosity. 'The
dispute within Yugoslavia', was, in the view of Foreign Office
Minister of State Douglas Hogg, 'largely ethnic and historic.'[11]
While even at that stage, the UK identified the Serbian leadership as the source of war and was advocating economic sanctions, particularly on oil,[12] the tendency was to highlight the
inter-communal aspect in the war, the element of villages and
neighbours fighting with one another.[13]

This vision was reinforced by reflections on the situation in
Northern Ireland. First, there was the belief that there were
strong parallels between Yugoslavia and Northern Ireland as
irremediable inter-ethnic conflicts. This led to the understandable notion that it would be unwise to volunteer for a second
experience like Northern Ireland. Whereas the deployment of
UK troops on sovereign territory was considered a necessity, a
similar deployment in Yugoslavia was very much a contingency
to be avoided.

Beyond the reluctance to embark on 'another Northern

Ireland', there was the critical sensitivity that any UK government might have had about Northern Ireland. There was, therefore, always a concern to seek to avoid diplomatic developments which might have adverse implications for the situation there. For example, any international role in the dissolution of the Yugoslav state had to be weighed against the possibility of parties or organisations outside the UK trying to take a role in resolving the troubles in Northern Ireland – that is, dealing with matters which are concerns of UK sovereignty. Thus, there was a reluctance to make moves on Yugoslavia which might raise difficulties about this area of domestic concern. This was not a very prominent factor in British thinking, but one which was always there implicitly in the background.

A second domestic objective was not to do anything which would call into question the Ministry of Defence policy plan entitled 'Options for Change'. This important Treasury-driven exercise derived from the government's programme to cut public expenditure, including that on defence. Under 'Options', various cuts were being made in the UK armed forces. An unstated imperative guiding action was the requirement not to do anything which might reverse these decisions.[14] However, this proved not to be an absolute as, first, the decision was taken, in September 1992, to deploy 2400 troops in Bosnia and Herzegovina with UNPROFOR,[15] then, later (in the summer of 1993), 'Options' itself was reviewed and ground force cuts restored at the expense of cuts in other services.

The Yugoslav break-up and war presented challenges to the UK in terms of its external security policy. Through membership of international bodies such as the UN, the EC and NATO, the UK secures its borders, its political community and its status by projecting itself on the international stage.[16] This strategy is based on the UK's 'punching above its weight' in the international arena. That meant the country taking a prominent role within each of the bodies of which it was a member. The importance to the UK of preserving its place as one of the Permanent Five (P-5) members of the UN Security Council, as well as having a leading role in both NATO and the EC, brings responsibilities and commitments. In particular, the position of the UK within the EC framework of Common Foreign and Security Policy (CFSP) was essential – the UK was strongly committed to acting within the EC context, although the evident disagreements with other members proved a strong challenge to the effectiveness of the proto-CFSP. The strategy of 'punching above its weight' led the UK to seek to maintain its status through leadership on these issues, as well as through its contributions of resources and personnel. Concerns for international order, stability in Central and Eastern Europe, including Yugoslavia (albeit sometimes less immediate than for some of Britain's partners and allies), added to the desire to retain status as a major international player, induced the UK to take a significant role in the Yugoslavian war of dissolution.

UK CONTRIBUTIONS TO THE INTERNATIONAL EFFORT

The UK made notable contributions in three areas – support of international diplomatic efforts, troops for the UN force in Bosnia and Herzegovina and the imposition of sanctions through UN Security Council resolutions. This contribution included facilitating the appointments of two former foreign secretaries (Lords Carrington and Owen) as EC envoys and mediators and the provision of small secretariats, as well as the back-up of the Foreign and Commonwealth Office (FCO), to support them.[17] Carrington ran the EC Conference on Yugoslavia in The Hague and Brussels after September 1991 and Owen jointly chaired its successor, the International Conference on Former Yugoslavia, launched with the London Conference in August 1992 and continuing since then in Geneva. (Owen's initial co-chair was UN Special Envoy Cyrus Vance, later replaced by former Norwegian Foreign Minister Thorvald Stoltenberg.) Indeed, it was the UK's commitment to the international diplomacy surrounding the Yugoslav break-up, as well as to both the EC and the UN, which led it, as President of the former, to convene the London Conference to harmonise relations between the two bodies after tensions in July 1992.

The UK deployed troops to Bosnia, conscious of its responsibilities as a country with one of the major military capabilities in Europe, as well as the country which had convened the London Conference where the decision to dispatch further contingents of troops to the former Yugoslavia was taken. There were two dimensions to this deployment. The first was the need to take the lead. The UK had convened the Conference and cautiously responded to pressures for military intervention (following the televisual revelation of Serbian-run detention camps in Bosnia) by calling for the deployment of troops to provide protection for the UNHCR in delivering food and medicines to communities under siege. It was therefore under pressure to make a sizeable contribution – the original reluctance to deploy 1100 troops giving way to the eventual dispatch of 2400 troops. A little noted measure of the seriousness with which this force was sent was the inclusion of heavy-calibre artillery ammunition for forward storage should there be escalation and reinforcement with the types of artillery to go with the ammunition.[18]

The UK was also strongly committed to the use of the UN to secure Security Council resolutions on the former Yugoslavia. These include those imposing mandatory comprehensive economic sanctions on Serbia and Montenegro (the 'Federal Republic of Yugoslavia'), Resolutions 757 and 820, as well as those concerning the issue of the use of force, 770, 781, 816, 819 and 824. UK engagement, in terms of UN Security Council resolutions has begun to have a practical dimension with regard to the creation of an international war crimes tribunal which it was agreed would be established under Resolution 808. As an initial step, the UK has begun an investigation into charges that during the Falklands campaign of 1982 atrocities were committed by British soldiers. This investigation was almost certainly conceived in relation to the issue of the war crimes tribunal – to give the UK clean hands and to offer a model. However, the UK's role particularly in one resolution, in retrospect, leaves space for questions. This was the first Security Council resolution, 713, which imposed a mandatory embargo on the transfer of arms to the territories of what was still legally the Yugoslav state at the time.

Although a Chapter VII resolution, requiring the security council to have determined a threat to international peace and security, 713 was in fact only passed because it was the then Yugoslav foreign minister, Budimir Lončar, who called for it. This was noted in the resolution itself, as well as by certain members of the Security Council in their statements – if this had not been the case, then there would have been countries voting against the resolution, including at least China of the P-5, which would have used its veto.[19] It was, however, the UK which had quietly suggested Lončar's appeal for the arms embargo to the Yugoslav foreign minister. That resolution fixed an imbalance in weaponry on the territory of the former Yugoslavia between the forces of the Serbian camp and all its opponents. It was passed with the intent of signalling the gravity with which events in Yugoslavia were viewed. In practice, it became one of the pillars of international policy, along with the deployment of UNPROFOR, which complicated discussions on the use of force.

THE USE OF FORCE DEBATE

The main issue of contention between the UK and its critics was the use of force. In spite of the dismal prospects for international order of allowing the use of force by the Serbian military (as well as the Croatian) and the volume of evidence on genocide,[20] there was a mixed response with regard to the use of force. As far as the UK's initial assessment went – that the Yugoslav war was one of ethnic and historic nature in which it would be unwise to intervene militarily – this was probably modified during 1992 and certainly by the spring of 1993, with regard to the use of air strikes, led by the US. It was the UK's vociferous reluctance to agree to air strikes while it had troops on the ground and its support for the commitment of ground forces to UNPROFOR, rather than a withdrawal in favour of allowing arms to the forces of the Bosnian Presidency, which brought most criticism of the UK.

A partial lifting of the arms embargo was considered by London at the same time as the contribution of troops to UNPROFOR was being planned. For a variety of reasons, this option was rejected. These included, among other things, the expressed fear that more arms would only encourage reciprocal bloodshed, that there would, anyway, be very considerable practical obstacles in getting supplies to the Bosnian Army, that there would probably be a Russian veto were the issue of a partial raising to be put to the Security Council and that, if it proved possible to get the embargo partially removed, there was no guarantee that the Bosnian army would be victorious, or that there would not be pressures at some later stage to send troops to its aid. Taken together, these points of analysis made the UK government reject the idea of lifting the arms embargo.

Instead, other ways in which assistance could be offered were considered. It is hard to gauge accurately where the weight lay in the balance between the reluctance to become embroiled militarily and the pressures to intervene. There was some debate about sending a large expeditionary force. The UK mandate was restricted, in the end, with rules of engagement only permitting return of fire if the source of fire had been clearly identified. There was resistance to an armed intervention, not so much because of the concerns about the complexity of the battle on the ground (although there were such concerns), but because there was no political will to mount an expeditionary force, either in the UK or elsewhere, as Douglas Hurd strongly counselled analysts to recall:

> The only thing which could have guaranteed peace with justice would have been an expeditionary force. . . . And no government, no government has at any time seriously proposed that. And that I think is a line which should run through any analysis because it cuts out so much of the rhetoric which has bedevilled this.[21]

While Hurd was correct to emphasise the reluctance of various governments to become engaged in a major intervention, it would be fallacious to suppose that in doing so he was implying that the UK wished to see action, but was restrained by the lack of enthusiasm for such a project elsewhere. If anything, Hurd and the British Government were backwards in coming forwards: rather than attempting to lead the international community and to persuade, in particular, the US to take action (as it was frequently supposed by commentators would have been the case had Margaret Thatcher still been Prime Minster), Hurd reacted swiftly to subdue discussion of using force whenever the issue arose.

With every government nervous of embarking on an adventure for which it had little stomach, the British troop commitment made some sense. Deployed, at least partly, with the implicit hope that the presence of UK and other NATO troops would be a symbolic deterrent, the troops with UNPROFOR in Bosnia were given a mission which could be carried out without serious risk of difficulties and heavy casualties. There was little doubt, however, that with the UK's greater inclination than most countries to use a military option, as well as the implicit sub-text of British security policy – tucked under America's wing – in the event of US ground troops being deployed in what would inevitably have been a US-led expedition, the UK would have joined in international action. Without US ground troops, the UK (and France, the other major – and larger – contributor of troops in former Yugoslavia) could only envisage intervention as an act of folly, given the reality that, without US involvement, the European allies in NATO simply did not have enough troops to ensure that a fiasco would be avoided.

As it was, the US was only interested in using its air power. Air power alone is generally regarded as likely to require a follow-up with ground troops. This raised two issues. One was the implication that the UK and other troops on the ground might have to take this role. The other was that the soldiers in Bosnia, as well as those in Croatia, perhaps would become targets and would certainly have to curtail their humanitarian operations. Advocates of the use of air strikes suggested that UNPROFOR could withdraw and that the Bosnian Army could provide the ground follow-up – but this led straight back to the debate on lifting the arms embargo, which was weighed against the lives being saved and the humanitarian work being done by the UN troops in the country.[22]

The UK did not rule out the use of selective use of air power, either close air support for UNPROFOR, or air strikes in pursuance of UN Security Council resolutions on 'safe areas'. Indeed, on six occasions in 1994, it was prepared to implement them. UK support for the US of using air power increased following the appointment of Lieutenant General Sir Michael Rose as head of Bosnia-Herzegovina Command in UNPROFOR. The UK authorities were both obliged to give backing to their own general and persuaded by him that there were things which could be achieved in very limited circumstances by the judicious use of air capability, either to give UNPROFOR credibility, or to prod the diplomatic process – as was demonstrated, on a smaller scale, by the approach of British troops on the ground throughout Bosnia,[23] and, on a larger scale, at Sarajevo, in February 1994, when the 22-month-old bombardment of the city was brought to an end with the threat of air strikes on Serbian positions around the Bosnian capital.[24]

Of course, both Rose and his political masters in the UK remained acutely aware of the limitations of using air power, particularly in the context of a UN operation – as was demonstrated in the events at Goražde in the following April.[25] Thus, the UK position on the use of force shifted slightly after the appointment of General Rose, admitting in practical ways the need, on occasion, for using force. This was also, it appeared, a way of improving relations with the US, which generally welcomed signs of more forceful action. However, the UK position continued to place the overwhelming emphasis on a consensual approach to dealing with the protagonists in the war, as far as possible.

The incidents involving use of air power showed clearly that the UK was not absolutely against using force. Nor, even, did it rule out the possibility of withdrawal and lifting the arms embargo. However, its judgement continued to be that more could be done through UNPROFOR than through the uncertain and difficult course of action which withdrawal and lifting the arms embargo would present. In short, the UK objective of resisting Serbian and, latterly, Croatian aggression, as well as stabilising the former Yugoslavia through the mix of international diplomatic pressure, sanctions and the deployment of troops in UNPROFOR was conditioned by two realities. One was the indisputable reality that the US reluctance to commit ground forces meant that there was no chance of a large enough international force being composed to meet force with force without unacceptable risk. The second was the perceived reality that lifting the arms embargo would not carry guarantees of success – some elements of which remain in question as far as the UK's critics are concerned.

CONCLUSION

The UK's 'objections' concerning the issues of the use of force (including that of the arms embargo), for the most part, were founded on sound analysis of the circumstances – although there remained areas in which questions might have been asked, depending on views of the strength and competence of the various forces in Bosnia and Croatia. This analysis had one critical feature: the determined reluctance of political leaders in all the major countries to be prepared to commit ground forces in the former Yugoslavia. In spite of the advice of some officials, British politicians, like their counterparts elsewhere, shrank from more decisive action. They may be criticised for their outright nervousness, for their failure to take a leading role in drumming up support for more forceful international action and for their acceptance of apparent half measures and symbolic gestures in the hope that these would be enough. The major fault with British policy was its pusillanimous realism.

For the most part, however, UK objections on certain questions concerning the use of force should not be confused with UK objectives. In terms of the Yugoslav war, these were to restore regional peace and stability and to resist the Serbian war campaign – albeit not through force of arms. In terms of UK security policy and global standing, the objectives were to ensure a prominent role and to prevent commitments being made by partners and allies that would be impractical, or unacceptably costly. However, the long-term cost of the UK's opposition to US policy to the so-called 'special relationship' between the two (and where that left the UK's tuck-under-the-American-wing policy) remained to be counted. While the UK's attitude was always negative, in practice, it did more than most other countries and its actions were usually commensurate with the international environment in which they arose. Unfortunately, they were never commensurate with the circumstances of the Yugoslav war of dissolution.

NOTES

1. The present analysis is based on continuing research and on material prepared for my book *Triumph of the Lack of Will: International Diplomacy and the Yugoslav War of Dissolution* (London: Hurst, 1995). An earlier paper on this topic was presented to the Liechtenstein Colloquium on International Affairs, Vaduz, November 1993; I am grateful to Wolfgang Danspeckgruber, co-ordinator of that event on behalf of the Crown Prince, for encouraging me to begin work specifically on UK policy and to the Colloquium for its support.

2. I should like to acknowledge the benefit I have derived from regular

discussions on UK policy with some of the those involved at various stages, in particular, Peter Gray and Jenny Little.

3. Mirza Hajrić, 'Mejdžorova posljednja jesen?', *Oslobodjenje*, 1–8 October, 1993.

4. Quoted in Jane M. O. Sharp, *Bankrupt in the Balkans: British Policy in Bosnia* (London: Institute for Public Policy Research, 1992), p. 1.

5. See ibid., pp. 19–20, where the recent record on Bosnia is judged 'comparable with Neville Chamberlain's appeasement of Hitler in the late 1930s'.

6. *The Independent*, 8 September 1993.

7. Quoted, ibid.

8. Hajrić, loc. cit.

9. See *The Independent*, 8 September 1993.

10. Niall Ferguson, 'We say we should stay out of it – we've seen it all before', *The Daily Telegraph*, 15 May 1993.

11. Evidence to the Foreign Affairs Committee, Foreign Affairs Committee, *Central and Eastern Europe: Problems of the Post-Communist Era*, First Report, Vol. II (London: HMSO, 1992), p. 58.

12. Ibid., p. 59.

13. I have argued elsewhere that this was only one of two roads to war in Yugoslavia – and the lesser of them. (For example, see James Gow, 'One Year of War in Bosnia and Hercegovina', RFE/RL *Research Report*, vol. 2, No. 23, 4 June 1993.) The other one, the ambitions of political elites, was by far the more significant, something the UK Foreign Office was later to acknowledge through its role in the imposition of comprehensive economic sanctions against the Serbian leadership.

14. Col. Bob Stewart, Commanding Officer of the first UK contingent to be sent to Bosnia was told that 'the absolute ceiling on our total personnel was to be 1822'. See Bob Stewart, *Broken Lives: A Personal View of the Bosnian Conflict* (London: Harper Collins, 1994), p. 15.

15. By summer 1994, the UK contribution to UNPROFOR was more than double the original ceiling, totalling 3688. (UNPROFOR 'Facts Sheet', Press and Public Information Office, UNPROFOR HQ, Zagreb, 29 June 1994.)

16. This is partially stated in the Foreign Affairs Committee, First Report, op. cit., pp. xvi–xvii.

17. Both, of course, obtained indirect and irregular support from other countries and organisations.

18. House of Commons Defence Committee, *United Kingdom Peacekeeping and Intervention Forces*, Session 1992–93 HC 188, 369 (London: HMSO, 1993).

19. UN Security Council Resolution 713, 25 September 1991, specifically noted Lončar's statement and a letter from the then Yugoslav Permanent Representative to the UN (UN Doc. S/23069).

20. For a vivid and credible account see Roy Gutman, *Witness to Genocide* (Shaftesbury, Dorset: Element, 1993).

21. Interview, Channel 4 TV, 'Diplomacy and Deceit', 2 August 1993, *Bloody Bosnia*, Media Transcription Service, M2578, p. 4.

22. On the US–UK differences, see Fiona M. Watson and Richard Ware,

The Bosnian Conflict – a turning point? (House of Commons Research Paper No. 93/56, 28 April 1993).

23.   The British battalion in Bosnia returned fire 67 times between November 1993 and May 1994. (This figure was cited in discussion with officers from the Coldstream Guards which served as the British battalion in this period.)

24.   For a more comprehensive treatment of these events, see Gow, *Triumph of the Lack of Will.*

25.   For a full UN analysis of these limitations, see 'Secretary-General's Report', UN Doc. S/1994/1389, 6 December 1994.

6 Serbian Perspectives
Ivan Vejvoda

Serbia and Montenegro became full-fledged, independent states in the modern age in 1878. On 1 December 1918 both states joined in the making of the Kingdom of Serbs, Croats and Slovenes, to be renamed the Kingdom of Yugoslavia in 1929. They thus relinquished their statehood for the sake of forming a broader country (encompassing other Southern Slav peoples – *narodi*) which would also comprise the Serbs who had lived until then under Austro-Hungarian rule. Since 1918, therefore, the great majority of the Serbian people have lived in one country, along with other ethnic nations.

After the outbreak of war in 1991, the ensuing breakdown of the Socialist Federative Republic of Yugoslavia, and recognition of Slovenia, Croatia, and Bosnia-Herzegovina as independent states, Serbia and Montenegro proclaimed the Federal Republic of Yugoslavia on 27 April 1992. This state still remains unrecognised by the international community and is often referred to simply as 'Serbia and Montenegro'.[1] As a result of the disappearance of Yugoslavia, Serbs are now living in separate states again. Those who have not left to go to Serbia and Montenegro or abroad remain within the territories of the Republic of Croatia and the Republic of Bosnia-Herzegovina. In addition, because of the secession of Croatia and Bosnia-Herzegovina, and the invoked right to self-determination, a significant number of Serbs have seceded from these newly recognised states and have formed two unrecognised states: for the Serbs of Croatia, the Republic of the Serbian Krajina (*Republika Srpska Krajina* – Serbs of Croatia); for the Serbs of Bosnia, the Serbian Republic (*Republika Srpska*). There are thus at least three Serbian perspectives on the break-up of Yugoslavia, on the conflict and its consequences, and on any future settlement.

This chapter addresses the issue of Serbia proper within the Federal Republic of Yugoslavia, as it is the most significant although by no means the only Serbian actor on the scene. In particular I dwell on the Serbian polity, as it informs the behaviour of Serbia on the international scene and its future role in the region.

Within Serbia, it must be stressed, Serbs make up some 66 per cent of the population. The remaining 34 per cent is principally composed of Albanians (17 per cent), Hungarians (3.5 per cent), (self-styled) Yugoslavs (3 per cent) and Muslims (3 per cent). Like Montenegro, it is an ethnically mixed republic. In fact the final political/constitutional crisis in the former Yugoslavia began (and many say will end) in Kosovo,[2] the former Socialist Autonomous Province of Serbia. The 1974 Constitution of the former Yugoslavia stipulated that the Socialist Federation was composed of five constitutive nations/peoples (Slovenes, Croats, Serbs, Muslims and Macedonians). It is on the basis of this right (of being a constitutive nation) that the various peoples composing the former Yugoslavia invoked the right to self-determination, as did the Albanians of Kosovo who were not in the same category but were a *narodnost* – neither a national minority nor a nation/people (*narod*) but something in between.[3]

In the former Yugoslavia the problem was not so much the demand for self-determination – although one must not underestimate the explosive potential of its vagueness of definition (who, where, in whose name, in which circumstances) within the crumbling, complex Yugoslav institutional construction[4] – but the way in which the leaderships of the republics composing the Yugoslav federation went about resolving their grievances and demands for separation.[5] A 'velvet divorce'[6] in the winter of 1990–91 was conceivable had there been a decision by the presidents of all six republics to agree a moratorium on their respective demands for constitutional and territorial change. They could have also agreed to accept the European Community's generous offer of approximately $4 billion credit for economic restructuring, to accelerate federal-level negotiations with Brussels over EC associate membership, and to sign a 'Civic Accord'[7] of all political actors, pledging to resolve conflict by peaceful means, negotiation, and compromise, respecting human rights and democracy.

This vision now appears utopian. In its place there has been loss and disaster, five years of war, a quarter of a million deaths, and countless numbers displaced or made refugees. As a result fear, shame and degradation are everywhere, and the well-understood national interest is a fantasy.

For many in Serbia and elsewhere over territories, borders,

the right to self-determination, the right of minorities, it has been a totally senseless war; a war that could have been avoided and that could have been 'fought' by other means, around a negotiating table, without the unnecessary loss of life – and all this in a Europe that had lived without a major armed conflict since 1945.

Many observers, however, particularly in the West, claim that the indigenous peoples wanted this result, and voted for it. The successor regimes in the former Yugoslavia are fundamentally legitimate, they say, and their actions are broadly endorsed by their citizenry. The results of the first elections in 1990 – before the outbreak of violent chauvinism – are taken as ratifying extreme nationalism, and even war. This argument is central to the way the conflict is understood in some quarters, and to the ideas for resolution that are proposed. It is, as the adage goes, the old Balkan story: 'ancient ethnic hatreds' – but now in modern parliamentary guise. In such circumstances, it is said, nothing can be done other than to wait for the internal actors to 'play it out'.

There is no use disputing the obvious: many people did indeed vote for national(ist) goals, including separation and independence. But the majority were seeking normalcy, peace and a gradual transition to a market economy. Judging from a range of elements and, in particular, studies of the first elections, from expectations present in the society at large and especially in the sphere of the economy at the time, the 'peace-scenario' described above could indeed have become reality. So it was in Serbia.

THE NATURE OF THE REGIME

As Milovan Djilas has written, 'Serbia is not a dictatorship. It is an authoritarian regime in which there are political liberties. . . . it is undemocratic because all other actors [except the ruling party] have been excluded from power and public political life. But this public political life has not been suffocated, there are [oppositional] political parties, one can express oneself freely – this is therefore not a dictatorship'.[8] Serbia and Montenegro – the Federal Republic of Yugoslavia – are the only entities in East Central Europe where the ruling communists have been

continuously in power since before 1989, a curious exception
to the other post-communist countries of the region. In Montenegro they have never lost their absolute electoral majority;
in Serbia they retained a relative majority and had to share
power with the extreme right between December 1992 and
December 1993.

Much has changed, however, mostly for the worse, since 1989.
War has already imposed enormous social, economic and political costs, in spite of the regime's persistent refrain that 'Serbia is not at war', and that 'peace reigns on its territory'. The
sanctions imposed on 30 May 1992 by the UN Security Council
(Resolution 757) and reinforced on 18 April 1993 (Resolution
820) have led to further degradation. When Milosevic's break
with the Bosnian Serb leadership in August 1994 appeared to
confirm his pacific intentions, sanctions relating to air traffic,
culture and sports were partially suspended (Resolution 943),
although key economic sanctions are still in place. As a consequence the Federal Republic of Yugoslavia has become a
pariah state in the middle of Europe.

One Serbian perspective (Milosevic's) thus clashed with
another (Karadžić's), while a third (the Krajina Serbs) went
along with Milosevic down the road towards a progressive normalisation of relations with Croatia. (A comprehensive ceasefire between the Krajina Serbs and Croatia was agreed in March
1994, followed by the re-establishment of certain economic
relations in December 1994.) The interface between the three
in all directions is complex and makes the search for a solution extremely complicated. To simplify, Milosevic and others
originally launched/provoked the 'trans-Drina' Serbs into their
'independence adventure'. Since then Milosevic has attempted
to reverse the process, abandoning the project of a 'Greater
Serbia' – which was always more of an instrumental goal, to help
him to retain power, though many of his nationalist confeder-
ates may have seen it differently.[9] The political problem from
Milosevic's point of view is that he has accumulated enemies
on every front: not only anti-nationalist, anti-war adversaries,
but the nationalist opposition.

The political struggle evolves against the backdrop of a
wrecked society. Already in 1992 the Belgrade economic and
business weekly titled its front page 'All has come to a halt'.[10]
Only a quarter of the 2.4 million labour force was working and

producing effectively. Vast numbers of workers were on 'forced holidays' (paid leave) for several years, receiving meagre salaries as their factories have been closed. From 1990 to 1994 the GNP was more than halved. Serbia, once semi-developed, has slid backwards into underdevelopment. In 1994 inflation exceeded that of the Weimar Republic. Ljubomir Madzar, professor of economics at Belgrade University, summed it up by saying that an inflation of this kind is tantamount to bombardment of an economy.

In a nutshell, the war and sanctions have had a disastrous effect on all walks of life. An enormous social price has been and is being paid because of a totally erroneous politics. A terrible loss has been sustained by a power-hungry leadership embarking on the 'final solution' of the Serb national question without any prior 'feasibility studies'. The result is that the Serbian outlook has darkened to such an extent that not only will it take years to re-enter the global economy but, in consequence of mass emigration, there will be few people to rebuild a more prosperous future.

IL PRINCIPE AND ACOLYTES

In an article written in one of the first oppositional papers in the early part of 1990 a young journalist asked a seemingly strange question: 'Did you know that Slobodan Milosevic was born the same year (1941) as Mick Jagger?'

Milosevic came to power in September 1987, during a Central Committee meeting of the League of Communists of Serbia in the typical authoritarian manner of one-party politics. Some have called it a 'bonapartist coup'. Milosevic overthrew his friend, the previous president Ivan Stambolic who had in fact brought Milosevic into the higher ranks of Serbian communist party politics in 1983 by making him President of the Party Committee for Belgrade. The way in which Milosevic took power during the (televised) Central Committee meeting offered a warning that things were not going to turn out well in Serbia.[11]

It has been said that Milosevic rose to fame as a political leader through the challenge of Kosovo not through the challenge of Europe. This might be an over-simplification, but it does capture an essential feature of all his later policy, namely that he has led Serbia towards a closed society instead of confronting the realities of the end of the century and responding to the challenge of creating an open society by radically democratising and reforming the existing one. He faced a real issue: the fact that Serbia did not have any competency within the two Autonomous Provinces existing on its territory, Voyvodina and Kosovo, while both Provinces had veto power within Serbia. This was the issue that marked the political beginning of the (later violent) resolution of the internal disputes in the former Yugoslavia. Milosevic completely mismanaged it, as he would do in future cases, by choosing the wrong means and by remaining within the old framework of the authoritarian communist-party state, avoiding any change, or postponing change until there was no other alternative.[12] This will prove to be the formula of his future politics.

This is for example the reason why Serbia was the last of the Yugoslav republics to have its first free elections (in December 1990). The end result of his actions has been to engender a more complicated and unresolved situation than the one that preceded it. However adept he may have been at rising to power and then surviving, he has slowly but surely diminished his own room for manoeuvre, until he finds himself forced into a corner. In this corner he still has immensely important levers of power and the potential to steer the situation almost alone; but at the same time the political, economic and social scope is much reduced. Ever since the summer of 1993 such survival tactics have led him down the path of peace-making, but in infinitely more complex circumstances than in 1991, when all could have been achieved around a table instead of looking down the barrel of a gun.

Having started out as a staunch defender of the authoritarian, self-managed, Titoist version of Yugoslav socialism, as someone who participated in various 'witchhunts' against intellectuals and their publications, he soon became the first communist politician in the former Yugoslavia to 'have realised that Tito was dead'. In other words that the field was clear for individual moves in the communist political arena.

Milosevic's diehard positions scared off the reformists and quickly antagonised the other republics. There was no flexibility in his stance, no will to compromise, no understanding of the realities of international political and economic relations. In January 1990 he desperately tried to keep the last 14th League of Communists Congress going after the Slovenian delegation had already left (some of them in tears), not realising that this was the end of the communist party in Yugoslavia at the federal level. He resisted the introduction of political pluralism in Serbia until the spring of 1990 advocating with his ideologists the nonsensical 'non-party pluralism'. All of the changes agreed in most East and Central European countries through various forms of round-tables were in Serbia exclusively defined by the old regime, by the old apparatus of the party, its apparatchiks, with the addition of some prominent figures, among whom was Mihailo Markovic, one of the (dissident) philosophers of the *Praxis* group.

How did Milosevic manage to gain support for his policies and widespread popularity as a political leader among the majority of the Serbian people, many intellectuals and much of the media?

Former Yugoslavia being a party-state federation, hence a non-federation in terms of modern political theory, suffered a violent breakdown (unlike the former Czechoslovakia and the former Soviet Union), because all of its constituent parts were dissatisfied in one way or another with their status within it. And yet, all of the ex-Yugoslav republics depended in many ways on the existence of the former Yugoslavia and therefore on each other. Serbia was one such republic and Milosevic knew how to play upon such grievances by creating a broad authoritarian, populist movement which roamed through the republic of Serbia and through the former Yugoslavia antagonising all that was not Serbian, with the declared aim of leading an 'anti-bureaucratic revolution' (a sort of cultural revolution). This homogenising of the population around the *ancien régime* that was slowly incorporating a nationalist idiom into its rhetoric and abandoning some of its communist language, while retaining its monopoly of power, clearly obstructed any possibility of a pluralisation of the political scene.

Many prominent intellectuals supported such policies, either tacitly or overtly, by arguing that the defence of the national interest (mostly defined by the need to secure the existence of all Serbs in one country at all costs) ranked above other priorities of democratisation and pluralisation. Thus before the crucial referendum of March 1990 in which Milosevic advocated 'first a new Constitution (obviously to be written by the Communist Party), and only then free elections' – a line strenuously opposed by the newly born opposition parties – someone like Dobrica Cosic (later to be Federal President from 1992 to 1993) stood behind the *ancien régime* option. Such support for Milosevic was catastrophic for the development of democracy in Serbia because it completely blocked the possibility of reform and also gave credit to the popular belief that Milosevic was what Serbia needed. Cosic later changed his mind, but at that time heralded Milosevic as the best politician Serbia had had since the early twentieth century, thus blurring the political boundaries that were being drawn between old and new politics.

In understanding the phenomenon of Milosevic's popularity one must include, apart from the support of the *nomenklatura* and a significant part of the intellectuals, the media that he managed to infiltrate and manipulate the way he wished. The most prestigious Serbian newspaper, *Politika,* became his *cheval de bataille* in the rise to power but the stronghold was, and still remains, state-run television with its three channels. The media were the necessary propaganda tools and later weapons (as was the case in the other republics as well) used to antagonise everybody and everything and turn Serbia and Serbs into the paragons of virtue, justice and truth. Without the media such a homogenisation could not have been conceivable.

Fortunately Milosevic's grip was not total. Paradoxically, it was under Milosevic that Milovan Djilas, the dissident who spent 13 years in prison, was able to speak in front of the (state) TV cameras for the first time, in 1990. A free press developed in Belgrade and remained more or less uncurbed until 1994, when a campaign first against the semi-independent TV station *Politika* and then against the daily *Borba* (now *Nasa Borba*) and the independent TV station Studio B demonstrated the regime's limited tolerance for plurality in the public sphere.

WHY THE LONGEVITY IN POWER?

In describing and explaining the success of Milosevic in Serbian politics, sociological analysis is important. The agrarian nature of pre-1939 Serbian society, the legacy of patriarchal family structures in the rural areas, a stifling period of communist rule, when all politics pertained to what Paul Ricoeur called the specific evil of politics, namely its instrumental and manipulative side – all of this defines the attitudes and opinions of a great many people. How many exactly?

The first more-or-less free elections of December 1990, conducted under the 'new' Constitution written and adopted by the rigidly communist parliament in April 1990, give one answer. This Constitution combined elements of parliamentary and presidential systems, effectively calling both into question, and creating conditions for rule by one person, the President of the Republic. The chosen electoral system was a double ballot majority vote. Milosevic won the presidential election with about 65 per cent of the vote in the first ballot. The interesting result came though in the parliamentary election in which his ruling Socialist party polled a mere 47 per cent, while all the opposition parties together polled 50 per cent. As the electoral system worked, Milosevic, with 77 per cent of the seats in Parliament, was able to rule in an absolutist fashion. Serbia was thus split politically into two, with half of the electoral body being completely unrepresented in Parliament. This created a legitimacy deficit from the very beginning. It is interesting to observe that this split suggests a latter-day version of the fundamental political division in modern Serbian history. Latinka Perovic has argued that the Serbian elite became polarised after independence. The larger element, organised in the Radical Party, wanted to build a society and state based on traditional Serbian institutions with a reliance on Russia. The smaller part, organised in the Liberal and Progressive Party, wanted to modernise Serbia by moving it away from a closed patriarchal culture to an open, modern, Europeanised society.[13]

Milosevic's convincing personal victory can be explained as a result of several factors. He was on the crest of the populist wave he had created; there was no convincing opponent to offer a serious alternative; and above all Milosevic's platform rested on a number of simple ideas: peace, prosperity, and a tempered, gradual transition to privatisation. The slogan of his campaign was: 'With us there is no uncertainty'. The biggest opposition party, the Serbian Renewal Movement (SRM), made the mistake of trying to outdo Milosevic in the field of nationalism, going to extremes which scared off potential opposition voters. After the election the leader of the SRM became one of the advocates of a peaceful and negotiated solution to the war and to the crisis, but his past fiery words still linger in some minds. The upshot was that Milosevic brought to the citizens of Serbia the exact opposite of what he had promised. The country plunged into war after six unsuccessful attempts of the presidents of the republics to come to terms with each other during the spring of 1991.

Despite Milosevic, Serbia as a whole could not be identified with the *ancien régime* after December 1990. The first elections proved that clearly, although the ruling order in many ways remained intact, the other Serbia, with its internal differences and options, was overwhelmingly convinced that Milosevic had to be defeated within the legal, political arena, however difficult that might prove for its citizens. The opposition – parliamentary and extra-parliamentary groups, citizens' initiatives, associations, the universities, the Serbian Orthodox Church – started to move towards a quicker or slower awakening from a bad dream. The demonstrations of March 1991 symbolised the beginning of the resistance to Milosevic and the regime that he represented. After the end of the demonstrations Milosevic unexpectedly agreed to talk to the students and their professors at the Rectorate of Belgrade University. In direct dialogue, the students (spiritual heirs of the nineteenth-century Serbian Liberals) told him in the simplest terms that he should resign because he was not defending the interests of the Serbian people, which they defined as democracy, pluralism, freedom and peace. Milosevic responded unconvincingly, managed to endure some extremely harsh criticism – and walked out as if nothing had happened.

On 17 March 1991 he met with President Tudjman of Croatia in one of Tito's villas, Karadjordjevo, where according to many an account they decided to divide up Bosnia and Herzegovina between Serbia and Croatia. Substantial opposition to the war began in May 1991 with a spontaneous, unorganised resistance to mobilisation by the armed forces.

The relationship between Milosevic and the armed forces cannot be dealt with here at any length. The Yugoslav People's Army (JNA) had lost its state – a rare occurrence. The army was looking for a new patron after its defeat in Slovenia and its early troubles in Croatia. Milosevic for his part needed a strong lever of military power to give effect to his policy of keeping all the Serbs within one state. A short-lived but lethal marriage was consummated. The army has since been relegated by Milosevic to a secondary position behind the police – Serbia has the highest number of policemen per capita in Europe.

Democratic resistance to the regime reached a peak in the spring of 1992, when various institutions spearheaded by the University held a huge sit-in, 'Student Protest '92', demanding Milosevic's resignation in an atmosphere reminiscent of the heady days of 1968.[14] It was against this background that in April 1992 yet another old regime Constitution was drawn up, this time a modified federal one (for the third, rump, Federal Republic of Yugoslavia), in an effort to conceal the failure to 'solve' the Serbian ethnic question by war and to try to maintain the legal continuity with former Yugoslavia. This Constitution represented the short-lived hope of a possible change of regime with the election of Dobrica Cosic, the well-known writer, a Federal President, and Milan Panic, the Serbian-born American businessman, as Federal Prime Minister. Panic brought a breath of fresh air, straightforward language, simple yet deeply thought-out ideas of a return to peace, democracy, privatisation and above all compliance with the demands of the United Nations. At the London Conference in August 1992 Panic and Cosic managed for a time to turn the tables on Milosevic. Panic's popularity rose enormously. Opinion polls showed that in Belgrade Milosevic was in dire straits. Open conflict broke out in September when Panic's government was put to a vote of confidence in the Federal Parliament. Cosic convincingly defended Panic and his peace-making policies. This was repeated once again in October. Milosevic attacked both men harshly, saying he knew that Panic's helmsman was in Washington, but that he did not know where Cosic's was. This *intermezzo* proved that, when it came to staying in power, Milosevic was a skilful tactician, and that it was going to take much more to bring about any fundamental political change.

POLITICAL APATHY AND ITS CONSEQUENCES

There are signs of exhaustion and political apathy in Serbia. Continuing uncertainty is a source of great stress. The population does not know in the morning what the evening will bring. There has been an unbearable acceleration of events. Very few people are really still in full employment. The President of the Democratic Party has said that: 'What happens here in our country in 24 hours, happens in Switzerland over 300 years.'

Political apathy has led to an extremely high rate of absenteeism in recent elections (37 per cent in December 1993). Opinion polls indicate that people are simply fed up with irresponsible and ineffectual parliaments – a mock parliamentarianism. Milosevic's disregard for institutions, procedures and democracy itself has alienated many from political engagement. After three elections in quick succession in the early 1990s (1990, 1992, 1993) few have the energy to engage in politics at all. Politics is conducted in Milosevic's drawing room, where every day international negotiators ply their daily trade.

Opposition political parties that had been in the making since 1989–90 were being created from the top down as 'catch-all' parties, with little or no social differentiation. Caught at an early stage of their development in the tangled web of nationalist politics, some tried (successfully) to outdo the ruling party in their zealotry. These parties alienated many potential 'rational voters', throwing them either into the expanding abstentionist camp, or back into the hands of the governing party – better the devil you know. Opposition parties simply did not have the capacity or energy to insist on a longer-term democratic alternative. When they tried, they were successfully neutralised by the state-run television monopoly.

The deeper retreat of the middle classes from the cause of public freedom gave way to the pursuit of private ends. Both are necessary for a polity and society seeking more stable grounds of democratic political culture. More dramatically, the flight of tens of thousands of people, among them many highly qualified professionals, leaves a void in any future reconstitution of a civil society.

For Serbia the result of war is a restricted, crippled polity, citizens without representation, and political life in the waiting. Political parties are bogged down by a single-issue agenda (war or peace); their membership is hypothetical; their leadership involved more in rhetoric than in reconstruction. There is no clear social or political compass for ordinary people baffled by the sudden plunge into impoverishment and disorder. There is a largely criminalised and increasingly lawless society (creating a stratum of immensely rich and powerful individuals and their coteries). There is also bafflement at the decisions, reticences, and meandering of the international community. This is not the stuff of a quick move to rational politics.

What then is the prognosis for Serbian democracy? At least until the war in Bosnia ends, until there is a *modus vivendi* developed in Croatia between Croats and Serbs, there will be no possibility of reintegration within the international community for the Federal Republic of Yugoslavia (Serbia and Montenegro). 'Creeping normalisation' must begin first, from within. It is in everyone's interest that it begin soon.[15]

CODA

The renowned German sociologist Claus Offe has talked of the political economy of patience during transition. As always in history – above all in the Balkans – transitions are slow, imperfect, meandering. The road to Claude Lefort's 'democratic invention' runs close by the road of Etienne de La Boétie's 'voluntary servitude'.

NOTES

1.   The Federal Republic of Yugoslavia is often called 'rump' Yugoslavia. Yet Serbia and Montenegro together accounted for roughly 40 per cent of the territory, 44 per cent of the population and 40 per cent of the social product of the former Yugoslavia.

2.   The last phase of the crisis in Kosovo began with the 1981 demonstrations, but there were demonstrations in 1968 and demands were already put forward for an upgrading of Kosovo's status from Autonomous Province to Republic. See, for example, B. Feron, 'La minorité albanaise de Yougoslavie souhaiterait obtenir le statut de république fédérée pour sa region', *Le Monde diplomatique*, January 1969.

3.   One of many 'novelties' that the communist party constitution-makers of former Yogoslavia invented in order to try to satisfy the various ethnic groups and thus to solve the national question.

4.   C. Tilly, 'National Self-Determination as a Problem for All of Us', in

Daedalus, vol. 122, no. 3 (Summer 1993) (Special issue on 'Reconstructing nations and states').

5. 'I consider that the disintegration of the Yugoslav state, more precisely, the manner in which the Yugoslav nations/peoples are separating, represents their historic defeat and the inability of their elites to find a formula for life within difference. To resort to the ultimate means – weapons – in a geographic space where one living generation still remembers five wars, is cynical if not infantile.' L. Perovic, 'Jugoslavija se osvetila svojim grobarima', in *Borba*, 16–17 January 1993.

6. M. Butora and E. Butorova, 'From the Velvet Revolution to the Velvet Divorce', in *The East & Central Europe Program Bulletin of the New School for Social Research*, vol. 4, no. 1.

7. As was done in Russia at the beginning of 1994, although this did not help to resolve the Chechen conflict. More importantly the 25 million Russians who remained outside the Russian Federation (within the newly independent states of the Baltic, Ukraine, Belarus, etc.) were no reason for armed conflict, war and a cascade of secessions (regardless of extremist nationalist demands).

8. M. Djilas, 'Depresija se plasi promena', in *Borba*, 25–6 December 1993.

9. Interview with Mihailo Markovic in *NIN*, 24 February 1995.

10. *Ekonomska politika*, Belgrade, 14 September 1992.

11. There have been two books published on Milosevic which give particularly interesting insights. The first is by the renowned opposition politician and professor of law, Kosta Cavoski, *Slobodan protiv slobode (Slobodan Against Freedom)* (Belgrade: AIZ Dosije, 1991). It is a political-theoretical analysis whose aim it is to show that the 'political myth of S. Milosevic is the birth of a false dawn . . . where freedom is endangered'. The second is by a prominent Belgrade journalist Slavoljub Djukic, *Kako se dogodio vodja – borbe za vlast u Srbiji posle Josipa Broza (How the Leader Appeared – Power Struggles in Serbia After Josip Broz Tito)* (Belgrade: Filip Visnjic, 1992). It gives a detailed biographical account of Milosevic's career and publishes interviews with people who knew him closely. A revised edition of this book has recently appeared under a new title: *Izmedju slave i anateme: politicka biografija Slobodana Milosevica* (1994). See Misha Glenny, 'Yugoslavia: the great fall', in *New York Review of Books*, 23 March 1995.
    Milosevic himself published a book of his speeches, *Godine raspleta (The Years of the Disentanglement)* (Belgrade: BIGZ, 1988). See also A. Djilas 'A profile of Slobodan Milosevic', in *Foreign Affairs*, vol. 72, no. 3 (1993), pp. 81–96.

12. A. Djilas (ed.), *Srpsko pitanje* (Belgrade: Politika, 1991). A comprehensive overview of varying political and intellectual positions on the 'Serbian question' in the wake of the end of former Yugoslavia.

13. L. Perovic, 'Politicka elita i modernizacija u prvoj deceniji nezavisnosti srpske drzave', in *Srbija u modernizacijskim procesima XX veka* (Institut za noviju istoriju Srbije, Belgrade, 1994), pp. 235–45. The debate in the Serbian Parliament at the end of the last century on the introduction of a railway network is particularly revealing: a Radical Party MP declared that it will introduce foreign ideas and people into Serbia,

that it will subsume Serbia into the spiritually alien capitalist West and that it is 'a cold snake . . . which will penetrate the heart of the Serbian people, a snake which will have to warm itself and which will in the end swallow it up', pp. 239–40. Needless to say the Liberal Party MPs were staunch supporters of the railway which finally arrived in 1888.

14.   One of the main slogans of the students addressed to Milosevic was 'Get out the way, we can't see the future because of you!'.

15.   See the interesting 'Balkan debate' between M. van Heuven, 'Rehabilitating Serbia', and H. Carter, 'Punishing Serbia', in *Foreign Policy*, no. 96 (Fall 1994), pp. 38–56.

7 Slovene and Croat Perspectives
Christopher Cviic

Yugoslavia's rapid disintegration amid violence and war in 1991 came as a shock to the outside world. The shock was all the greater because the collapse was caused by an internal implosion rather than, as in 1941, an external invasion. Nobody wished Yugoslavia any ill in 1991 – unlike in 1941, when several of its neighbours had designs on parts of its territory and helped themselves to it when Hitler and Mussolini gave them a chance to do so. Nor were there in 1991 any international 'imperialist' conspiracies to break up the confederation. On the contrary, Yugoslavia's immediate neighbours as well as other states in Europe and beyond, including the United States and the (then) Soviet Union, were in full agreement among themselves that the continued existence of Yugoslavia was assured and that this was in everybody's interest. The last thing anybody wanted at that time of momentous change was a destabilising disintegration of a multinational state in the Balkans, not least because it was feared that it could set a precedent for other such disintegrations elsewhere. But just as the world had convinced itself that Yugoslavia was here to stay, it broke up amid general consternation and wringing of hands coupled with a lot of puzzlement.

The consternation was understandable: Yugoslavia had been a popular country. But there was no justification for the puzzlement. It had been clear for some time that Yugoslavia's main nations had for their own very different reasons become disillusioned with it – at least in its current form – and had come to reject it as not measuring up to their needs and aspirations. To that extent, the violent and bloody parting among Yugoslavia's peoples in 1991 was only the culmination of a gradual process of cooling off towards their common state that had begun a long time before.

The conception of Yugoslavia as an artificial creation made up of parts of Austria-Hungary and of the pre-1914 Kingdoms of Serbia and Montenegro and put together by the victorious Entente Powers at the end of the First World War is erroneous. In fact, both Britain and France had hoped until quite close to the end of the First World War to keep a version of Austria-Hungary in being – provided it could be detached from Germany and negotiated with separately. But when this proved impossible, and Austria-Hungary began to collapse from within following its military defeat in 1918, the Entente gave its political, military and diplomatic encouragement to local Serb, Croat and Slovene politicians who had been trying to set up a Southern Slav state since the outbreak of the war against considerable local opposition from their own fellow-nationals. (Nobody bothered to ask the ethnic Albanians, the Bosnian Muslims or the Macedonians – their recognition as separate ethnic groups came only later, in post-1945 Yugoslavia.) Subsequently the Kingdom of the Serbs, Croats and Slovenes, as the state was originally called, did become one of the (admittedly shaky) pillars of the 'anti-revisionist', pro-French Little Entente (Czechoslovakia, Romania and Yugoslavia), designed to support the status quo against a resurgent Germany and a revolutionary Russia. Within the new state, tensions among its main nations and national minorities – principally between the Serbs, the largest nation, and the Croats, the second largest – began to show almost immediately and later grew into dangerous conflicts that helped destroy both the first and the second Yugoslav states. But that was later. At its inception in 1918 the new state had many attractions for the Croats and the Slovenes, its two westernmost peoples who were later to become its chief critics.

THE SLOVENES

Until they became a part of the Yugoslav state in 1918, the Slovenes had for many centuries been ruled by various foreign feudal dynasties, longest of all by the Catholic Habsburgs. Squeezed among far more powerful neighbours, they nevertheless managed to survive as a distinct ethnic group absorbing in the process numerous other smaller ethnic groups that had settled on their territory. The Slovenes' development from ethnicity to nationhood was influenced by the Protestant

Reformation, the brief French rule in a part of Slovenia during the Napoleonic era (1809–14) and the European 'Spring of Nations' in 1848 (during which time the name 'Slovenia' first surfaced).

In the closing years of the nineteenth century and the early years of the twentieth, the Slovenes, who lived scattered about in separate regional units in the Austrian half of the Habsburg Empire, were increasingly exposed to assimilationist pressures, particularly from the strongly nationalist and anti-Slav pan-German movement in Austria led by Georg von Schönerer. Other threats came from militant Italian nationalism seeking to assimilate the Slovenes of the Trieste region and from Hungarian nationalism in the Prekomurje region in the north. Demands for a redrawing of the internal borders of the Austrian 'crownlands' (*Kronländer*) where the Slovenes represented a majority so as to create an autonomous, culturally homogenous Slovene unit were rebuffed by Vienna. The same happened to the demand for a Slovene-language university. This led the Slovene elite to consider other options. Though to a lesser extent than their Croat counterparts, the Slovene intelligentsia – particularly on the left – had in the second half of the nineteenth century embraced, at least in principle, the idea of South Slav unity, but only within certain bounds and not necessarily as an alternative to Habsburg rule. In fact, right up to the end of 1918 the predominantly Catholic Slovene political establishment continued to work firmly within the Habsburg framework. Thus, for example, though the unity of Serbs, Croats and Slovenes was called for in the so-called May Declaration of 30 May 1917, whose main instigator was Anton Korosec, a Slovene Catholic leader and chairman of the Yugoslav Club of deputies within the Imperial Council, the parliament of the Austrian half of the Monarchy, it was to be unity within the Habsburg realm.

Once Austria-Hungary had broken up and Yugoslavia was formed on 1 December 1918, with Serbia's Prince Regent, Alexander Karadjordjevic, as its ruler, the pragmatic Slovenes adapted to the new situation and sought to extract the maximum advantage from their geographic, linguistic and political position within the new state. Some of the benefits were immediate and tangible. The association with the other Southern Slavs in the old Empire and the Kingdom of Serbia helped the

Slovenes to stop the Italian military conquest in 1918 and to secure the northern border in local military clashes with the German-speaking Austrians. In the end, only 1 050 000 Slovenes found themselves within the borders of the new state, with 400 000 left behind in Italy and 90 000 in Austria. However, within Yugoslavia the Slovenes' position became far more influential than it had ever been – or could have ever become – in Austria-Hungary. Situated in the far north-western corner of Yugoslavia and also separated, by virtue of their separate language, both from the next-door Croats as well as the more distant (but also more powerful) Serbs, the Slovenes did not feel threatened in their identity by either of the two nations, though their wariness had been traditionally greater towards the geographically close (and three times more numerous) Croats. In Yugoslavia the Slovenes obtained several important national institutions they did not have under the Habsburgs – among them their own university, their academy of sciences and, not least, their own intelligentsia and officialdom. Both the main Slovene political parties, the Catholic People's Party and the anti-clerical Liberals, benefited from the Belgrade government's need for partners against the Croats whose main party, the Croat Peasant Party, remained in opposition for virtually the entire period of pre-1941 Yugoslavia's existence. In contrast to the Croats, the Slovenes, represented either by the People's Party or by the Liberals, took part in all Yugoslav cabinets right up to 1941. In January 1929, King Alexander proclaimed a personal dictatorship and, deliberately ignoring historic units, divided Yugoslavia into nine so-called *banovinas* (provinces) each named after the main rivers. One of them, the Dravska *banovina*, took in all of the country's Slovenes. As a result, there was little antagonism towards Belgrade and little desire to split off from Yugoslavia in the period between 1918 and 1941.

Hitler's *Anschluss* of Austria in March 1938 reawakened among the Slovenes their old fear of German imperialism. At the same time they also felt threatened by Mussolini's expansionist plans in the south. In 1941, following Yugoslavia's occupation and dismemberment by the Axis powers, Slovenia was divided into three parts: one annexed to Hitler's *Reich*; one, including the capital, Ljubljana, occupied by Italy; and a small region in the north under Hungarian rule. Under the occupation – especially in the part under German Nazi rule –

the Slovenes were threatened with forced assimilation and, if they resisted, with annihilation.

In this situation, Slovene Communists, until then a small and relatively insignificant force, took advantage of the confusion within the deeply divided 'bourgeois' camp and seized the leadership of the anti-Axis resistance movement in a coalition (totally dominated by themselves) with left-wing Catholics and remnants of pre-war Liberals. They thus took on the mantle of the patriotic defenders of the nation while also ruthlessly pursuing their ultimate 'class' objective of eliminating their bourgeois rivals.

For the duration of the occupation and the war, Slovene Communist Partisans, although part of a wider Yugoslav Partisan movement under Tito's overall direction, fought a more or less autonomous struggle on Slovene territory in units whose commanders were ethnic Slovenes and whose language of command was Slovene.[1] This was to prove highly significant: it meant that Slovenia entered Titoist Yugoslavia in 1945 in a far more self-confident mood than when it had entered royalist Yugoslavia in 1918. In Tito's Yugoslavia, Slovenia became for the first time in its history a state with defined borders – albeit within a Yugoslav federation ruled by a Politburo presided over by Marshal Tito. It is true that the Slovenes had been frustrated in 1945 in their attempt to wrest from Italy Trieste (Trst) and the region surrounding it, with its sizeable Slovene population, and from Austria Villach (Beljak) and Klagenfurt (Celovec) in Carinthia. (Western Allies supported Austria and Italy against Tito's Yugoslavia, then still a close associate of Stalin's Soviet Union.) But this time only 120 000 ethnic Slovenes were left in Italy and about 80 000 in Austria – far fewer than after the First World War. Importantly, Slovenia managed to obtain direct access to the Adriatic Sea with its own port in Koper. The promotion of Slovene national interests within Yugoslavia was also helped by the presence of influential Slovenes in the top Communist Party leadership in Belgrade – including Edvard Kardelj, Tito's chief ideologist and long-standing second-in-command. Kardelj, though something of a Communist dogmatist and by no stretch of the imagination a Slovene nationalist in disguise, understood that – whether the Communists liked it or not – the majority of their fellow Slovenes still gave priority to 'national' over 'class' questions and the Party had to take that into account in its political tactics. It was in that spirit that the Yugoslav Communist Party had in 1937, shortly before the outbreak of the Second World War, set up separate Party organisations for Slovenia and Croatia, a symbolic gesture then but an important one.

The remarkable Slovene consensus in favour of Yugoslavia was shared by Communists and non-Communists alike. In contrast, supporters of an independent Slovenia such as Professor Ciril Zebot, a prominent Catholic academic and politician who left Slovenia for Rome in 1943 to escape both the Communists and the German Gestapo and eventually settled in the United States, were a small minority.[2] The majority view among the Slovenes was far more accurately reflected by Msgr Joze Pogacnik, the Roman Catholic Archbishop of Ljubljana, who – though no friend of Tito's Communist regime – was in favour of Yugoslavia and was fond of saying that, for Slovenia, even a bad Yugoslavia was better than none.

Slovene doubts about Yugoslavia started to be voiced openly in the early 1960s. Various factors, some of them going back a long time, played a role in this *volte face*. One of the earliest public manifestations of Slovene misgivings about Yugoslavia was sparked off by the revival in the late 1950s and early 1960s of the idea of 'Yugoslavism' (*jugoslovenstvo*). This idea was inspired by the Yugoslav Communist Party programme adopted at the Party Congress held in Ljubljana in 1958, which envisaged an eventual merging of separate national cultures into a single 'Yugoslav' culture within the context of a 'Yugoslav' patriotism that would transcend individual national loyalties. The *jugoslovenstvo* campaign was taken extremely seriously in Slovenia because it was led by Dobrica Cosic, a Serbian writer close to Aleksandar Rankovic, the hard-line Serb head of the Yugoslav secret police and Party cadre secretary who was thought likely to succeed Tito. To Slovenes – and Yugoslavia's other non-Serbs – this looked like a new version of King Alexander's dictatorial regime's effort after 1929 to create a hybrid 'Yugoslav nation' – which in reality meant Serbianisation under another name.

As a small nation which owed its survival principally to its culture, notably its language and literature, Slovenia – even under Communist rulers – was not having any of that. With the tacit support of the Slovene Communist Party Central Committee (and, it is said, Edvard Kardelj himself), the concept of 'Yugoslavism' was attacked in *Borba*, the main Yugoslav Party daily, by Dusan Pirjevec, a well-known Party intellectual. Cosic replied and a long and bitter controversy followed. It ended without a clear victor due to the fact that both had highly placed backers in the Party. But the Slovenes had made their point, and the *jugoslovenstvo* campaign was discontinued. Another cultural controversy, which also touched the Slovenes' raw nerve in the early 1980s, was about plans for an all-Yugoslav 'core' educational curriculum in all secondary schools, for subjects like history and literature. This project – like the earlier *jugoslovenstvo* one – was dropped owing to strong Slovene opposition but only after passionate polemics between Serb and Slovene intellectuals.

Other factors contributed to the Slovenes' disillusionment with Yugoslavia, which grew apace in the 1970s and 1980s, and which led to a fundamental reappraisal of their 'Yugoslav connection'. One was the stubborn opposition, coming chiefly from Serbia, to political and economic reforms, a popular cause in Slovenia partly because of its geographical proximity to Austria and Italy, and partly because of the growing evidence that political democracy combined with a market economy seemed to be a recipe for prosperity. At the same time, the old Slovene fear of German and Italian expansionism, for so long the main reason for Slovenia clinging to Yugoslavia, had diminished. It was the prospect of a 'European connection' that now attracted the Slovenes while the 'Belgrade link' was increasingly seen as a burden. One of the early advocates of a closer European connection was Stane Kavcic, Slovenia's Prime Minister from 1967 to 1972, who was purged at the end of 1972. A Slovene Central Committee resolution of 4 November 1972 condemned Kavcic for advocating 'an independent Slovenia linked to and relying on Central Europe' and for attempts to 'devalue Slovenia's connection with the other nations and nationalities of Yugoslavia.'[3]

With only 8 per cent of the total population of Yugoslavia, Slovenia in the 1980s accounted for more than 20 per cent of Yugoslavia's gross domestic product (GDP) as well as a quarter of its total exports. It demanded but failed to obtain a reduction in the large (and constantly rising) federal budget where the biggest items were expenditure on Yugoslavia's large federal army and civil service. Another Slovene grievance was the forcible Serbian reannexation in 1988–89 of the ethnic

Albanian-majority Kosovo province which had, under the last Tito Constitution in 1974, achieved a high degree of autonomy from Serbia and a status close to that of a federal republic on a par with Croatia, Slovenia or Serbia itself. The huge financial as well as political costs of that operation were borne by Yugoslavia as a whole but with only Serbia having any say in Kosovo's affairs. Trade boycotts were imposed on Slovene goods in retaliation for moral support offered in the Slovene media to Kosovo's Albanians. To crown it all, there was the monetary 'coup' in December 1990, in which the financially embarrassed Serbian government, anxious to cover pre-election wage and salary increases, used Serbia's National Bank to take possession of US $1.7 billion worth of money from the Yugoslav National Bank – the bulk of the fresh money supply earmarked by the federal government for 1991.

Ultimately, however, the Slovenes' main concern was not economic but political. It was the looming threat of the imposition of a new, strongly Serbian-flavoured centralist regime in Belgrade that would curtail Slovenia's autonomy as well as blocking its further democratisation. Many Slovenes began to fear for their national survival if Slovenia stayed in a Serb-dominated 'Kosovised' Yugoslavia. The only formula acceptable to most Slovenes was that of a loose confederation of sovereign Yugoslav republics. That, however, was rejected by the Serbs who demanded recentralisation of Yugoslavia, strong presidential rule and the abolition of internal borders between the republics. That was not at all acceptable to Slovene public opinion. Considerable influence among not only the intelligentsia but also beyond was exerted by such journals as *Nova Revija* and magazines like *Mladina*. In the mid-1980s *Nova Revija* began to work, with tacit approval from the Slovene Party leadership, on the preparation of a political and economic programme for a sovereign Slovenia within Yugoslavia if possible, outside it if not.[4] For its part, *Mladina* – also with support from certain top Slovene leaders – targeted the top leaders of the Yugoslav People's Army (JNA) like the Minister of Defence, Admiral Branko Mamula, by nationality a Serb from Croatia, as corrupt individuals and the strongly centralist and Communist army as the chief danger to the republic's democratisation. *Mladina* also campaigned for the Slovenes to do their national service in Slovenia, and for Slovene to replace Serbian as the language of command in at least some JNA units in Slovenia. Another demand was the placing of Slovene inscriptions on army barracks in Slovenia. The JNA retaliated by accusing *Mladina* of 'anti-state activity', including disclosure of military secrets, and staged in 1988 a trial before the military court in Ljubljana of its editors. The trial inflamed public opinion not only against the JNA but also against Yugoslavia which it represented. Such conflicts provided the setting for the final showdown between Slovenia and Belgrade in 1990–91. The really new and important element in the situation then was that Slovenia felt not only that it would like to cut loose from Yugoslavia but that it could actually afford to do so. It no longer saw Yugoslavia as indispensable for national survival.

THE CROATS

For the Croats, too, Yugoslavia held at one time numerous advantages. At the end of the First World War, the Croats were glad to sever their eight-centuries-old association with Hungary under the Crown of St. Stephen because militant Hungarian nationalism had attempted in the closing decades of the nineteenth century and the beginning of the twentieth to assimilate the non-Hungarians (including the Croats) living in the Hungarian half of the Habsburg Monarchy. But by then, new dangers loomed from the south. Italy had been promised by the Entente Powers (Britain, France and Russia) in the so-called Treaty of London in 1915 most of Croatia's northern Adriatic coast (including most of the off-shore Adriatic islands) as an inducement to join the war on the Entente's side. At the end of 1918, in the wake of Austria-Hungary's military defeat and political collapse, Italy was occupying not only the territories that had been promised to it by the Treaty of London but also others – such as the port of Rijeka – which had not. In those circumstances, for the Croats – as for the Slovenes – union in a new South Slav state with Serbia, itself a victorious Entente coalition member, seemed like the best protection against these Italian claims.

But disillusionment with Yugoslavia came to the Croats far sooner than to the Slovenes. This was not only because the government in Belgrade had failed, as Croat opinion saw it, to stop Italy from, finally, acquiring most of the territory promised to it under the Treaty of London. There were deeper reasons. One was that Croatia, a relatively well-developed and prosperous part of the new Yugoslav state, saw itself from the start economically discriminated against and financially exploited by a rapacious ruling class in Belgrade popularly known by the Turkish word *carsija* with the excuse that Serbia needed to be compensated for its losses in the First World War. Among the big Croat grievances was the manner in which the currency reform was carried out in Croatia after 1918 and the subsequent deliberate, as the Croats saw it, undermining of Croat financial institutions directed from Belgrade. Another charge was that of serious under-representation of Croats in the Yugoslav state and local administration, the army, the police and the diplomatic service.[5]

Behind all this lay the Croats' realisation that, by joining together with the Serbs, they had leapt from the Habsburg frying-pan into the Karadjordjevic fire. In the new state Croatia was not only far less well governed than it had been under the Habsburgs, but it had also lost the autonomous status it had enjoyed up to 1918 as one of the 'historic' nations of the Habsburg Empire under the so-called *Nagodba* (Compromise) that Croatia signed with Hungary in 1868, a year after a similar Austro-Hungarian compromise deal. The *Nagodba* also provided Croatia with representation in the joint parliament in Budapest. (The *Nagodba* had, however, left Dalmatia within the Austrian half of the Empire administered from Vienna and represented in the imperial parliament there.) But even before the 1868 arrangement with Hungary, Croatia had through centuries always had its own *Sabor* (parliament) and *ban* (viceroy).

An improvement for the Croats came but rather late in the day. In August 1939, just over ten years after the introduction by King Alexander of a Fascist-style personal dictatorship and five years since the King's assassination by Croat and Macedonian terrorists, Croatia was offered a measure of autonomy. The offer came from Prince Paul Karadjordjevic, who ruled Yugoslavia after Alexander's death, as Regent on behalf of Alexander's young son, Peter. Under the so-called *Sporazum* (Agreement) concluded between the Prime Minister, Dragisa Cvetkovic, a Serb politician close to Prince Paul, and Vladko

Macek, leader of the Croat Peasant Party, the largest political party in Croatia, as well as leader of Yugoslavia's united opposition, Croatia became an autonomous unit (*Banovina Hrvatska*), pending a further, final reorganisation of the state under a new constitution. The arrangement gave Croatia less actual autonomy than it had before 1918 in Austria-Hungary but it also gave it extra territory – a substantial chunk of Bosnia and Herzegovina with most predominantly Croat areas (but also some Muslim ones) and the city of Mostar. The Cvetkovic–Macek agreement was supported by the Serb minority in Croatia, the so-called *precani* ('people from the other side', as the Serbs from Serbia called them), who had grown to mistrust the corrupt government in Belgrade and saw their interests better protected by Zagreb. However, the Cvetkovic–Macek agreement was undermined by its vehement rejection by the Serb public in Serbia. The broad anti-*Sporazum* alliance in Serbia included the democratic opposition parties and the Serbian Orthodox church. This echoed the vehement reaction of Serbian public opinion in 1937 against a proposed concordat with the Vatican, which would have given the Roman Catholic church equality of status with the Serbian Orthodox church. Large-scale public protests organised and led by the Serbian Orthodox Patriarch had forced the government to give it up. A similar fate awaited the *Sporazum* which had hardly had time to be put into practice before the war broke out in April 1941: one of the first things the predominantly Serb royal Yugoslav government-in-exile did on reaching British-controlled territory in 1941 was officially to refuse to confirm the *Sporazum*.

At the root of the Croats' sense of insecurity within royalist Yugoslavia lay their fear of assimilation by the twice more numerous Serbs. As the Croats saw it, not only did the Serbs deny them – except briefly on the eve of the Second World War – their political autonomy but also, and even more important, their right to separate national identity. The threat was no narcissistic illusion by a paranoid people. In 1844 Ilija Garasanin, Serbia's Minister of the Interior, prepared a document called *Nacertanije* (Outline), which was the national programme for a Serbian state that would be the successor of the short-lived fourteenth-century state of King Stefan Dusan, and would take in all the Serbs. But Garasnin did not mean only the Serbs (and the Montenegrins, who were Orthodox like the

Serbs and traditionally regarded as part of the Serbian nation), but also the Croats, the Bosnian Muslims and the Macedonians.[6] A theoretical justification for Garasanin's programme for a Greater Serbia was provided by the nineteenth-century Serb linguistic reformer, Vuk Stefanovic Karadzic, a contemporary of Garasanin's. He defined as Serbs all those who speak the central-south Slavic dialect (*stokavian*) – among them the vast majority of Catholic Croats and Bosnian Muslims.[7] Vuk's ideas served to reinforce the official 'unitarist' concept adopted after 1918 of a single 'Yugoslav' people made up of three 'tribes' (*plemena*) – the Croats, the Slovenes and the Serbs. Paradoxically, the linguistic closeness of the southern Slavs – notably the Croats and the Serbs – instead of forming a basis for a more harmonious common life than with the not-so-close non-Slavs – such as the Germans, the Hungarians, or the Italians – turned out to be a divisive factor, since it made assimilation easier. It was bound to be so in a politically charged context involving two unevenly matched protagonists. It is this fear of relatively easy assimilation by language that explains the Croat linguists' repeated and – to the uninitiated outsiders – bizarre attempts to put as much linguistic distance as possible between the Croats and the Serbs by, for example, publishing dictionaries documenting the differences between the languages spoken by the Croats and the Serbs. Significantly, the serious playing up of Croat–Serb differences began for the first time when the Croats and the Serbs first started living in a common state in 1918.

In Tito's Communist federation, the Croats not only got back important territories lost to Italy after the First World War but also a federal republic of their own. Nevertheless, the Croats felt after 1945 an acute sense of alienation, a 'nation on probation' within their own republic of the Yugoslav federation, forever suspected of not being wholehearted in their attachment to the system and – even more important – to the Yugoslav state. Equality was what, at least on paper, the post-1945 Tito Yugoslavia offered to its republics, in contrast to the pre-1941 arrangement that had been based on Serb supremacy. The promise of national equality had helped Tito's Partisans gain extra support during the Second World War, but after their victory in 1945 reality proved to be different. Yugoslavia was to be a centralist state run by the Communist Party and its leader, Tito. But elements of Serb supremacy reappeared in the new, supposedly internationalist-minded Yugoslav regime. This resulted from Tito's need to appease the Serbs in the immediate post-1945 period. As part of that policy, Tito played down his own Party's pre-1941 denunciations of Serb 'hegemonism'. The reason for Tito's tactics was clear.

During Germany's wartime occupation of Serbia, the majority of Serbs backed General Draza Mihailovic, leader of the royalist *cetniks*, who hoped to restore the pre-war, strongly Serbian-flavoured kingdom and vehemently opposed the idea of a Yugoslav federation proposed by Tito's Communists. Tito never won the allegiance of the Serbs in Serbia during the war (in contrast to the mainly rural Serbs in Croatia and Bosnia who joined the Partisans to escape the murderous quisling regime of Ante Pavelic that the Nazis and the Fascists had installed). Tito, therefore, needed to build a power base in a largely hostile Serbia after he came to power in 1945. The Serbs held against him the fact that he had dethroned King Peter, the son of Alexander killed in 1934, and that he had had Draza Mihailovic executed in 1946 as a Nazi collaborator. To appease the Serbs, Tito espoused Yugoslav 'unitarism', which directly and indirectly favoured the revival of Serbian influence – especially in the army, the police, the federal civil service, and the diplomatic service. This policy was reflected in apparently small but highly significant decisions such as publishing the official Party daily *Borba* in Belgrade in the *ekavian* (Serb) version of the official Serbo-Croat language (though in Latin, not Cyrillic, script). Also in 1945, the Serbian variant of Serbo-Croat was made the official language of command in the Yugoslav army.

But the bargain did not last. The late 1950s and early 1960s saw Yugoslavia obliged to look for alternatives to Soviet-style centralism in all spheres of public life. The fight against centralism was led in the economic sphere but was also led in the political arena by the industrialised republics of Croatia and Slovenia, with Croatia taking the lead.[8] After 1966, during a brief period of liberalisation ushered in by the sacking of Aleksandar Rankovic, the hard-line Serb head of the secret police and Party cadre secretary, the post-1945 'unitarism' came under strong attack from most of Yugoslavia's non-Serbs – but the Croats in particular.

In that fight, however, Croatia was politically handicapped

by the appalling heritage of the wartime quisling Ante Pavelic regime. There was an element of irony in that in view of the Croats' massive participation in the wartime anti-Fascist struggle Pavelic's *Ustasa* (Insurgent) movement was minuscule before it was put in power by Hitler and Mussolini in 1941, and only a minority of Croats sided with the *Ustasa*.

Nevertheless, the embattled centralists (as well as those among the Serbian non-Communist nationalist opposition who hoped for the restoration of Serbian hegemony) found it politically convenient to undermine the position of the Croats by not only harping on, but even exaggerating, the numbers of the Pavelic regime victims. For example, the notorious Pavelic death camp in Jasenovac, where some 60 000 to 70 000 people (not all of them Serbs) were killed between 1941 and 1945, was said to have claimed the lives of 700 000 Serbs alone. The exaggerations had a clear political purpose: they were meant to prove that Pavelic and his *Ustasa* movement enjoyed mass support among the 'genocidal' Croats.[9]

The advantage of this tactic was that it made it possible to characterise various anti-centralist *démarches* from Zagreb – whether political, economic, or even cultural – as 'separatism', 'nationalist extremism' and a threat not only to the official regime policy of 'brotherhood-and-unity', but also, because it allegedly harked back to the Second World War, to all Serbs. This was demonstrated in the case of the famous 'Language Declaration' of 1967. Signed on behalf of 18 Croat cultural institutions by 140 prominent scholars, writers and other intellectuals, the Declaration demanded constitutional recognition and full equality for four languages – Croatian, Macedonian, Serbian and Slovene. Most Croats rejected Serbo-Croatian as a manifestation of official 'Yugoslav unitarism', a 'political language' *par excellence.* The declaration caused a bitter public row and many of its signatories were expelled from the Party. An orthographic handbook produced in 1971 by leading Croat grammarians for use in schools and offices was branded as 'chauvinist' and 'separatist' the following year and the entire printing of 40 000 copies was ordered to be burned.

That action happened at the height of the purge in Croatia, ordered at the end of 1971 by President Tito, and which formed part of a larger Yugoslav crackdown on 'liberals' and 'technocrats'. The purge was particularly harsh in Croatia. The new leaders installed by Tito completely crushed the 'Croatian Spring', a political and cultural revival that started in 1966 after Aleksandar Rankovic's sacking. The massive purge had a stultifying effect in Croatia – similar in impact to the suppression of the 1968 'Prague Spring'. This prolonged systematic repression, in the course of which thousands of Croats were expelled from the Party and lost their posts, with only a few matching losses among the (admittedly few) Serb supporters of the 'Croatian Spring', earned Croatia the title of a 'silent republic'. It strengthened pro-independence sentiment in Croatia but also fuelled anti-Serb feeling in Croatia. Behind this growth of anti-Serbianism lay the fact that the deeply unpopular and insecure leaders Tito had put in power in Croatia after his crackdown were obliged to rely heavily on the 'faithful' Serbian Party cadres in Croatia in the implementation of their repressive policy.

One of the most negative long-term effects of Tito's 1971–72 purge was the deepening mistrust between the majority Croat population and the Serb minority, which destroyed the possibility of reviving the pre-1941 alliance between Croats and *precani* Serbs. Perhaps inevitably, the Croats' instinctive response to Tito's purge, which they saw as a full-scale attack on their basic national identity, was to concentrate on defending those things that seemed to be in particular danger – such as national symbols, the Croat language and culture, and so on. Unfortunately, there was little or nothing there for Croatia's Serbs to identify with. They felt left out and, with memories of Pavelic's extremist brand of Croat nationalism still fresh in their minds, apprehensive about the future. This growing Croat–Serb rift, set against the background of increasing Croat rejection of Yugoslavia, was one reason why there was no joint Croat–Serb struggle for democracy and civil rights in Croatia or, indeed, Yugoslavia as a whole. While more and more Croats were coming to reject Yugoslavia, most Serbs (including supporters of democratic change) continued to take its continued existence for granted – whatever their own particular criticisms of Yugoslavia from the Serb national point of view. Among the Croats, unfortunately, the increasing emphasis on the purely 'national' aspects of the anti-regime struggle led to a de-emphasis of democracy, pluralism and civil rights as the struggle's principal aims. This was in contrast to the situation in the nationally homogenous Slovenia where early democratic initiatives in favour of greater Slovene autonomy in Yugoslavia were matched by 'non-national' ones arising from concerns with the environment, anti-militarism, sexual freedom and other 'civil' issues.

The Croats' growing preoccupation with the 'national question' in the wake of the 1971–72 purge, accompanied by a steady growth of anti-Yugoslavia and pro-independence sentiment, found delayed but all the more powerful expression in the first multi-party election in April/May 1990, with the overwhelming victory of the Croat Democratic Union (*Hrvatska Demokratska Zajednica* or *HDZ*), a right-of-centre movement emphasising the national issue and presenting itself to the electorate as 'the most Croat' party. Its leader, Dr Franjo Tudjman, a historian and former general in the JNA, appealed to his fellow Croats to look on him as the indispensable champion of Croatia in the struggle to refute various anti-Croat 'black legends' in recent history, notably the one about the Croats as a 'genocidal nation'. Sacked in 1967 as head of the Party history institute in Zagreb for his attempts to correct what he saw as anti-Croat bias in official Yugoslav pronouncements about the Second World War, Tudjman was later twice arrested and imprisoned.

CONCLUSION

It was the advent of Slobodan Milosevic, with the spectre of revived Serbian hegemonism allied to a version of populist Communism, that turned both the Croats and the Slovenes totally against Yugoslavia. On 2 July 1990 Slovenia's National assembly, following the example of the Baltic republics of the Soviet Union, adopted a declaration of sovereignty which stipulated that Yugoslavia's federal constitution would apply to Slovenia only if it did not conflict with Slovene laws. It was also announced that Slovenia would develop its own foreign and defence policies. In September 1990 the Slovene government brought under its own peacetime control the republic's territorial defence force. At a referendum on 23 December 1990 an overwhelming majority voted to empower the government to proclaim an 'independent and sovereign' Slovenia, failing agreement (within six months) among all six Yugoslav republics for the restructuring of the federation. The culmination of this process was Slovenia's declaration of independence on 25 June 1991.

Croatia held its own independence referendum in May 1991, with an outcome similar to that in Slovenia the previous December but with one significant difference which showed that, for Croatia, cutting the umbilical cord linking it to Yugoslavia would be more difficult than for Slovenia. By the time the referendum took place, militant Serbs in the Knin area north of the Adriatic coast as well as in western and eastern Slavonia in the north had, with the support of the Yugoslav army, staged rebellions against the Croat authorities which were unable to stop it. Unlike in Slovenia, where the government managed to retain control over at least 40 per cent of the arms assigned to the local territorial defence forces, these forces had been totally disarmed by the army in Croatia at the time of the changeover in May 1990. It was Croatia's vulnerability to the combined military and Serb pressure that made the Tudjman administration in Croatia hesitate longer over its quest for independence than Milan Kucan's in Slovenia, which has a 90.5 per cent ethnic Slovene population and thus no sizeable hostile minority to oppose and sabotage independence and, just as important, no common border with Serbia. The multi-party election in Slovenia in April 1990 had brought to power a coalition of non-Communists and former liberal Communists under the presidency of Milan Kucan, Slovenia's Communist leader throughout the late 1980s. In the end, both Croatia and Slovenia declared their independence on the same day, 25 June 1991.

It is sometimes said that Slovenia and Croatia had shown neither sufficient patience with, or understanding for, the Serbs, nor readiness to take into account the vital interests of the Bosnian Muslims and the Macedonians, and that, to this extent, the two 'secessionist' republics bear a heavy share of responsibility for the war that subsequently followed. But on 4 October 1990 Croatia had proposed, jointly with Slovenia, a 'confederal' model for Yugoslavia as a loose grouping of states modelled on the European Community, with a single market and common foreign policy and common armed forces – though the republics would also have their own forces. The proposal was summarily rejected by Serbia. So were subsequent proposals by

Bosnia and Macedonia as well as another by Croatia and Slovenia in the spring of 1991. By their unwillingness to negotiate a new deal for a confederal Yugoslavia or a peaceful parting on the model of Norway and Sweden in 1905 or, closer to our own time, that among the republics of the Soviet Union at the end of 1991 and between the Czechs and the Slovaks at the beginning of 1993, Milosevic and the army high command left Ljubljana and Zagreb no other option than that of a unilateral declaration of independence. The alternative was total surrender which the public opinion in the two republics would not have accepted even if Croat and Slovene leaders had decided to bow to pressure and threats from Belgrade. Of the two republics, Croatia certainly has had to pay a far higher price for independence than Slovenia but so far there are no signs of regret over their exit from Yugoslavia either in Croatia or in Slovenia, which suggests that this parting may be final. A third South Slav state, taking in the Croats and the Slovenes, is – at least in the foreseeable future – unlikely.

NOTES

1. An interesting insight into the Slovene Partisans' mode of operations and frame of mind is offered in Franklin Lindsay's *Beacons in the Night: With the OSS and Tito's Partisans in Wartime Yugoslavia* (Cambridge: Cambridge University Press, 1993). An interesting view of Slovenia under the occupation and the subsequent Communist rule is offered by Ljubo Sirc in *Between Hitler and Tito* (London: Andre Deutsch, 1989).
2. His book *Neminljiva Slovenija* (Eternal Slovenia), half-historical analysis and half-personal memoir, published by the Slovene Catholic publishing house Druzba sv. Mohorja in Klagenfurt/Celovec in 1988, is an important source for contemporary Slovene history from somebody close to events.
3. See Dusan Bilandzic's *Historija Socijalisticke Federativne Republike Jugoslavije. Glavni procesi* (History of the Socialist Federative Republic of Yugoslavia: The Main Processes) (Zagreb: Skolska knjiga, 1978), p. 438.
4. See special issue of *Nova Revija*, vol. VI, no. 57 (1987), entitled *Prispevki za slovenski nacionalni program* (Contributions towards a Slovene National Programme) and the book by one of the editors of *Nova Revija*, Tine Hribar, *Slovenska drzavnost* (Slovene Statehood) (Ljubljana: Cankarjeva zalozba, 1989). See also *Samostojna Slovenija* (Independent Slovenia), a special issue of *Nova Revija*, vol. IX, no. 95 (1990).

5. Some of the Croat economic and political grievances were set out in a politically influential book published in Zagreb in 1938 and called *Ekonomska podloga hrvatskog pitanja* (The Economic Basis of the Croat Question), and much attacked in Belgrade. Its author, Professor Rudolf Bicanic, a young left-wing economist linked to the Croat Peasant Party, was in London during Yugoslavia's occupation from 1941 to 1945 working for the Yugoslav government-in-exile but returned to an academic career in Yugoslavia after the war. For an authoritative analysis of the national controversies in pre-1941 royalist Yugoslavia, see Ivo Banac's excellent monograph *The National Question in Yugoslavia. Origins, History, Politics* (Ithaca and London: Cornell University Press, 1984).

6. A French translation of Garasanin's *Nacertanije* is available in a collection of historical documents, see Mirko Grmek, Marc Gjidara and Neven Simac (eds), *Le nettoyage éthnique. Documents historiques sur une idéologie Serbe* (Paris: Fayard, 1993), pp. 57–80.

7. For Karadzic's views, consult extracts from his work in Grmek, Gjidara and Simac (eds), op. cit., pp. 27–53.

8. A full treatment of the economic controversies linked to the national question, particularly as far as Croatia was concerned, is to be found in Jakov Sirotkovic, *Hrvatsko gospodarstvo 1945–92. Ekonomski uzroci sloma Jugoslavije ioruzane agresije na Hrvatsku* (The Economic Causes of Yugoslavia's Collapse and of the Armed Aggression against Croatia) (Zagreb: The Croatian Academy of Sciences and Arts, The Institute for Economic Research, 1993).

9. The controversial question of the exact number of people killed in occupied Yugoslavia during the Second World War could not for a long time be treated objectively. One of the reasons was that Tito's government, in support of its post-1945 claim for reparations, had fixed upon an arbitrary and heavily exaggerated figure of 1 700 000, of which the Pavelic regime's victims formed the bulk. No questioning of the figure was allowed for many years. It was not surprising, therefore, that the first objective examination of the issue was undertaken by an exiled Serbian scholar. See Bogoljub Kocovic, *Zrtve drugog svetskog rata u Jugoslaviji* (Victims of the Second World War in Yugoslavia) (London: Nase Delo, 1985). According to Kocovic's calculations, Yugoslavia lost a total of 1 014 000 million people (5.9 per cent of the total population) between 1941 and 1945. Serb losses, including not only the Serbs killed in Pavelic's camps, but also those who perished in battle either on the side of Mihailovic or of Tito, were 487 000 (6.9 per cent of the total number of Serbs), Croat 207 000 (5.4 per cent), Bosnian Moslem 86 000 (6.8 per cent), Jewish (77.9 per cent) and Gypsy 27 000 (31.4 per cent).

   Kocovic's estimates correspond closely to those arrived at independently by a Croatian population expert, Vladimir Zerjavic in his *Gubici stanovnistva Jugoslavije udrugom svjetskom ratu* (Losses of the Population of Yugoslavia During the Second World War), published under the auspices of the Yugoslav Victimological Society in Zagreb in 1989. Zerjavic returned to the issue in his *Yugoslavia – Manipulations with the Number of Second World War Victims* (Zagreb, 1993).

8 The Macedonian Question
Misha Glenny

The dissolution of the former Yugoslavia into a number of smaller states, provoked by Slovenia, Serbia and Croatia and then encouraged by the international community, placed two Yugoslav republics, Bosnia-Herzegovina and Macedonia, in an invidious position. No state emerging from the ashes of Yugoslavia could be guaranteed because all were confronted with a minority problem which could become a security problem. In the case of Croatia, the Serbs remain an insurmountable difficulty; in the case of Bosnia-Herzegovina, the loyalty of the Serb and Croat minorities was demonstrably absent; Serbia cannot count on the support of its Muslim, Hungarian or Albanian populations, and so on. Obviously some minorities are more equal than others by dint of the particular size or military strength of the broader nation to which they belong, but the difficulties faced by Bosnia and Macedonia were especially acute. These were reflected by the activities of the respective presidents, Alija Izetbegović and Kiro Gligorov, in the period leading up to the outbreak of full-scale war between Serbs and Croats in June 1991. Both men understood that in the event of a violent collapse of Yugoslavia, their two republics would come under the greatest pressure and, in all probability, be the two central theatres of war. Bosnia was the more vulnerable because it formed a wedge between the two main belligerents – the Serbs and the Croats, neither of whom disguised their territorial claims on Bosnia-Herzagovina. But the former Yugoslav Republic of Macedonia (for the sake of convenience, FYROM) is still threatened for the same reasons.

THE INVIDIOUS POSITIONS OF BOSNIA AND MACEDONIA

The central problem facing both republics is one of internal stability. Neither can be assured of the loyalty of a substantial part of its population. In FYROM's case, it is the Albanian population in the west and the capital, Skopje, which may undermine the state's cohesion. In both cases, the question of external aggression is secondary to the issue of internal stability although it places an enormous additional burden on these states as they attempt to assert their independence. In FYROM's case, it is almost inconceivable that any of its four neighbours (notably the three with latent territorial claims, Albania, Serbia and Bulgaria) would infringe the country's sovereignty until after a collapse of relations between the Albanians and Slav Macedonians (hereafter Macedonians).

The core populations in both Bosnia and Macedonia are relative newcomers to the Balkan national game. In the past half a century, the Bosnian Muslims have discarded their guilt as the inheritors of Ottoman imperialist traditions and assumed many characteristics of a modern European nation. This was recognised by Tito, albeit for his own Machiavellian purposes, by the granting of nationhood to the Muslims in 1971. The Macedonians, too, have only recently succeeded (again in part due to Tito's policies) in asserting themselves as a self-contained national entity. Anybody who has enjoyed extensive contact with the Macedonians will confirm that these people are not Bulgarians, Serbs or Greeks even if a century ago almost all their ancestors would probably have described themselves as one of the three.

The aspiration towards statehood among Muslims and Macedonians was accelerated quite dramatically by the break-up of Yugoslavia. Prior to 1991, there were not even any underground political organisations advocating an independent Bosnia or Macedonia (although Macedonian emigré organisations of Macedonians cherished what was at the time an unrealisable dream). Both political elites initially recognised their relative weakness and inexperience by opposing independence until the last minute. Once Croatia was recognised, the Bosnian Muslims were faced with a terrible choice – remain in a Yugoslavia dominated by the Serbs, and by Milosevic in particular, or apply for international recognition as an independent state and brace themselves for the Serb and then Croat onslaughts both of which had been well advertised, though the Croats had been more discreet about their intentions. The Muslims chose the latter course which may have made sense had they received cast-iron guarantees from President Tudjman that the Croats would give their full backing to an independent Bosnia. Unfortunately, Tudjman was as bent on smashing Bosnia as was Milosevic. Only the promise of American support (particularly in Croatia's struggle to re-establish sovereignty over the Krajina) and the relegation of Muslims to a subordinate position in their relations with Croatia (which is what the Washington Agreement amounts to) was enough to persuade Tudjman to cease Croatian aggression against Bosnia.

The elevation of the Muslims and Macedonians from their role during the Second World War as spear-carriers to co-stars in the present conflict has further complicated the Balkan tangle. Serbs and Croats alike wish to return the Muslims to the ranks of the extras. Potentially, the Macedonians face even greater hostility. Of their four neighbours, only the Albanians have recognised both the Macedonian state and the Macedonian nation (although recognition of the former is conditional upon certain variable concessions being granted to the Albanian minority in FYROM).

The fear of independence in virtually land-locked Bosnia and Macedonia points to the final similarity. Both territories occupy key strategic and economic positions on the Balkan peninsular. A Greater Serbia including most of Bosnia-Herzegovina hangs over the Adriatic coast like an impatient vulture. A Greater Croatia, including the Krajina and most of Bosnia, would overcome the communications difficulties which Croatia's awkward topography presents and block Serbian territorial aspirations. FYROM for its part is both blessed and cursed as the only territory of the southern Balkans where the Balkan mountain range can be traversed both north to south and, with more difficulty, west to east. Should any of FYROM's neighbours control the territory, they would determine whether the main transit route in the region runs from Belgrade to Thessaloniki or from Durres to Istanbul. Such are the geostrategic realities which lie behind such apparently mindless disputes over Macedonia's name and flag.

FYROM PAST AND PRESENT

FYROM succeeded in escaping the Yugoslav federation without bloodshed. It also negotiated the voluntary withdrawal of the Yugoslav People's Army (JNA) by the end of April 1992 (which coincided with the beginning of major offensives in Bosnia-Herzegovina). FYROM's impressive diplomatic victory should be tempered by the knowledge that the JNA took all its weaponry with it, leaving the new state almost completely unable to defend itself.

So far it has survived, it must be said, against the odds. On the level of representation in government, President Gligorov has worked hard to integrate the Party for Democratic Prosperity (PDP), the main Albanian party. Due to a combination of poverty, bureaucratic indolence and the fear of a Macedonian nationalist backlash, the state has been less successful in addressing the two central grievances put forward by the Albanian community – the development of Albanian-language schooling and representation in the police force (currently negligible).

The politics of the Albanians in western FYROM are complicated. Despite the evident efforts of Gligorov and the government to integrate them (by no means all Albanians are convinced of these efforts), the Albanians are reluctant to trust the Macedonians. Especially during the 1980s, the Serbophile leadership of the Macedonian Communist Party (CP) dealt with the Albanian population even more harshly than its Serbian counterpart did in Kosovo. For Albanians, it will take more than two years of a verbal commitment on the part of Macedonians to reassure them that their jailers and persecutors of previous decades have really lost their influence.

In addition, the Albanians hold a peculiar place in the complex constellation of inter-Albanian relations, an area of study which has been regrettably ignored by journalists, academics and policymakers alike. Albanians are split into two tribes which have developed distinct political preferences this century – the Gegs and the Tosks – and three political units, Albania, western Macedonia and Skopje, and Kosovo, which have been stable geographically since the end of the Second World War. The line dividing Gegs and Tosks bisects Albania and Macedonia (and a little further south the confessional divide between the Muslim and Orthodox Albanian communities) but Kosovo is entirely Geg and almost exclusively Muslim (the Albanian Catholics are Gegs living largely in the Shkoder region). Since the League of Prizren was formed in 1878, political competition between the three factions from central and south Albania, north Albania, and Kosovo has been a key issue in intra-Albanian relations. Within this framework, the western Macedonian Albanians have never enjoyed an autonomous political status. Depending on historical circumstances, their political activity has been subordinate to either Tirana or Pristina.

The collapse of Yugoslavia and the relative weakness of the Macedonian state is changing this. The Kosovars remain relatively impotent because of the repressive power of Serbia while President Berisha has relied upon a number of authoritarian mechanisms which have lightly damaged his democratic credentials but until now ensured him a free hand in intra-Albanian affairs. Ironically, the FYROM Albanians in certain respects enjoy the greatest political freedom among all the Albanians and this has increased their relative weight in intra-Albanian struggles. The programmes and divisions within the Albanian community of FYROM cannot be properly understood without reference to the Albanian question in the southern Balkans as a whole.

On one occasion, on 6 November 1992, FYROM's stability came close to being undermined when police shot dead three Albanian men and a Macedonian woman at the Bit Pazar market in Skopje. One scholar has claimed that the Bit Pazar incident was exclusively an economic incident resulting from the activities of the Albanian mafia, noting that the clash produced no political echo either from the Albanians of western Macedonia or the leaderships of the PDP and the NDP (the National Democratic Party, the other much smaller Albanian grouping). Immediately after the incident, however, most of Skopje and Tetovo was in a state of war psychosis. The streets emptied at night and much of the population (Albanian and Macedonian) appeared to be bracing itself for a greater struggle. Both communities agree that it was only the authoritative intervention of Mirhat Emini, the then chairman of the PDP who enjoyed the confidence of the Macedonian leadership, that prevented a deterioration of the situation. Speaking in Albanian for almost half an hour (itself unprecedented), Emini appealed to all Albanians not to take to the streets.

The assumption that both communities are now committed to a peaceful coexistence misses the point. As the wars in Croatia and Bosnia have demonstrated, external factors can alter the national consciousness of the masses in a matter of days (in July 1991, in a mixed village in eastern Slavonia, I observed how the mildly Yugoslav identity of both Serbs and Croats was transformed into what in this case may be properly described as a Chetnik and Ustasa identity in the space of a week as the war closed in around them). Just as in Bosnia-Herzegovina, only the tiniest minority actually desire conflict. The war in Bosnia did not begin because of a breakdown in social relations between the three national communities but because the national principle dominated the elections of 1990. It was the collapse of political relations between the three communities which was the internal cause of the war. Similarly, FYROM's democracy functions according to national divisions. Although a greater party political differentiation is apparent within the Macedonian and Albanian communities than in the three Bosnian communities (although as the war developed, serious splits developed among all three), their MPs always vote along national lines on critical issues.

The danger facing FYROM is that the Albanian community might withdraw its commitment to state structures and establish alternative political institutions in Tetovo. Were this to happen, FYROM will have taken a large step on the road to war. A number of developments give cause for concern. In late October 1994, two rounds of parliamentary and presidential elections were held (the latter easily won by Gligorov). During the first round the main opposition parties of the Macedonian community alleged that widespread fraud had been perpetrated by the electoral commission which favoured the government coalition of Social Democrats and Liberals. Their claims were not without substance. The government committed a crucial error by not organising the elections properly as this offered the opposition an excuse to boycott the elections and engage in extra-parliamentary politics. As a result they are much more dangerous than they would have been inside parliament with few seats.

Partly as a consequence, the new government has hardened its position both in the dispute with Greece (Gligorov is no longer prepared to make any concessions to encourage Papandreou to lift the blockade), but even more disturbingly with the Albanians. The Prime Minister, Branko Crvenkovski, did succeed in persuading the moderate Albanian party, the PDP, to take three cabinet seats and one Deputy Prime Ministership in his government. However, after the announcement by a radical Albanian grouping that it intended to establish an Albanian university in Tetovo, relations between the PDP and Crvenkovski have become strained. The dispute over the university, which enjoys virtually 100 per cent support among Albanians, now threatens to destabilise Albanian–Macedonian relations as a whole, conceivably bringing into question the Macedonian state. It is imperative that this issue is resolved as soon as possible before the government decides to use force to halt the work of the university.

War in FYROM is not inevitable. Nonetheless, for the moment the country is trundling steadily towards political stagnation and breakdown which could preface war. It may not happen this year or next, but unless FYROM is knocked off its present trajectory, the threat is ever present. The political mechanism which alone may solve the constitutional chaos in the former Yugoslavia remains elusive. As for FYROM, the international community has had bigger or more urgent fish to fry.

FYROM AND ALBANIA

By dint of the Albanian minority, Albania's position on FYROM is perhaps the most important of all Macedonia's four neighbours. Just as the Macedonians and Bosnian Muslims have for the first time demonstrated their aspirations towards statehood, so too have the Albanians progressed on their historical journey as a consequence of the collapse of communism and Yugoslavia. Despite Hoxha's unbearably repressive system (much worse than Ceaucescu's, for example, and only just pipped at the post by Stalin's purges), his regime consolidated an independent Albanian state at a time when no others looked even remotely like succeeding. Albania is now a firm entity in the Balkans, even if the south may be threatened by Greek territorial aspirations if war were to break out in the region.

The stated goal of all three Albanian units is unification, with the important proviso that this should take place within the general process of European unification; that is, not through war and territorial acquisition but through an overall relaxation of border regimes. Nonetheless, one may question to what degree the values of European integration as understood in

Bonn or Paris pertain anywhere in the Balkans, especially since the process in the advanced countries of Europe is running into such trouble. In addition, the idea of an independent Kosovo (supported by Tirana), would seem to contradict the Albanians' commitment to the policy of unification through integration.

This reflects a real ambiguity in Albanian politics borne of a dilemma. Just as the Serbs and Croats have moved from their initial goal of establishing independent states to a policy of expansion to incorporate a majority of Serbs and Croats in their territories, so too do the Albanians now nurture Greater Albanian aspirations – especially perhaps in the potentially soft target of Western Macedonia. However, the threat to Albanian national interests posed in particular by the Serbs in Kosovo, but also by the Greeks in Albania proper, has forced the Albanians to temper this aim. Were they, for example, to encourage the outbreak of war in Kosovo with the eventual aim of securing the bulk of that territory as Milosevic did in the Krajina, they risk an appalling massacre of their people at the hands of Serbs. Albania has a very restricted military potential and its ultimate security lies in Albanians' birth rate (which is three times higher than that of its immediate neighbours). Unfortunately for the Albanians, this offers very little immediate protection and encourages racist attitudes among the Greeks and Serbs, in particular, but also among some Macedonians. The exceedingly low level of economic development in Albania itself is an important factor limiting expansionist ideology among the political elite. In contrast to Greece, Serbia and Croatia, its constituents place a higher importance on economic matters than on nationalist goals. As we shall see President Berisha has attempted to compensate for the country's military weakness by courting powerful international allies.

FYROM AND GREECE

Greek policy towards FYROM and other countries in the southern Balkans is informed primarily by domestic political considerations, the result being that Athens is pursuing a dangerous course which may well turn out to be self-defeating.

The collapse of Yugoslavia and communism in the Balkans has presented Greece with some very serious problems. The immediate economic impact which sanctions on Serbia have had on the northern Greek economy (effectively cutting the main transit route from northern to southern Europe) is serious enough. Graver still, however, has been the identity crisis which the collapse has provoked in Greek society. The Cold War enabled Greeks to discard their Balkan identity (except as it pertained to Turkey); with the departure of the Colonels in 1974, the country started to make great strides especially after it was accepted into the European Community in 1981.

The dissolution of Yugoslavia and the return of Albania from isolation has unsettled Greece enormously. An independent Macedonia conjures up disturbing memories of the Greek Civil War. But as a member of the European Union (EU) and NATO, Greece's local struggles in the Balkans also have a significant impact on the European Union's ability to deal with the situation. In some respects, this is positive as the EU has occasionally been able to use Athens' friendly relations with Belgrade as a conduit when other channels have been closed. But in general it has been negative as Greece may apply its veto to Balkan policy which the other eleven members have agreed on as for example in the case of loans to Albania.

As FYROM has been struggling to maintain peace between its two largest national communities, it has been forced to suffer outrageous economic fortune. The UN sanctions' regime on rump-Yugoslavia was imposed in total disregard to the economies of the surrounding countries. Six of these (Albania, FYROM, Bulgaria, Romania, Hungary and Ukraine) are attempting the painful transformation from state socialism to market structures. They are forced to carry the losses sustained by adhering to sanctions entirely alone. This is particularly damaging for FYROM, threatened as it is by instability which, as the Bit Pazar incident demonstrated, can be linked to economic tensions between the Albanians and Macedonians. As an index of hardship, an estimate published by the United Nations (UN) in November 1993 put the losses sustained by Macedonia due to the sanctions at US $2 billion. Since then, the UN has given up trying to calculate the extent of the damage because its experts have admitted that they can no longer estimate the knock-on effect which direct losses are having on the rest of the Macedonian economy.

Furthermore, a total trade blockade against FYROM was

imposed by Greece in February 1994. This is now beginning to bite. According to government statistics, FYROM has been losing US $58 million a month because of it. Macedonia's only rail links are with Serbia to the north and the Greek port of Thessaloniki to the south. The country used to receive all its oil imports through the northern Greek capital. Now it is dependent for its oil on road transportation from Bulgaria and Albania (which is five times as expensive). The UN fears that a social explosion in Macedonia would quickly assume the characteristics of nationalist unrest.

This is why Greece's policy towards FYROM is self-defeating. As a consequence of its intransigence, the country's reputation inside the EU has been torn to shreds. More specifically, their actions have both stiffened resistance to change in FYROM on the issues of the name, the flag and the constitutions, and also contributed greatly to a possible internal collapse of the country. If war were to break out, the eventual outcome (after fighting more bloody than in Bosnia) would probably be the consolidation of a Greater Albania and a Greater Bulgaria on Greece's northern border and a concomitant increase in Turkish influence (via Albania) in the region. This is the worst Greek nightmare and yet, by throttling FYROM in the way it is, Athens is hastening the day.

FYROM AND THE INTERNATIONAL COMMUNITY

There have been three major international players (whose roles occasionally overlap) in the southern Balkans: the US, the UN and the EU. The last is chiefly represented by the structures of the Geneva Conference on the Former Yugoslavia. Where the EU has attempted to intervene on its own, it has failed abjectly. The deployment of the preventive UN force to FYROM in May 1992 – a force including 500 American marines – was the first time that peace-keeping troops had been stationed in an area before a conflict has broken out. The office of peace-keeping operations in New York is well aware that the deployment cannot address the central question of Macedonia's internal stability which requires not a military but a political solution. The Security Council decided on the deployment as a way of demonstrating to FYROM's neighbours that it is both in practice and in principle committed to the country's territorial integrity. Confidence in the commitment is eroded by the knowledge that the troops are ready to pull out at the first sign of trouble in the republic. However, the UNPROFOR units have given an important psychological boost to the Macedonians and apart from one or two unpleasant incidents between locals and off-duty blue helmets in some Skopje bars, relations between the population and the UNPROFOR troops are very warm.

To a degree, senior government ministers in FYROM recognise that the American deployment is not entirely altruistic. Since the collapse of communism in the Balkans, the United States has invested much diplomatic capital in the region, particularly in Bulgaria and Albania although latterly in Romania as well. Much coherence, however, has been lost in the policy confusion surrounding Bosnia-Herzegovina and at present the Clinton administration's southern Balkan policy is a sometimes contradictory hotchpotch developed by the regional embassies (who rarely appear to consult with one another), the State Department, the Defense Department, and the White House who, for obvious reasons, take more notice of the Greek and Albanian lobbies in formulating their policy than the other agencies.

Rhetorically, and to a degree practically, the United States is indeed committed to the maintenance of FYROM. However, under the influence of an energetically Albanophile embassy in Tirana, the US has given substantial support to the Albanian government and Sali Berisha in particular. The relationship smacks a little of the clientism practised by the United States in the developing world during the 1960s and 1970s. Just as Greece's Balkan policy appears driven primarily by domestic considerations, so too is Berisha's in Albania. Panicked by the Socialist Party's successes in last year's local elections, Berisha has turned to increasingly authoritarian measures backed by support for an unscrupulous economic mafia which is profitably supporting Albanians' desires for the fruits of western consumerism. The conviction of five leaders of the Greek minority in Albania in September 1994 bore all the hallmarks of Berisha's politics. Despite being offered reasonable deals by the American embassy, the Albanian president refused to back down and insisted they must go to prison. Berisha's refusal may lead to a reassessment of American support for him which until now has been extremely warm.

Along with this political support, Washington is developing closer military cooperation with Tirana (this appears to be a largely solo effort of the Defense Department). Berisha gave Washington permission to station two automatically-piloted GNAT spy planes on Albanian territory from where the Americans monitor Bosnian and Serbian troop movements. In March 1994 the State Department announced that it was lifting the arms embargo (routinely imposed on all communist countries) on Albania, allowing Tirana to purchase NATO cast-offs. These policies have been executed outside the framework of NATO, indicating the Americans' intention of developing a security policy in the southern Balkans which excludes the Europeans to a degree (British and Italian military advisers initially cooperating with the Defence Ministry in Tirana have since been dropped in favour of US officers). America's other military commitment in the region, the 500 marines belonging to the UN preventive peace-keeping force in FYROM, are in theory under Scandinavian command, but their movements are strictly controlled by the Defense Department.

Whereas American policymakers may consider the lifting of the arms embargo a relatively small matter, the Albanians and others in the region interpret its significance very differently. The government in FYROM was especially alarmed by the decision given its own military impotence. As a result, it dropped its support for the maintenance of an arms embargo on the republics of the former Yugoslavia and appealed directly for the embargo against Skopje to be lifted. If there is a unilateral lifting of the embargo against Bosnia (which would mean a *de facto* lifting for Croatia), Slovenia, Yugoslavia and Macedonia would be the only republics still affected by the block on arms exports. Slovenia, as the main smuggling conduit of arms to Bosnia and Croatia, is drowning in weaponry; Yugoslavia still produces weapons and controls large stockpiles; so FYROM (the most vulnerable state in the region) would be the only country without the possibility of buying arms, surrounded by Albania busy purchasing NATO material with Saudi money, Greece whose northern border is brimming with high-tech weaponry, and Bulgaria with its Warsaw Pact equipment still intact.

In the event of Albania becoming embroiled in a conflict

in the southern Balkans, its politicians are encouraged by its warm relationships not just with Washington and NATO but with Turkey (under a Defence Treaty signed in May 1993 between Ankara and Tirana, Turkey is committed to supporting Albania with weapons supplies and logistics if war breaks out in Kosovo). Of course, Tirana has many security concerns, not the least being that the three Albanian communities are squeezed between Serbia and Greece, two countries joined by their Orthodox religion, by solid track records of hostility to Muslims and Albanians, as well as by their modern historical development. They also happen to be two of the region's three mighty military powers (the other being Turkey).

But instead of reducing military competition in the region therefore, American policy tends to encourage it. It is important to consider this policy within the overall framework of Russian–American strategic relations in the northern Balkans and elsewhere in Eastern Europe. The entire region of central and south-eastern Europe, stretching from the Baltic States down to Macedonia, Albania and Bulgaria is currently doing a security limbo dance, with the height of the stick set at different levels ranging from on the ground in Bosnia's case to tolerably high in the case of the Visegrad countries. The United States and Russia appear to be trying to establish the rules of the game rather than actually developing a joint security policy. Each side is hampered by domestic considerations. The American political elite is split by the old division between isolationists and interventionists while NATO has clearly lost the unity of purpose which existed prior to the collapse of communism (as Bosnia has demonstrated well), highlighting different security perceptions between Europe and the United States. President Yeltsin's resolute resistance to some American policy ideas (for example, arming the Muslims in Bosnia or extending NATO membership to the Visegrad countries) is borne partly of fear of a nationalist backlash inside Russia. Yet it is equally informed by Russian security needs. American or NATO support for the Muslims is perceived in Moscow as a direct threat to Russia's security.

The unevenly matched Great Powers, Russia and America, have thus both established a military presence in the Balkans. This should be seen purely in strategic terms and certainly not with respect to economic interests. In private conversation,

Macedonian government officials maintain that the American military presence in their country should be seen as a counter-balance to the Russian troops stationed in the Krajina and above all in Sarajevo. For our purposes, it is important merely to note that both have now a certain military commitment in the area although it is striking that Russia has shown little interest, diplomatic, economic or military, in FYROM.

There are too many political missions being sent to Macedonia. Aside from the envoys of the OSCE, the European Union, the Geneva Conference on Yugoslavia, the United Nations, and the United States, numerous think-tanks send delegations to FYROM who ask the same basic questions of Macedonian politicians, academics and journalists who have better things to do with their time. Of the above mentioned, the EU, the UN and the US have had some concrete, positive influence on the politics of FYROM. But the Macedonians have lost patience with the others.

Despite considerable effort, neither Cyrus Vance, working on behalf of Boutros-Ghali, nor Matthew Nimetz, President Clinton's special envoy mediating in the Athens–Skopje dispute, has made any progress. The United States did force a shift in Albanian policy towards FYROM and the European Union has played an important role in organising the 1994 census (although this will only be regarded as a success once the Albanians have recognised its results). Beyond this and the piecemeal establishment of low-level diplomatic relations between FYROM and EU member states, Russia, China and the US, there has been little activity. It has taken three years of war in Croatia and Bosnia to glimpse even the beginnings of a constitutional settlement. The likelihood of war in FYROM is impossible to calculate but it is undoubtedly a serious threat. A conflict on this territory has more serious implications than even the Bosnian one as it would spring the boundaries of the former Yugoslavia. As the current conflict between Albania and Greece indicates, it is not just the former Yugoslavia which requires new constitutional and political settlements in the Balkans. Yet the international community appears unprepared to invest political capital in preventive work – it merely responds to conflicts once they have broken out. In the case of FYROM, this is simply not good enough.

9 Law and War
Françoise Hampson

When we arrived it was called a war; now it is called a breach of the agreement.[1]

INTRODUCTION

The conflicts in the former Yugoslavia pose a challenge not just to international lawyers but to all those concerned with the role and function of law in international relations. Have the rules of international law affected in any way the conduct of the parties or played any part in shaping the response of the international community? If so, what has that role been and could more have been achieved?

Legal rules may have a variety of functions. At one end of the spectrum, they may be absolute norms in the light of which the conduct of the parties is to be judged. A rule may be characterised in this way because it is seen as fundamental to the existence of an international legal order. To that extent, the entire community has an interest in seeing that the principle is upheld. The parallel in domestic law is with criminal law. The condemnation and punishment of the guilty party takes precedence over the compensation of the victim.

At the other end of the spectrum, the law simply provides a framework for the expectations of the parties. It is the context in the light of which they may assess their relative bargaining positions. The interest of the international community lies in their reaching agreement and not in the content of that agreement. The parallel in domestic law is in the law of contract or, if the dispute arises after an event which has caused harm, the law of tort or delict.

While international law recognises this spectrum, states do not in fact act in accordance with its implications. Were they to do so, any violation of a rule at the absolute norm end of the spectrum would be met by unanimous condemnation and collective action being taken, by force if necessary, to undo the

148

wrong.[2] Such a reaction followed the Iraqi invasion of Kuwait in 1990 but was the exception which proves the rule.

If a norm were absolute, its content, application and enforcement would be certain and least open to political manoeuvrings. In fact, the political sensitivity of the response to a use of armed force is such that what should be non-negotiable is most subject to manipulation. One only has to consider the range of response to events in the former Yugoslavia amongst European Union states – states which aspire to a common foreign policy.

This results in the worst of both worlds. International law employs a language which implies that it is an independent system of rules but, in practice, provides no more than a context for the settlement of disputes.[3] The gulf between rhetoric and reality is greatest where there is most need for absolute, non-negotiable principles. A different difficulty arises where it appears that, in a particular field, no legal principles at all may exist. When such a field encompasses issues to do with the organisation of states and the stability of existing state structures, international institutions have no tools for navigating in potentially very disturbed waters indeed. Such a situation appears to exist in relation to the disintegration of independent sovereign states, particularly where the splits occur along national or ethnic lines, raising issues explored by Adam Roberts in this book.

INTERNATIONAL LAW AND THE DISINTEGRATION OF STATES

During the 1960s and 1970s, the status of self-determination emerged clearly as a principle of both customary law and treaty law.[4] The practice of the international community established that the kernel of the rule was that colonial peoples and those in non-self-governing territories were entitled to independence. Certain issues were left unresolved, such as the applicability of the principle to other groups and whether those entitled to self-determination were also entitled to external military support to achieve it.[5] Newly independent states seemed as averse to any form of secession by minority groups within their state as were older states. For both legal and political reasons, state boundaries were treated as sacrosanct.

This structure might have survived the shock waves from the disintegration of the Soviet Union and the inrush of nationalism or any other -ism to fill the post-communist vacuum had norms of internal governance evolved and achieved the status of international law. Whilst the 1960s and 1970s saw respect for human rights increasingly recognised as a matter of legitimate international concern, Article 2(7) of the UN Charter was still invoked to keep internal situations outside the purview of the Security Council.[6] Only where a domestic situation represented a threat to international peace and security could Article 2(7) be by-passed. Within the human rights field, the norms tended to be concerned with the relationship between the individual and the state, rather than with principles of good government or the relationship between groups or communities. Even within these limitations, human rights law was subject to political manipulation. The nature and/or scale of the alleged violations was a relatively insignificant factor in determining whether a situation was raised in a human rights forum.[7]

No body of legal principles was in place on minority rights, when pressures were experienced within sovereign states in the late 1980s. What was needed was not merely the right of a minority to use its language or manifest its culture. As a *quid pro quo* for denying a right to secession and insisting on non-recognition of seceding entities, with the possible exception of 'divorce' with the consent of all the parties, what was needed was a right to autonomy and some mechanism independent of the state for determining the existence of a relevant type of minority. Such proposals were and are anathema to states in general and not merely to the newly independent states of eastern Europe.

One cannot say whether, if such a package had been in place in the 1980s, it would have prevented or limited the devastation in the former Yugoslavia. One can say, however, that the lack of any such consensus as to the legal norms applicable enabled states to take different positions on recognition, which in turn prevented the international community from acting in a concerted fashion. It also weakened any collective measures which were taken. The 'special cases' of Germany and the Baltic States perhaps created false expectations. Those seeking a solution to the conflicts were denied the benefit of a non-negotiable 'bottom line'. Any attempt to draw such a line failed to get the committed support of states. The failing here is not of the enforcement of international law, nor yet of rules which should be regarded as fundamental being manipulated for political ends. The problem is that, in this area, international law is at best negligible, if not actually non-existent.

The difficulties surrounding the creation of new states are different. There are legal rules on the recognition of statehood. They have been developed to deal with a variety of situations. There are even precedents for the creation of states upon the dissolution of empires. In many cases, they followed major international wars, with or without peace treaties, or the independence of former colonies. In the case of the former Yugoslavia, other conditions were added by the Badinter Commission to the grant of recognition by European Union member states.

It has been suggested that no attempt should be made to base the creation of new states on legal principles.[8] Recognition should be accepted as the manifestation of a political process determining whether an entity can be admitted to the club. Insofar as the objection is based on the rigidity of legal requirements, this may be inherent in the nature of legal rules. They aim for certainty at the expense of flexibility. There can be no rules if every situation is to be treated on an *ad hoc* basis. In that case, it would seem futile to argue that the rules on the creation of states need to be modified. If each situation is to be determined on its own merits, or on the basis of the interests of the recognising state, it cannot be subject to legal rules, but merely to a political process.

INTERNATIONAL LAW AND CONFLICT MANAGEMENT

One of the most significant threats to any legal order is the use of force. The community interest in avoiding or curbing the threat would lead one to expect norms of an absolute, rather than a contractual, character and the certainty of enforcement. Perhaps the best example was the response to the Iraqi invasion of Kuwait. An act of aggression was undone and the perpetrators of the invasion and of serious violations of the laws and customs of war were threatened with prosecution. Yet to state the situation so baldly is to disguise the degree to which political

factors shaped that response. The apparent reliance on the law
was an expedient. The conflicts in the former Yugoslavia have
shown the inability of the international community to act with
any consistency, even in a field of such importance to the very
existence of an international legal order.

Conflict prevention

The UN Charter gives the world body a responsibility for the
maintenance of peace and security, and therefore conflict prevention, within certain legal parameters.[9] States are prohibited
from engaging in acts or threats of force against the territorial integrity of other states. This led to the need to define the
threshold at which involvement became intervention. While
assistance, upon request, to a state confronted with an external
threat was generally seen as lawful,[10] more difficult questions
arose with regard to assistance given to 'rebels'. The Third
World's desire not to preclude assistance to those fighting in
the name of self-determination, combined with the reluctance
of the Cold War superpowers to have the form of their involvement labelled as 'intervention', resulted in a principle whose
scope was uncertain. The International Court of Justice (ICJ)
clarified the legal position in the Nicaragua Case.[11] That could
not, however provide certainty as to the application of the law
in any given situation.

The United Nations was also constrained, in its attempts to
prevent the resort to force, by the requirement that it not raise
situations internal to a state. The limitation in Article 2(7) of
the UN Charter did not preclude the taking of Chapter VII
enforcement measures, but that required a threat to *international*
peace and security, which implied trans-border effects arising
from the internal situation. One way round the problem was
for some form of consent to be engineered for the matter to
come before the Security Council. In this instance, the federal authorities of Yugoslavia were eventually persuaded to
bring the situation before the Security Council.[12] The Council
responded by imposing sanctions and an arms embargo. Economic sanctions are the first response envisaged under the
Charter. Whilst it might be possible to think of imminent action
in relation to which they would be an adequate response, they
are unlikely to deter the resort to armed force. Furthermore,

by the time they are imposed, all too often that which they are supposed to deter has already happened. The track record of sanctions in undoing harm suggests that without other measures they are ineffective, even where their implementation is nearly one hundred per cent successful.[13] It is small wonder that they have not achieved the desired result in the former Yugoslavia, where sanctions breaking is widespread.

The other traditional response, an arms embargo, was no more successful in deterring fighting, not least because the Federal Republic was almost self-sufficient as an arms producer. There have, in fact, been reports of the parties obtaining certain weapons externally. The arms embargo has had a varying impact on the different parties, as it has remained in place notwithstanding political developments on the ground. Imposed on the entire territory of the Federal Republic, it has borne most heavily on Bosnia-Herzegovina, the only UN-recognised independent sovereign state denied the means to defend itself.[14]

If the mechanisms provided in international law to reinforce the search for a peaceful solution before the outbreak of fighting not merely did not work in this particular situation but could have been predicted to be ineffective, one needs to look for the creation of new devices. The existing regime may be characterised as too little and too late. The obvious solution is the massive preventive deployment of UN or UN-authorised forces. As Adam Roberts underlines, *An Agenda for Peace* proposed a much more robust form of preventive diplomacy than exists at present.[15] With the passage of time since the proposals were made (1992), it is clear that the political will does not exist to create the necessary infrastructure. It is not only that there are no permanent UN forces but there is also no sign of the will to deploy such forces on a sufficient scale to prevent conflict.[16] It seems inconceivable that the Secretary-General would be given the authority to order the deployment. Without that, the decision is subject to the political manoeuvrings in the Security Council. The increase in the number of UN peace-keeping operations and their complexity and duration has led to a crisis in their financing. We are more likely to see a retrenchment than an expansion in such operations.

While the United Nations, whether acting through the good offices of the Secretary-General or the Security Council, is seen as the principal legal mechanism for the prevention of conflict, the Charter itself envisages a role for regional organisations, under the supervision of the Security Council. Initially European states sought to maintain that the situation in the Federal Republic of Yugoslavia was a European problem and should be dealt with as such. The available institutional mechanism was the Conference on Security and Cooperation in Europe (CSCE), of which Yugoslavia was a member. In legal terms, that organisation is *sui generis*.[17] Its 'agreements' are supposed to be politically but not legally binding. It has been suggested that this in fact increases compliance with commitments. The institutions created by the CSCE include the Conflict Prevention Centre, still very new at the outbreak of the Yugoslav crisis.[18] The issue was in fact transferred to the more authoritative Committee of Senior Officials. The CSCE did not have the infrastructure to take action on the ground but the European Community Monitoring Mission (ECMM) was deployed, in the name of the CSCE, originally in Slovenia but eventually throughout the territory of Yugoslavia, until the Serbian authorities refused to extend its authorisation to monitor the situation in Sandzak, Kosovo and Vojvodina.

The issue of conflict prevention cannot be concluded without some reference to early warning indicators of potential conflict. It is most unusual for a conflict to spring from nowhere. In the case of the former Yugoslavia, news reports had indicated for some time not merely a worsening situation but one which was deteriorating in ways likely to lead to conflict. The fragmentation of the previously centrally controlled media under the revised constitution of 1974 had enabled the articulation of grievances in nationalist, rather than Republican, terms.[19] The election of 'nationalist' political parties, particularly in Slovenia and Croatia, had exacerbated this tendency. The mystery for the educated layman is not that the disagreements degenerated into armed conflict but why other governments seemed surprised.

Conflict resolution

Once the fighting has started, the focus of the United Nations shifts from conflict prevention to conflict resolution. In theory at least, this ought to involve a different legal issue, the *ius ad bellum*. It would be naive to imagine that the lawfulness of a resort to armed force would be the determining factor in the response of the international community. Nevertheless, the relative degree of unlawfulness might be expected to play a significant role in creating the context in which a solution is sought, particularly given the importance of the prohibition of the use of armed force in upholding some form of international order.

At once there is a tension between two different elements. On the one hand, a speedy end to the fighting requires agreement at any price. Conciliation needs the maximum space or the minimum of legal restrictions.[20] Conciliation also precludes one party being wholly in the right. On the other hand, the very concept enshrined in the UN Charter, a victim of aggression, implies that the law may apportion blame in clear-cut ways. To insist on upholding the law, however, means to impose a solution. This gives rise to something of a paradox. The legal rights and wrongs of a situation may exercise a positive effect in shaping the negotiating position of the parties but the very fact that it is no more than a bargaining chip undermines a legal principle whose content is, or ought to be, non-negotiable.

If there are problems enough where the law is certain, the significance of international law in the conflict resolution process is further weakened where the law is uncertain. This is compounded where the situation on the ground evolves in legally significant ways. At the outset, were the Federal authorities resisting secession or opposing a legitimate claim to self-determination? Can such a claim be founded on domestic constitutional provisions which provide a right to independence, which was not supposed to be acted upon? At what point did the Federal forces become occupying forces? Was it when independence was asserted, *de facto* achieved or only upon recognition? Is the conflict in Bosnia-Herzegovina a war of aggression led by Serbia and assisted by local forces or an uprising with external assistance? Eventually, judicial answers may be provided to some of these questions by the ICJ and the Ad Hoc War Crimes Tribunal. At the time when it matters, the answers are provided by sovereign states, some of which may be genuinely seeking to do no more than uphold their view of the law but others of which will be manipulating the legal uncertainty for political ends.

The manipulation of labels has been one of the most disturbing features of the situation in Yugoslavia, particularly with regard to Bosnia-Herzegovina. To use the label 'civil war' as if there were no argument is to distort the perception not merely of the facts but of the options. Outside parties must assist the victim of aggression, or at least allow it to arm itself. Outside parties are not, however, supposed to get involved in civil wars, for that would be intervention and unlawful. Some go one stage further and refer not merely to a civil war but to the parties, as if they were of equivalent status. This assumes that Serbs, Croats and Muslims are fighting one another. The governmental forces include Bosnians of every ethnic label and some who would prefer none. The command of those forces has not always been in the hands of Muslims. The government contained ministers from different groups. Assistance to fighting groups may represent intervention but assistance to a lawfully elected, recognised government is not usually viewed in that way.

Another area in which the search for peace leads to a setting aside of legal considerations is in the choice of people with whom the envoys or negotiators talk. If their object is to bring an end to the fighting, they must talk to the leaders of those engaged in the fighting. This leaves voiceless those who wish to live in peace with one another. It does not treat the situation in the territory as a whole but looks only at the fighting. This must inevitably affect the outcome. Any 'solution' in Bosnia-Herzegovina will not reflect in any way the desire of those who wished to live together in a unitary state.[21] Where the international community has no bottom line which it is prepared to impose, if necessary by the use of force, the fighting parties determine the terms of the settlement. In this way, aggression, crimes against humanity and other violations of fundamental rules of international law may be rewarded. Those negotiating on behalf of the EU and the UN have taken a good deal of criticism. Whether or not they have any responsibility for 'selling out', the fault is not theirs alone. They could only invoke non-negotiable principles, such as cantons not based on ethnic criteria, if the Security Council were willing to impose them if necessary. They have never had that type of support.

The Security Council has not only been seeking a political solution to the fighting but has also been trying to provide humanitarian assistance to the victims of the conflict and to maintain the peace-keeping operations. Each of these activities carries its own problems but, in addition, each also has an impact on the attempts to stop the fighting. Legally speaking, these activities may be unrelated but, in practice, that is far from being the case. All too easily, the delivery of humanitarian assistance becomes a bargaining counter and the peace-keepers become potential hostages. This not only prevents their functioning as they are supposed to do but inhibits the Security Council from taking resolute action, particularly if members have forces on the ground.

It is hard to discern any positive contribution which international law has made to conflict prevention or conflict resolution in the former Yugoslavia. Rather, the invoking of legal precepts to no visible effect may have done serious damage to the status of international law and reduced its potential for shaping events in other areas. Insofar as this may be attributable to the conjunction of a politically sensitive subject matter, the use of armed force, and gaps in the law, notably with regard to the disintegration of states, one might expect international law to have had more impact in other fields, where the law is more certain and less subject to political manipulation. Three such fields are the peace-keeping operations, the provision and delivery of humanitarian assistance and imposing limits on the conduct of hostilities.

THE PEACE-KEEPING OPERATIONS

The types of situations in which traditional peace-keeping operations occurred enabled the development of established practices.[22] Peace-keepers were usually deployed following the end of active hostilities in an inter-state armed conflict. All the parties consented to the presence, mandate and activities of the force. It usually constituted a buffer between zones under the control of different parties. Its main function was monitoring the ceasefire. Its mandate made it clear that the forces could only open fire if they were the target of attack. They could not use force to prevent any other violation of the ceasefire. In those circumstances, they only needed to be lightly armed and they did not need to be highly trained career soldiers. The limitations on the scope of traditional peace-keeping were, in part, a product of their uncertain status under the UN Charter.

They could range from operations authorised under the Uniting for Peace Resolution of the General Assembly to Security Council 'Chapter VI and a half' operations.[23]

The new problems which have appeared to confront such UN operations recently are not simply due to their being different in kind. Some of the difficulties are inherent in all such deployments but did not emerge before because the consent of the parties hid from view some unresolved issues. One example would be effective machinery for command and control within the Department of Peace-keeping Affairs and the Office of the Secretary-General. Another example would be the problems which could arise in the interpretation of rules of engagement (ROE) by different forces.

That said, the increase in the number and complexity of UN operations has also brought new problems in its train.[24] The very factors which make the task of the forces more difficult lead to political tensions in the Security Council, with legal consequences. Different strategic interests will shape support for the parties to the conflict and the terms of the mandate. The mandate determines the ROE. The basis on which the forces are to be deployed will affect the consent of the parties, which in turn shapes how the forces operate, the type of forces which need to be deployed and the equipment they will need. In terms of international law, the mandate of the force is the connection between the force and its authorising body, the Security Council. The UN infrastructure appears either to have failed to recognise or else inadequately to have appreciated the significance of the three categories of UN operations. There are not merely traditional peace-keeping operations and enforcement actions under Chapter VII of the Charter. The category in between, sometimes called peace-enforcement, is not like peace-keeping.[25] It may not involve the imposition of an overall solution but the UN is giving the forces the obligation to achieve something specific and not merely to be there. The forces may be more at risk than those involved in a peace-keeping operation, since they will consist overwhelmingly of ground forces, deployed in areas where the consent of the parties can vary over time. This requires a different type of command and control infrastructure within the UN. The Department of Peace-keeping Affairs simply does not have the appropriate systems in place for this type of operation.

Any element of enforcement changes fundamentally the nature of the operation. Traditional peace-keeping is a neutral type of activity. It fits within the conciliation end of the spectrum. Enforcement, on the other hand, can appear to involve the taking of sides, even if that is no more than the upholding of international law. The law can be enforced even-handedly but that does not mean that a specific act of enforcement is seen as neutral by the party at the receiving end of it.

Two of the groups of UN forces in the former Yugoslavia reflect clearly these differences. UNPROFOR I, operating in the four UN Protected Areas in Croatian Serb-majority areas in Croatia, most resembles a traditional peace-keeping operation.[26] It was deployed following a ceasefire and the agreement for the withdrawal of the JNA. Its military purpose was to prevent a resumption of the fighting. Its other purposes include the prevention of further killings and 'ethnic cleansing', and creating the conditions in which refugees or the internally displaced could return home. The peace-keepers have not been given the authority to impose such conditions by force. They are lightly armed and do not expect to have to fight. UNCIVPOL (UN Civilian Police) was to assist the local, in practice Croatian Serb, police force but does not have the power to detain, to try or to run courts.

UNPROFOR I has largely achieved what traditional peace-keeping operations achieve and failed to achieve every other objective. The general resumption of fighting has been prevented. This achievement should not be underestimated. It has not, however, brought a political solution to the problem of the status of Croatian Serb-majority areas in Croatia. What was intended to create the space for the reaching of political agreement has merely frozen the *status quo*. Moreover UNPROFOR I and UNCIVPOL have not been able to prevent ethnically motivated killings, further 'ethnic cleansing' and the destruction of property.[27] Nor have people been able to return home. This can hardly be blamed on those forces. Their mandates do not give them the power to intervene to prevent such actions or to take effective action afterwards. That would change the nature of the operation.

UNPROFOR II, deployed in Bosnia-Herzegovina, is more like a peace-enforcement operation. Its patchwork of mandates includes the protection of humanitarian assistance, the keeping open of Sarajevo airport for relief supplies and what is supposed to be the protection of designated 'safe areas'.[28] The mandates raise a variety of legal and political problems. They are not always clearly defined, which runs the risk of being transferred into ambiguous ROE.[29] The ROE are themselves subject not only to interpretation but to translation. If different forces open fire in different situations, this sends confused signals to the indigenous parties and creates the risk of unnecessary incidents. A mandate to defend, by force if necessary, humanitarian assistance poses a problem for those contingents whose national law does not authorise the use of force in defence of property.[30] This could easily be solved by mandating the force to protect civilians but, except in the case of 'safe areas', that would be seen as far too interventionist by the Security Council. The original approach to the protection of the designated 'safe areas', that is to say without a demilitarised buffer zone, was shown to be seriously flawed in the case of Goražde. The contrast with the precedent, the 'Safe Haven' in Iraqi Kurdistan, was striking. In the case of Bosnia-Herzegovina, the mandate was more restricted, the means were not available to take the necessary action, UN–NATO coordination did not function as it should have done, and contributing states (which include UN veto powers) were worried about the safety of their forces. The fear of forces becoming hostages or targets has affected every aspect of the operation, from the decision on the lifting of the arms embargo to the scope of the mandates.

Both UNPROFOR I and II reveal possible difficulties with Status of Forces Agreements (SOFAs). Even if the state in whose territory they are operating is willing to conclude a SOFA, that is of little assistance when forces are dealing with non-state entities. Any attempt to conclude a similar agreement with such a party might appear, particularly to the host state, as a form of recognition.[31]

While the problem of coordination, both within the UN machinery and between the UN and other organisations such as NATO, might appear to be exclusively practical, it can have legal implications. The authority for different types of enforcement action is very much a legal question. Confusion between NATO, whose resources are needed for air strikes, and the UN Secretary-General or his designated representative, who are supposed to authorise air strikes, can exacerbate the situation on the ground and send dangerous signals to the parties posing the threat. The UN has also had problems in coordinating the relief effort, notwithstanding the creation of the Department of Humanitarian Affairs.[32] The various roles of the UN have also complicated matters for those seeking to provide humanitarian assistance under the protection of UN forces.

HUMANITARIAN ASSISTANCE

International law provides for relief actions for the civilian population in a conflict zone. Different provisions apply, depending on whether the area is occupied territory or the conflict is international or non-international. The rules are to be found in the Geneva Conventions of 1949 for the Protection of the Victims of War, notably Convention IV, and the two Protocols to the Conventions of 1977, the first dealing with international and the second non-international conflicts.[33] The Federal Republic of Yugoslavia had ratified all of these treaties and implemented them by means of domestic legislation. Slovenia, Croatia and Bosnia-Herzegovina claim to have succeeded to these treaty obligations.

While it is clear how treaty provisions may bind state authorities even in the case of a non-international conflict, it is at first sight less clear how they can bind non-state fighting groups. The Geneva Conventions, however, contain not only the usual type of provision on domestic implementation. They also provide, in Article 3 common to each Convention, 'In the case of armed conflict not of an international character occurring in the territory of one of the High Contracting Parties, *each Party to the conflict* shall be bound to apply, as a minimum, the following provisions . . .'.[34] Protocol II of 1977 develops and supplements Article 3. It appears, however, to apply to a more limited range of non-international conflicts. They have to be of a higher intensity than the minimum threshold required for Article 3 and the Protocol only applies to conflicts between governmental and dissident armed groups, not between two dissident armed groups.[35]

In whatever way the conflicts in the former Yugoslavia are to be characterised, there are rules applicable to the delivery of humanitarian assistance. If a conflict is international, 'relief actions which are humanitarian and impartial in character and conducted without any adverse distinction shall be undertaken, subject to the agreement of the Parties concerned in such relief actions'.[36] The Parties to the conflict, 'shall allow and facilitate rapid and unimpeded passage of all relief consignments... even if such assistance is destined for the civilian population of the adverse Party'.[37] It will be noted that the language is mandatory but the obligation is subject to the consent of the Party concerned. Similarly, in non-international conflicts, relief actions 'shall be undertaken subject to the consent of the High Contracting Party concerned.'[38] Significantly, the provision does not require the consent of the non-state Party, because it is addressing the issue of sovereignty.

In practice, relief operations must have the consent of all the parties to the conflict, whether states or dissident armed groups. The providers of relief are both inter-governmental and non-governmental organisations (IGOs and NGOs). In the case of the former Yugoslavia, the United Nations High Commissioner for Refugees (UNHCR) was given the task of coordinating the relief operation. Apart from fluctuating donor interest, UNHCR has suffered from two major difficulties. In common with every other relief organisation, it needed a neutral, non-politicised space in which to operate.[39] Its only chance of meeting needs lay in persuading the parties that the relief operation posed no threat. The escort of relief by UN forces is likely to be perceived as calling the neutrality and impartiality of the operation into question. While relief organisations have complained, particularly with regard to Somalia, that the cure (armed UN escorts) may be worse than the disease (attacks on relief convoys and their personnel), it is not clear how they would solve the problem. They already have to assume that a significant proportion of the assistance will go to feed the fighters on each side. Secondly, UNHCR, as an IGO, has a quite specific problem insofar as it is perceived to be part of the UN intergovernmental machinery. Even if a neutral space for humanitarian action existed for the likes of the International Committee of the Red Cross (ICRC) and *Médecins Sans Frontières*, it is not clear that it would benefit UNHCR. When the exasperated High Commissioner for Refugees, Mrs Sadako Ogata, sought to suspend deliveries in central Bosnia until the parties agreed not to hinder operations, she was rebuked by the UN Secretary-

General and forced to resume the attempt to deliver assistance. This hardly helped her claims to independence.[40]

UNHCR has had to stretch its mandate beyond breaking point in relation to the displacement of people. The adjacent states and western European states made it clear they would accept no more people from Bosnia-Herzegovina. It was easy for non-adjacent states to avoid any responsibility by relying on the principle of first country of refuge. This led adjacent states in turn to prohibit entry into their territories because they knew the refugees would not be allowed to move on. After a time, only those with onward travel documents were allowed to leave Bosnia-Herzegovina for Croatia. This meant that thousands were faced with the choice of being killed where they were or 'ethnically cleansed' into overcrowded areas in central Bosnia. The one thing they could not do was to leave Bosnia-Herzegovina. Until they left their country, however, they were not technically refugees. UNHCR did try to cut through the red tape by attempting 'preventive protection'. By being present in areas such as Banja Luka, it sought both to reassure the non-Serb population and to deter further acts of 'ethnic cleansing'. While in some places for a time UNHCR officers may have had a beneficial effect, overall they have not been able to prevent continued 'ethnic cleansing'; a process they themselves are alleged to have either assisted or condoned.[41]

Finally, the ICRC has experienced repeated lack of respect for and even abuses of the Red Cross/Crescent emblem.[42] That represents a serious undermining of neutral humanitarian space. The ICRC has negotiated agreement upon agreement between the parties on the protection and transfer of prisoners and on measures to assist civilians. The agreements are broken as quickly as they are made.

THE CONDUCT OF THE CONFLICTS

The conflicts have been marked by the targeting of civilians, by both direct and indiscriminate means; the targeting of hospitals and medical facilities; the targeting of religious and cultural monuments; atrocities; mutilation of corpses; the forced movement of people on 'ethnic' grounds; in some places attempts to eliminate evidence that the expelled population was ever there; wanton destruction of civilian property belonging to the 'other' side; torture and killings in places of detention; appalling conditions of detention and allegations of the use of widespread and systematic rape as a weapon of war.[43] No party to the conflicts is free of such charges but those fighting on behalf of the Bosnian Serbs have the weightiest evidence against them in terms of the number and scale of the atrocities alleged and the degree of organisation involved. Some of these activities when grouped together have resulted in the practice that has become known as 'ethnic cleansing'. There have been charges that the practices, taken together, amount to genocide.

Popular reaction in the world at large seems to combine in equal measure scepticism as to whether conflicts can be subject to legal limitations and outrage as to the actual conduct in question. The attempt to regulate the conduct of conflict is as ancient as war itself but the modern rules may be seen as having their origins in the *Lieber Code* and the *Declaration of St Petersburg.*[44] The law developed in two streams, the one regulating the actual fighting and known as the law of The Hague and the other dealing with the protection of the victims of war and known as the law of Geneva. A body of treaty law was developed in both fields which, given the nature of treaties, regulated inter-state conflicts. Only Article 3 common to the four Geneva Conventions of 1949 and Protocol II to the Conventions of 1977 expressly deal with non-international conflicts. Alongside treaty law, there was also a body of customary international law.

In essence, the rules require that a distinction be drawn between civilian and military objectives. Only the latter may be targeted and indiscriminate attacks are prohibited. While combatants may kill one another, they may not inflict unnecessary suffering or superfluous injury on one another. Victims of war, such as the wounded and sick, prisoners of war and civilians in occupied teritory, must be respected and protected.

Breaches of the laws and customs of war represent war crimes.[45] They entail both state delictual responsibility and, in the case at least of 'grave breaches', individual criminal responsibility. 'Grave breaches' of the Geneva Conventions of 1949 and Protocol I are crimes of universal jurisdiction, rendering the defendant liable to trial before the courts of any country.[46]

Protocol I of 1977 clarified the law with regard to command responsibility.[47] The Charter of the International Military Tribunal at Nuremberg included the concept of a crime against humanity. The Tribunal held that actions coming within that formula had to be related to the war but the concept may have acquired an autonomous existence since then. It seems apt to cover conduct in a non-international conflict.[48] 'Grave breaches' as defined in the Geneva Conventions can only occur in international conflicts. It is also argued that war crimes can only exist in such conflicts. In that case, if the conflicts are characterised as non-international, courts outside the territory could only prosecute individuals for actions which amount to crimes against humanity or genocide. Those within the territory can prosecute for breaches of domestic criminal law, but that implies a functioning court system and the ability to obtain both defendants and evidence which may be in territory under the control of another Party.[49]

Prior to 1990, the international community generally analysed atrocities in terms of human rights law. Then the Iraqi forces were warned, in Security Council resolutions and the speeches of political leaders, that they would be held personally accountable for their actions.[50] After the liberation of Kuwait, evidence was gathered by certain forces but no trials were held, other than those held by the Kuwaitis. In the case of the former Yugoslavia, the first response was through human rights mechanisms but this was followed by the creation of a Commission of Experts whose mandate was specifically to enquire into the commission of war crimes.[51] That group was deprived of the resources necessary to gather the right type of evidence itself and complained that it was not receiving the requisite assistance from states. The evidence it required was very different in character from that required to establish a violation of human rights law. The latter requires evidence of a victim, the wrong suffered and the responsibility of the state for causing or, in some circumstances, failing to prevent the harm. The former requires evidence that can withstand cross-examination as to the identity of the perpetrator.

The Security Council subsequently established the Ad Hoc War Crimes Tribunal to prosecute those allegedly responsible for certain defined actions.[52] The Tribunal was established under a Chapter VII Security Council resolution. It appears to have a problem of resources and for a considerable period was without a Prosecutor. The problems confronting the Tribunal include getting custody of the accused, as trials *in absentia* are precluded, determining whether the conflicts are international or non-international, if war crimes *strictu senso* can only be committed in the former type of conflict, and defining the scope of the offences.[53] The problems for the Prosecutor include, most importantly, the gathering of the right type of evidence to bring criminal prosecutions.

It has been argued that to have proceeded so far along this road will be worse than useless if it does not result in a reasonable number of prosecutions and convictions. One fear is that the Tribunal may be abolished if that is the price for a peace agreement. Alternatively, a more limited form of amnesty may be insisted upon by the belligerents. This raises the familiar tension between upholding the law and achieving a political agreement. It has been argued that, even used as a bargaining chip, the tribunal will have served a purpose. The party with most to fear from the Tribunal will have to make the most concessions to have the Tribunal abolished. In this way, war crimes will be seen to be counter-productive.[54]

HUMAN RIGHTS LAW

In addition to the existence of treaty bodies, the UN Commission on Human Rights has a general supervisory role in relation to human rights law. It is a political body composed of the representatives of states. In August 1992, it held its first ever emergency session and appointed the former Polish Prime Minister Tadeusz Mazowiecki as the Special Rapporteur on Yugoslavia.[55] The calling of an emergency session was an innovative response and subsequently proved to be a useful precedent in the case of Rwanda. However, it again shows the international community doing too little, too late. Human rights violations had been reported long before. They were not used as a warning indicator. Rather, the Special Rapporteur's role has been to document the violations that have already taken place.

This is not to deny all significance to his reports. They do represent an official record. They not only contain information on well-publicised incidents, such as the Ahmici massacre, but also material on fields relatively neglected by the press, such as the role of the media in inflaming acts of violence and on the situation in Serbia and Montenegro. The detailed examination and assessment of the allegations of the widespread and systematic use of rape is a useful balance to the Warburton Commission Report for the EC, which was handicapped by a discriminatory mandate, inadequate time and a questionable methodology.[56] That said, the reports do not actually lead to the taking of any specific remedial action. The Commission deplores the situation and calls on the parties to do better. Breaches of human rights law engage the responsibility of the state but not of individuals or non-state groups, unless the actions in question represent war crimes.

The Human Rights Committee, established under the International Covenant on Civil and Political Rights, summoned Croatia, Bosnia-Herzegovina and Yugoslavia (Serbia and Montenegro) to report on how they secured respect for the provisions of the Covenant.[57] When the first two disclaimed responsibility for what happened in areas of their territory outside their *de facto* control and Yugoslavia disclaimed responsibility for what happened outside its territory, the exercise was somewhat limited. The Committee, however, required Yugoslavia to use its influence with Serbs in Croatia and Bosnia-Herzegovina or else to dissociate itself from human rights violations for which they were responsible.

The human rights NGOs, notably Amnesty International and Helsinki Watch, have documented the human rights violations in relation to which they have been able to obtain reliable information.[58]

The UN human rights machinery has, therefore, been involved and it has produced more than might have been expected, thanks to the holding of an emergency session and the appointment of an effective Special Rapporteur. Nevertheless, the lack of teeth in the system has resulted in the creation of a record but no effective action arising out of it. Information being fed into the UN system gets transformed as it makes its way to the seat of the decision-making. With some justice *The Times* has referred to 'the castrated neutrality of the reports being drawn up by the UN'.[59]

USE OF FORMAL LEGAL MECHANISMS

In addition to a few domestic criminal proceedings in Croatia, Serbia and Bosnia-Herzegovina and the creation of the Ad Hoc War Crimes Tribunal, civil proceedings have been instituted against Radovan Karadžić in the United States, and Bosnia-Herzegovina has brought a case against the Federal Republic of Yugoslavia (Serbia and Montenegro) in the International Court of Justice, *inter alia* alleging genocide.[60] It might have been thought that engaging in judicial proceedings represents the ultimate form of upholding the law, whether the proceedings are domestic, as in the case of Karadžić, or international. This is to over-simplify what parties think they are doing in going to law in such circumstances.

Nowhere is this more clearly seen than in the human rights law/war crimes field. The advantage to a state which believes that it will succeed in a case in that field is that it can claim the moral high ground on account of the nature of the norms invoked. This casts the other state not merely in the role of a party to a dispute but in that of villain. The decision to pursue such a course of action is clearly politically motivated. It is in that context that one must view the case brought by Bosnia-Herzegovina against the Federal Republic of Yugoslavia (Serbia and Montenegro). However well-founded on the merits and whatever the outcome, the case cannot be divorced from the broader political context. While the law may be being used for political ends, it does at least mean that the law is seen as a potentially useful tool. To that extent, it is better that it should be used than that the ICJ should not have anything to do with the Yugoslav conflicts. It is only to be regretted that the nature of international legal process means that, by the time the judgment on the merits is delivered, it will probably only serve as a postscript to the resolution of the situation which caused the case to be brought.

CONCLUSION

It would be unrealistic to expect international law to play the same role as the law plays in regulating affairs within a domestic legal order. In the latter context, the law can be the determining factor in decision-making. Within the international system, the law only provides a framework. The degree to which action departs from what is required under international law will at most affect the negotiating position of the parties.

If no more than this were claimed for international law, it would be seen to have fulfilled its role in the conflicts in the former Yugoslavia. The waters have, however, been muddied. The law has been invoked as if it could achieve more but it has not been seen to do so. In the very process of using the law as a bargaining chip, it has been seen to be negotiable. The principles at issue have been deprived of any absolute status as legal rules. This is particularly serious where the norm is at the criminal law end of the spectrum; that is to say, the international community as a whole has an interest in seeing that the principle is upheld, as being necessary to the existence of any legal order. The most obvious candidates for inclusion at this end of the spectrum are principles on the resort to armed force, war crimes, crimes against humanity and genocide. They ought not to be negotiable but the international community has not had the will to enforce them.

The status of international law has suffered as a result of the way in which the conflicts in the former Yugoslavia have been handled. Ultimately, the degree to which its ability to influence the conduct of states and other groups will suffer in the longer term will depend on the final outcome of the conflicts and on the achievements of the Ad Hoc War Crimes Tribunal.

NOTES

1. British officer serving with UNPROFOR, quoted in *The Times*, 30 June 1994.
2. A treaty which violates a principle of *ius cogens* is void; Articles 53 and 64 of the Vienna Convention on the Law of Treaties 1969. There is a significant overlap between such norms and those activities which the International Law Commission has labelled international crimes; ILC Draft Articles on State Responsibility, *YBILC*, 1980, II (Part Two), Article 19.
3. R. Higgins, *Problems and Process* (Oxford: Clarendon Press, 1994).

4.   Ibid., Ch. 7.
5.   General Assembly Declaration on Principles of International Law Concerning Friendly Relations and Co-operation among States in Accordance with the Charter of the United Nations 1970, G. A. Resn 2625 (XXV), 24 October 1970. See generally J. Crawford (ed.), *The Rights of Peoples* (Oxford: Clarendon Press, 1992).
6.   N. Rodley (ed.), *To Loose the Bands of Wickedness* (London: Brassey's, 1992), Chs. 1, 2 and 5.
7.   The international community took no effective action in response to the activities of the Khmer Rouge in Cambodia or the gassing of thousands of people, particularly in Halabja, by the Iraqi military authorities.
8.   See generally, J. Crawford, *The Creation of States in International Law* (Oxford: Clarendon Press, 1979). See also idem, *Rights of Peoples*.
9.   P. Calvocoressi, 'A problem and its dimensions' in Rodley, p. 5 *et seq.*; M. Howard, 'The Historical Development of the UN's Role in International Security', in A. Roberts and B. Kingsbury (eds), *United Nations, Divided World*, 2nd ed. (Oxford: Clarendon Press, 1993).
10.   D. W. Bowett, *Self-Defence in International Law* (London: Stevens, 1958); R. Pinto, 'Les Règles du Droit International concernant la Guerre Civile', *Hague Recueil* (1965), Vol. I, p. 452; but see L. Doswald-Beck, 'The Legal Validity of Military Intervention by Invitation of the Government', 56 *BYIL* (1985), p. 189.
11.   *Military and Paramilitary Activities in and against Nicaragua (Nicaragua v. United States of America)*, Merits, Judgment, ICJ Reports 1986, p. 14.
12.   N. Rodley, 'Collective intervention to protect human rights and civilian populations: the legal framework', in Rodley, p. 25. On the evolution of the crisis in Yugoslavia, see B. Magaš, *The Destruction of Yugoslavia* (London: Verso, 1993) and N. Malcolm, *Bosnia: A Short History* (London: Macmillan, 1994), Chs. 15 and 16.
13.   For example, the imposition and implementation of sanctions against Iraq, following the invasion of Kuwait; D. Bethlehem (ed.), *The Kuwait Crisis: Sanctions and Their Economic Consequences* (Cambridge: Grotius, 1991). See also A. B. Siegel, 'Enforcing Sanctions: A Growth Industry', 46 *Naval War College Review*, No. 4 (Autumn 1993), pp. 130–4.
14.   The right to self-defence is described in Article 51 of the UN Charter as being 'inherent'. It therefore arises independently of Article 51 and exists independently of the procedural and/or temporal limitations, which are dependent upon Security Council action. In the case of the Gulf conflict, the UK and the US argued for the independent and continued existence of Kuwait's right of self-defence, even though the Security Council was seized of the issue. The UK had taken a similar position in relation to the Falklands conflict. One of the American objections to the effect of the arms embargo on Bosnia-Herzegovina is that it deprives the state of the ability to exercise its right of self-defence. Even within the terms of Article 51, it could be argued that the Security Council has never taken action which satisfies the criteria for limiting the exercise of the right (that 'the Security Council has taken measures necessary to maintain international peace and secur-

ity') or that the passage of time has proved the measures taken to have been inadequate.

15. *An Agenda for Peace,* SC Doc. S/24111, 17 June 1992, 31 *ILM* 953 (1992); see also B. G. Ramcharan, 'New Models of Human Rights Protection: Preventive Peacekeeping', *ICJ Review,* No. 50 (1993), p. 101.

16. While the United States envisages a more active involvement in peace-keeping operations, it is reluctant to place its forces under UN command, particularly in the field of 'peace enforcement', where forces are more likely to have to engage in combat; United States: Administration Policy on Reforming Multilateral Peace Operations, 33 *ILM,* 705 (1994) and Department of Defense Statement on Peacekeeping, 33 *ILM,* 814 (1994). See generally, R. Connaughton, 'Military intervention and UN peacekeeping' in Rodley. For the proposal for the establishment of an immediately available elite UN force, see B. Urquhart, 'For a UN Volunteer Military Force', *New York Review of Books,* 10 June 1993; 'The UN and International Security after the Cold War', in Roberts and Kingsbury.

17. J. Gow and L. Freedman, 'Intervention in a Fragmenting State: the Case of Yugoslavia', in Rodley. On the CSCE generally, see D. McGoldrick, 'From "Process" to "Institution" – the Development of the Conference on Security and Cooperation in Europe', in B. Jackson and D. McGoldrick (eds), *Legal Visions of the New Europe – Essays Celebrating the Centenary of the Faculty of Law, University of Liverpool* (London: Graham & Trotman and Nijhoff, 1993); D. McGoldrick, 'The Development of the Conference on Security and Cooperation in Europe (CSCE) after the Helsinki 1992 Conference', 42 *ICLQ* (1993), p. 411.

18. Gow and Freedman, pp. 104–5. On recognition of statehood, see M. Weller, 'The International Response to the Dissolution of the Socialist Federal Republic of Yugoslavia', 86 *AJIL* (1992), p. 569.

19. Article 19, *Forging War: The Media in Serbia, Croatia and Bosnia-Hercegovina* (London: Article 19, 1994); F. J. Hampson, 'Incitement and the Media', *Papers in the Theory and Practice of Human Rights,* No. 3, Human Rights Centre, University of Essex, 1993.

20. J. G. Merrills, *International Dispute Settlement* (London: Sweet & Maxwell, 1984).

21. M. Glenny, *The Fall of Yugoslavia* (London: Penguin, 1992). For the expression of a variety of such views see *War Report,* formerly *Yugofax,* published in London.

22. See generally, R. Higgins, *United Nations Peacekeeping 1946–1967: Documents and Commentary,* 4 Vols. (Oxford: Clarendon Press, 1969–81); S. Morphet, 'UN Peacekeeping and Election-Monitoring' in Roberts and Kingsbury.

23. 'Chapter VI and a half', a phrase coined by Dag Hammarskjöld, refers to operations lying between Chapter VI peace-keeping and Chapter VII enforcement. The Uniting for Peace Resolution, first used to circumvent deadlock in the Security Council, has not been used as the basis for a peace-keeping operation since 1962.

24. Connaughton, op. cit., and *Military Intervention in the 1990s* (London: Routledge, 1992).

25. In the fifth draft of the British army's field manual, *Wider Peacekeeping*, the army uses that concept to describe operations in volatile environments in which there may not be tactical (i.e. local) consent but there is operational (i.e. general) consent. The manual terms 'peace enforcement' operations or activities in which there is neither form of consent. There is also a significant distinction between 'peace enforcement' and 'traditional' enforcement under Chapter VII of the UN Charter. In the case of the latter, the multinational forces are acting as a belligerent party in the name of the UN, a duly authorised regional organisation or a UN member state and are, to all intents and purposes, fighting a war, with the traditional type of war aims (for example, expulsion of an aggressor from territory which it has invaded). In the case of 'peace enforcement', the forces have been mandated to achieve a specific purpose not directly related to the war aims of the fighting parties (for example, the delivery of humanitarian assistance or the protection of 'safe areas') and may be doing so without tactical or operational consent. Army Field Manual, *Wider Peacekeeping*, Fifth Draft (Revised), 1994.

26. Security Council Resolutions 743 (1992), 758 (1992), 761 (1992), 762 (1992), 764 (1992), 769 (1992), 770 (1992), 771 (1992), 776 (1992), 779 (1992), 781 (1992) and 871 (1993).

27. International League for Human Rights, Mission to the former Yugoslavia, November 14–22, 1992, Preliminary Findings & Recommendations; New York, 1992; periodic reports of the Special Rapporteur on the Situation of Human Rights in the Territory of the Former Yugoslavia; Amnesty International, 'Torture and deliberate and arbitrary killings in war zones' (EUR 48/26/91), London, November 1991, and 'Further reports of torture and deliberate and arbitrary killings in war zones' (EUR 48/13/92), London, March 1992. E. G. Primosch, 'The Role of United Nations Civilian Police (UNCIVPOL) within United Nations Peacekeeping Operations', 43 *ICLQ* (1994), p. 425.

28. On 'safe areas', see Security Council Resolutions 819 (1993), 824 (1993), 836 (1993), 844 (1993) and 913 (1994); Report of the Secretary-General pursuant to Resolution 844 (1993), S/1994/555, 9 May 1994.

29. F. J. Hampson, 'Legal aspects of interoperability in multinational military operations', paper presented at the second interoperability conference, Stuttgart, June 1994.

30. A possible problem for Canadian forces, for example, unless an argument can be constructed based on customary international law.

31. Hampson, 'Legal Aspects of Interoperability'. There are currently negotiations taking place at the UN for a treaty which seeks to protect peace-keepers by making it an international crime to attack them. Whilst this would get round the problem of binding members of non-governmental groups, it is not clear how the perpetrators would be identified and arrested without the consent of their own side and without exacerbating the situation. It is also unclear whether a distinction should be drawn between peace-keeping forces, who are in no sense a party to the conflict, and peace-enforcement forces, who might be viewed that way.

32. UN General Assembly Resolution 46/182 (1991).
33. For texts see A. Roberts and R. Guelff, *Documents on the Laws of War*, 2nd ed. (Oxford: Clarendon Press, 1989).
34. J. Pictet, *Commentary on the Geneva Conventions of 1949*, Vol. 1 (Geneva: ICRC, 1952), pp. 51–2 (emphasis added).
35. Bothe, Partsch and Solf, *New Rules for Victims of Armed Conflicts* (The Hague: Nijhoff, 1982), pp. 622–9; Sandoz, Swinarski & Zimmermann (eds), *Commentary on the Additional Protocols of 8 June 1977 to the Geneva Conventions of 12 August 1949* (Geneva: ICRC & Nijhoff, 1987), pp. 1343–56.
36. Article 70.1, Protocol I of 1977.
37. Ibid., Article 70.2.
38. Article 18.2, Protocol II of 1977.
39. F. Jean (ed.), *Life, Death and Aid* (London: Médecins Sans Frontières & Routledge, 1993); Save the Children (UK), Position Paper: The United Nations and Humanitarian Assistance, March 1994; D. Sarooshi, *Humanitarian Intervention and International Humanitarian Assistance: Law and Practice*, Wilton Park Paper 86 (London: HMSO, 1993).
40. Sarooshi, op. cit., pp. 18–19.
41. This appears to pose less of a problem to UN forces; see B. Stewart, *Broken Lives* (London: Harper Collins, 1993), pp. 261–5.
42. See ICRC Bulletin throughout 1992 and 1993. In May 1992 the ICRC had to suspend its Sarajevo operation for two months following an apparently intentional attack on an ICRC convoy in which a delegate was killed.
43. Helsinki Watch, *War Crimes in Bosnia-Hercegovina* (New York, 1992; Vol. II, 1993); Amnesty International, 'Bosnia-Herzegovina: Gross abuses of basic human rights', EUR 63/01/92, London, 1992; 'Rape and sexual abuse by armed forces', EUR 63/01/93, London, 1993; 'Rana u duši: A wound to the soul', EUR 63/03/93, London, 1993; the reports of Mr. Tadeusz Mazowiecki, Special Rapporteur on the Situation of Human Rights in the Territory of the Former Yugoslavia; Reports of the Commission of Experts, Sec. Gen S/25274, February 1993; S/26545, October 1993 and Final Report S/1994/674, May 1994.
44. On the history of the laws of war, see G. Best, *Humanity in Warfare* (London: Methuen, 1983) and on the more recent history G. Best, *War and Law since 1945* (Oxford: Clarendon Press, 1994). On the laws of war generally, see F. Kalshoven, *Constraints on the Waging of War* (Geneva: ICRC, 1987); T. Meron, *Human Rights and Humanitarian Norms as Customary Law* (Oxford: Clarendon Press, 1989) and on the laws applicable in non-international conflicts, see R. Abi-Saab, *Droit Humanitaire et Conflits Internes* (Geneva: Institut Henry-Dunant, 1986) and T. Meron, *Human Rights in Internal Strife: Their International Protection* (Cambridge: Grotius: 1987).
45. T. J. Murphy, 'Sanctions and enforcement of the humanitarian law of the four Geneva Conventions of 1949 and Geneva Protocol I of 1977', 103 *Military Law Review* (1984), p. 3; B. V. A. Roling, 'Aspects of the criminal responsibility for violations of the laws of war', in A. Cassesse (ed.), *The New Humanitarian Law of Armed Conflict* (Milan: Editoriale

Scientifica, 1979); J. L. Fernandez Flores, 'Repression of breaches of the Law of War committed by individuals', *IRRC*, no. 282 (May–June 1991), p. 247; F. J. Hampson, 'Liability for War Crimes', in P. Rowe (ed.), *The Gulf War 1990–91 in International and English Law* (London: Routledge and Sweet & Maxwell, 1993).

46. On the practice within the former Yugoslavia, see F. J. Hampson, 'Violation of Fundamental Rights in the Former Yugoslavia, II. The Case for a War Crimes Tribunal', David Davies Memorial Institute, Occasional Paper No. 3, February 1993.

47. Articles 86 and 87, Protocol I of 1977.

48. Calvocoressi, pp. 6–7; Reports of the Commission of Experts, note 43; T. Meron, 'War Crimes in Yugoslavia and the Development of International Law', 88 *AJIL* (1994) p. 78; J. O'Brien, 'The International Tribunal for Violations of International Humanitarian Law in the Former Yugoslavia' 87 *AJIL* (1993) p. 639.

49. One of the problems at the trial in Sarajevo of Borislav Herak was that the crimes to which he had confessed had taken place in areas under the control of Bosnian Serbs; see Hampson, 'Violation of Fundamental Rights in the Former Yugoslavia, II'.

50. Hampson, 'Liability for War Crimes', p. 257.

51. The Commission of Experts was established under Security Council Resolution 780 (1992); its mandate was to examine and analyse *inter alia* information submitted pursuant to Security Council Resolutions 771 (1992) and 780 (1992) with a view to providing the Secretary-General with its conclusions on the evidence of grave breaches of the Geneva Conventions and violations of international humanitarian law committed in the territory of the former Yugoslavia.

52. Established under Security Council Resolution 827 (1993), under Chapter VII of the UN Charter.

53. 'Procedural and Evidentiary Issues for the Yugoslav War Crimes Tribunal', *Helsinki Watch*, Vol. 5, Issue 15, New York, August 1993; Amnesty International, 'Memorandum to the United Nations: the question of justice and fairness in the international war crimes tribunal for the former Yugoslavia' (EUR 48/02/93), London, April 1993; 'Moving Forward to Set Up the War Crimes Tribunal for the Former Yugoslavia' (EUR 48/03/93), London, May 1993. See also Meron, op. cit., and O'Brien, op. cit.

54. A. D'Amato, 'Peace v. Accountability in Bosnia', 88 *AJIL* (1994) p. 500.

55. Commission on Human Rights 1992/S-1/1, 14 August 1992.

56. EC Investigative Mission into the Treatment of Muslim Women in the Former Yugoslavia (the Warburton Commission); report of the Special Rapporteur on the Situation of Human Rights in the Territory of the Former Yugoslavia, E/CN.4/1993/50, Annex II, pp. 63–75; Report of the Secretary-General (E/CN.4/1994/5).

57. CCPR/C/SR.1200, 1201, 1202, 1202/Add.1 and comments adopted at 1205th meeting (46th Session), 6 November 1992.

58. See note 43.

59. *The Times*, 30 June 1994.

60. *Jane Doe I & Jane Doe II v. Radovan Karadžić*, US District Court,

Southern District of New York, Civil action No. 93 CIV 0878 (PKL); by Opinion & Order dated 7 September 1994, the court ruled that it lacked subject-matter jurisdiction. *Order on request for the Indication of Provisional Measures in Case Concerning Application of the Convention on the Prevention and Punishment of the Crime of Genocide (Bosnia and Herzegovina v. Yugoslavia (Serbia and Montenegro))*, Order of April 8, 1993, 32 *ILM* 888 (1993); *Order on Further Requests for Indication of Provisional Measures*, Order of September 13, 1993, 32 *ILM* 1599 (1993). There is an Arbitration Commission (the Badinter Commission) under the UN/EC (Geneva) Conference which has addressed questions relating to state succession with regard to assets and liabilities, including the date(s) on which succession occurred, and whether any war damages payable would affect the distribution. The Federal Republic of Yugoslavia (Serbia and Montenegro) does not recognise the competence of the Commission; 32 *ILM* 1572 (1993).

10 Communal Conflict as a Challenge to International Organisation[1]

Adam Roberts

Towards the end of the First World War, when allied leaders were considering the future structure of what was to become the League of Nations, Jan Christian Smuts of South Africa wrote:

> The animosities and rivalries among the independent Balkan States in the past, which kept that pot boiling, and occasionally boiling over, will serve to remind us that there is the risk of a similar state of affairs on a much larger scale in the New Europe, covered as it will be with small independent States. In the past the Empires kept the peace among the rival nationalities; the League will have to keep the peace among the new States formed from these nationalities. This will impose a task of constant and vigilant supervision on it.[2]

In 1918–19 there was much heated discussion as to whether or not membership of the League of Nations would require heavy commitment in the Balkans. This discussion was especially intense in the United States, whose geographical isolation and strong anti-colonial traditions militated against accepting distant and debatable responsibilities of this kind. In 1918 President Woodrow Wilson's Fourteen Points had offered a vague but optimistic prescription that the relations of the Balkan States should be 'determined by friendly counsel along historically established lines of allegiance and nationality.'[3] In his passionate but doomed advocacy of the League, he naturally denied that membership would involve the USA in endless policing of troubled regions. As he said in a speech in September 1919: 'If you want to put out a fire in Utah you do not send to Oklahoma

176

for the fire engine. If you want to put out a fire in the Balkans
... you do not send to the United States for troops.'[4] The fear
of involvement in the Balkans was among the factors that made
the US Senate oppose joining the League of Nations.

Thus once before in this century the question of how to
tackle ethnic/communal conflict, notably in the Balkans, dealt
a crippling blow to an attempt at global political organisation
– the League of Nations. Now, three-quarters of a century later,
conflict in that same region as well as elsewhere has exposed
weaknesses in the international community's efforts to maintain international order. Such conflict poses a challenge to the
United Nations, and also to regional institutions, every bit as
serious as was posed to the League of Nations so many years
ago.

This short survey of communal conflict in general, and the
former Yugoslavia in particular, focuses on the challenge posed
to international organisations, mainly the United Nations. It
glances at the language that is used in connection with such
conflict; outlines a few different national and intellectual perspectives; and draws attention to the special problems posed
by the collapse of the communist federations of Yugoslavia and
the Soviet Union. It then considers some of the UN's techniques
for addressing this type of conflict, and concludes with an examination of their strengths and weaknesses. It is largely limited
to responses to ongoing conflicts, and only touches tangentially
on preventive action.

QUESTIONS OF TERMINOLOGY

The words used to characterise a conflict matter deeply. They
often imply the type of interpretation to be placed on it, and
even the policy prescription to be followed. For example, calling the conflict in former Yugoslavia a case of 'ancient ethnic hatred' and 'civil war' has often been code language for
recommending a policy of partial or total non-intervention;
while calling it a case of 'aggression', and defence of a multiethnic Bosnia, has been associated with support for a more
militant outside response. Two terms that are used remarkably
loosely, with considerable policy implications, are first, 'ethnic
conflict'; and secondly, 'nation'.

'Ethnic' v. 'Communal' Conflict

In the history of conflict, ethnicity has been a central and fateful factor. However, there are hazards in labelling a conflict 'ethnic'. To characterise an entire conflict in this way is to imply that the adversaries are biologically distinct peoples, who are at war with each other purely because of such 'objective' factors as different racial origins, skin colours, and languages. In many conflicts, even those to which the word 'ethnic' is commonly applied, such a view is too simple. It may involve accepting too easily the semi-mythological, but nonetheless powerful, belief of particular groups that they have a common ancestry, distinct from that of their adversaries.[5] Some conflicts occasionally labelled as ethnic, far from being between rival ethnic groups, are between people of common ethnic origin. The civil war in Somalia has been for the most part a conflict of clans, not of distinct ethnic groups: indeed, Somalia is more ethnically homogeneous than most African states. In the former Yugoslavia, some of the most bitter fighting has been between groups – most notably Bosnian Serbs and Bosnian Muslims – which have largely common ethnic origins, but centuries ago adopted different faiths identifying them with different outside powers.

'Communal conflict' is often a better term for hostilities between peoples who live in close proximity but have different allegiances and strong mutual fears. The term was familiar in Britain in the days of the Empire, and has been commonly applied to Northern Ireland. It has its faults: it has a superior and world-weary sound, and does not completely capture the international complexities of at least some of these conflicts, nor their significance in the process of state formation. Yet it does better encompass not just ethnic, but also linguistic, regional, class and religious divisions.

A problem with all such terms is that they pigeon-hole conflicts that may have many dimensions. As the Ambassador of Slovenia put it in an address to the UN Security Council in January 1995, there were

> ethnic or religious elements in many conflicts of the past and other, non-ethnic and non-religious elements in present military conflicts, including those which are described as ethnic. As a matter of fact, it is possible to speak of the ethnic

coefficient in most military conflicts in human history. What is really necessary is a careful identification of actors in each conflict and of their actual agendas. Only if this is possible and done can one hope that the response by the United Nations and by other international mechanisms will correspond to the actual needs.[6]

In Croatia, and in Bosnia and Herzegovina, undoubtedly communal aspects of these conflicts have been overlaid with other elements, including the involvement of the Yugoslav Army in support of local Serbs in a role which has often been seen as a case of international aggression. While the case for characterising these wars as 'communal conflicts' remains strong, for some purposes it may be more accurate to refer to the communal (or ethnic) factor (or coefficient) in such conflicts.

'Nation' v. 'State'

The disjunction between 'nation' and 'state' has been among the major causes of practically every war in this century. Yet the language habitually used in international relations actually conceals the disjunction. The frequent use of such terms as 'nation-state' is misleading. So is the media habit of calling states or countries 'nations', a habit that seems to be growing, and that needs to be actively discouraged inasmuch as it is a barrier to understanding.

There is a long tradition of distinguished works, mainly by historians, on the place of nationalism and self-determination in the troubled politics of the European continent and the world.[7] Some of these have dealt particularly with Yugoslavia.[8] Such works have been widely known and taught in departments of International Relations in the United Kingdom, and their themes have been taken up by many scholars in the field.

Some American writers who have stressed the importance of group identity and so-called ethnic conflict have felt that they were swimming against the intellectual tide in their country.[9] Undeniably, many of their colleagues, including some leading International Relations theorists, have neglected a wide range of problems associated with nationalism and ethnic identity. Hans Morgenthau's *Politics Among Nations* followed the common American practice of using the term 'nation' uncritically, as if it were synonymous with existing states, their boundaries and their inhabitants. The potential of nationalism as a divisive force which could lead to the break-up of existing states was badly underestimated.[10]

Part of the explanation for this American usage arises from the unique character and experience of the federal system of the USA. Americans use the word 'nation' to refer to a country because in their political lexicon the word 'state' refers to the States of the Union. As Louis Henkin has put it:

> Throughout I frequently refer to 'nations' even where, strictly, the lawyer and the political scientist would insist on 'states.' ... (This is common usage, and avoids confusion between the states of international society and the states of the United States.)[11]

The usage in another great federal republic, former Yugoslavia, was the exact opposite. There, the term 'nation' referred to each of the major national groups that formed Yugoslavia, and the federation was the 'state'. As Article 1 of the 1974 Constitution put it: 'The Socialist Federal Republic of Yugoslavia is a federal state having the form of a state community of voluntarily united nations and their Socialist Republics...'

Today, the language used in much journalistic, political and even sometimes academic discourse treats 'nation' and 'state' as identical, and fails to comprehend that each term means different things in different societies. The deplorable conflation of 'nation' and 'state' is built into such basic terms as 'international relations' and indeed the 'United Nations'. Such linguistic confusion, which is an impediment to understanding many contemporary conflicts, cannot be eliminated, but attempts can be made to contain it.

SOME PERSPECTIVES ON COMMUNAL CONFLICT AND ON FORMER YUGOSLAVIA

Different individuals, states, and regional bodies have fundamentally diverging perceptions of communal conflict in general, and of particular crises involving such conflict, including former Yugoslavia. There are notable differences on such key questions as whether such conflict is a widespread threat, or one confined to particular situations and countries; whether it is susceptible to integrative solutions, or requires the surgery of secession; and whether outside powers, individually or collectively, can play a useful part in helping to end it, and if so at what stage and by what means. The perspectives of countries and individuals are shaped by their own attitudes and experiences: those with recent experience of civil war and communal conflict often view matters differently from those that have been more preoccupied with inter-state problems.

Reactions to the Yugoslav conflict illustrate all too well the general truth that people in different states see the world differently. For example, Russia has naturally had much sympathy with the Serbian cause, or causes: this is not just for the reason commonly advanced (traditionally close ties with Serbia), but also because Russia and Serbia have shared the trauma of collapse of a communist federation. Similarly, if for different reasons, Greece is much more favourable to Serbia than are any of its NATO allies. Many Muslim states, and those with substantial Muslim minorities, have identified closely with Bosnia. Germany has renewed old connections with Croatia, and has shown only limited understanding of the messy complexities of communal conflict.

The various perspectives on former Yugoslavia have not been well articulated. There have been short statements and sound-bites galore, but no Western political leader has made a major statement analysing in depth the causes and character of the war, and the policy options for outside powers. There have been obvious reasons for this, but there are also costs: not least the elements of incomprehension in much international, including transatlantic, debate.

The UN Secretary-General

It is an open secret that few in the UN Secretariat wanted the organisation to be saddled with the problems attendant upon Yugoslavia's break-up. They rightly perceived the problems as extremely difficult, and the UN's possible involvement as hazardous. Today, UN officials sometimes hint that, but for the terrible intra-state conflicts with which the organisation has had to deal, the UN might have realised at least part of the vision, widespread in 1991–92, of its post-Cold War role.

In many statements at the UN, including those by leading members of the Secretariat and Security Council, nationalism, warlordism and ethnic conflict have been treated as modern versions of original sin: to be deplored, and to be restrained and controlled from outside. UN Secretary-General Boutros Boutros-Ghali has addressed the subject of ethnic/communal conflict in a number of documents and statements. He said in 1992 in *An Agenda for Peace* that 'the cohesion of States is threatened by brutal ethnic, religious, social, cultural or linguistic strife.'[12] This presents communal strife exclusively as a threat to the cohesion of states, rather than (as sometimes happens) as part of a process of state formation.

In a speech in 1993, Boutros-Ghali discussed ethnic conflict at some length, including the key question of whether, or when, it constitutes a threat to the peace calling for action under the UN Charter: 'All ethnic conflict is deplorable. But not all ethnic conflict threatens world peace. The United Nations cannot and should not try to solve every such problem.' However, another passage in the same speech, using a biological analogy, presented ethnic conflict as a general threat:

> ... ethnic conflict poses as great a danger to common world security as did the cold war. The character of the challenge and the time-frame involved are not the same – but the threat to security is no less real. No country today, and particularly multi-ethnic countries, can afford to ignore ethnic conflict. Borders and oceans can no longer insulate people at home from the consequences of such violence abroad ... Just as biological disease spreads through a body, and as an epidemic spreads geographically, so also a political disease can spread through the world. When one State is endangered by ethnic conflict, others will be endangered as well.[13]

Boutros-Ghali called ethnic conflict a 'new reality'.[14] While it is indeed new in some areas and forms, it is basically an old phenomenon – and one that has often been viewed by outside powers nervously, as something in which to avoid direct involvement. One of the UN's problems in respect of such conflicts, including in former Yugoslavia, has been this sense of nervousness: states have been able to use the UN as a means of limiting their own direct involvement.

Some Western States and Organisations

In the early stages of the war, many Western leaders underestimated the depth and seriousness of the Yugoslav crisis. The hubris of a regional organisation in claiming to be able to handle a tragic conflict without outside help was exemplified by the remark of Jacques Delors, President of the European Commission, in the summer of 1991, when fighting broke out in Yugoslavia: 'We do not interfere in American affairs. We hope they will have enough respect not to interfere in ours.'[15]

The US policy in the crucial year, 1991, illustrates the difficulty of resisting the tide of nationalist events. Even after Croatia and Slovenia had adopted declarations of independence in June 1991, the US policy remained one of supporting whatever unity of Yugoslavia could be salvaged – which was not a lot. In early August 1991, in his 'chicken Kiev' speech, President George Bush warned the Ukrainian people of the dangers of 'suicidal nationalism', and stated that his administration intended to 'maintain the strongest possible relationship with the Soviet government of Mikhail Gorbachev'. The fate of these policies suggests that, however flawed the doctrine of national self-determination may be, to resist it as a matter of general principle is not an option for the international community.

Following the outbreak of the wars in former Yugoslavia, official speeches by Western leaders generally described the conflict in terms of ancient hatreds unleashed, and of a cauldron of hot liquid which boils over when the lid is removed. In August 1992 President Bush said that Balkan strife grew out of 'age-old animosities'. Therefore, Bush went on to say, 'let no one think there is an easy or a simple solution to this tragedy . . . whatever pressure and means the international community brings to bear.'[16] A similar view was offered in what is arguably the fullest statement of American policy on former Yugoslavia – that by Warren Christopher on 10 February 1993. His image of the war was summed up in this statement:

> The death of President Tito and the end of communist domination of the former Yugoslavia raised the lid on the cauldron of ancient ethnic hatreds. This is the land where at least three religions and a half-dozen ethnic groups have vied across the centuries. It was the birthplace of World War I. It

has long been a cradle of European conflict, and it remains so today.[17]

Warren Christopher's interpretation of the Yugoslav conflict contains much truth. It is indisputable that there have long been deep and exceptionally bitter ethnic divisions in Yugoslavia: indeed, these have been noted by countless writers. Yet the history of Yugoslavia is not exclusively one of 'age-old animosities'. Such imagery ignores evidence of extensive ethnic co-existence (including widespread intermarriage) over a period of decades and even centuries.

The 'ancient ethnic hatreds' view of ex-Yugoslavia has predominated in US foreign policymaking, but is too pessimistic to capture the high ground in American political and public debate. There, another compelling framework of thought has held sway: that which sees international problems in terms of (Serb) aggression v. (Bosnian) defence, and which is quick to condemn European powers for their selfishness and incapacity. This perspective leads naturally to 'lift and strike' – that is, opposition to the arms embargo on former Yugoslavia, so that Bosnia can defend itself better; and advocacy of that traditional US long-distance and low-risk instrument, bombing.

In view of the existence of many different perspectives on the Yugoslav conflict, only a few of which have been mentioned here, it is remarkable that international organisations, including the UN Security Council, have been able to reach agreement on action; and it is not surprising that the action recommended has often been only a limited and partial response to a peculiarly difficult challenge.

THE END OF EMPIRES AND FEDERATIONS

The central feature of many post-Cold War conflicts, including ones which have engaged the UN, is not so much the nature of the contending groups as the complete collapse of an existing system of government. The original causes of the collapse may involve many factors besides ethnic/communal issues. The process of collapse, however, may exacerbate communal tensions: all kinds of groups – ethnic, religious, territorial, or linguistic – may have their own ideas and folk memories of who their friends are, who their enemies are, what kind of state they aspire to create, and within what frontiers.

Yugoslavia and the Soviet Union are not 'normal' cases of imperial dissolution. They are disintegrations of large and complex socialist-cum-federal states, which had been akin to empires, albeit in socialist colours and with some special features. For the most part, the internal borders of these two great states did not follow clear ethnic, economic, or strategic lines, and were not intended to be possible international frontiers. Their previous regimes' official nationalities policies had for better or for worse emphasised nationality as one basis of political units, had patronised ethnic cultures, and at the same time had sought to constrain and discredit serious ethnic claims. When the chance came to break with the old communist order, its only half-real sub-order of republics and of ethnic groups suddenly became the main surviving foundations for political construction. The theoretical right to secession became actual, and the steadying hand of the old communist system was no longer there to hold centrifugal tendencies in check. The old communist political language of absolute right and wrong was transferred catastrophically to an ethnic framework.

Once the break-up of the Soviet Union and Yugoslavia became inevitable, the international community, and some local political forces, sought to accept the existing republics of the federation as the successor states. This meant accepting the internal frontiers of the federation, however artificial or arbitrary, as the international frontiers of these new or reconstituted states.[18] In both cases, the federal collapse took place so quickly that the republics had little or no time to prepare for independent statehood. Many of the new states thus formed contained significant sectors of the population which were reluctant to come under their rule. The biggest and most populous units (Russia and Serbia respectively) of these old federations had large numbers of fellow nationals in nearby republics; but also faced potential for further fission, due to the existence within them of republics or autonomous provinces with distinctive populations and good reason to fear domination and to desire independence. The Russian Federation includes 20 Autonomous Republics and 11 Regions, containing an impressive variety of language groups and populations in almost every possible proportion and combination.

In many parts of the former Soviet Union, much effort was devoted to preventing the outbreak of ethnic conflict, and trying to build new states 'on the basis of co-citizenship and on the policy of cultural pluralism'.[19] Despite such efforts, it is not surprising that many wars began there: in Armenia and Azerbaijan, Moldova, Georgia, Tajikistan, and within the Russian Federation itself, in Chechnya. In ex-Yugoslavia wars broke out in Slovenia, Croatia and Bosnia; and there was fear of conflict in Macedonia, and in Vojvodina and Kosovo, both of which are within Serbia.

The rapid moves toward national self-determination in the former socialist world in the 1990s have not had the dubious benefit of any Lenin- or Woodrow Wilson-style advocacy. As indicated above, in 1991 the USA was notably cautious, even conservative, in respect of the break-up of both Yugoslavia and the Soviet Union. In Russia there were some exponents of national self-determination as a general principle, including, notably, Dr Galina Starovoitova, who in 1992 was a member of the Russian parliament and an adviser on ethnic matters to President Yeltsin. However, there has been little international political debate on the merits and defects of self-determination as a basis for order. It is as if, after the collapse of communist empires and their ideologies, national self-determination was the default position – the principal remaining basis for political organisation. It has largely ceased to be a theory for international order, but it remains an effective battle-cry for ambitious local leaders and their followers.

TECHNIQUES FOR ADDRESSING ONGOING CONFLICTS

International institutions can respond to conflicts involving ethnic/communal dimensions with a wide variety of types of action. Boutros-Ghali has listed four: 'education, economics, human rights, military.'[20] The order is interesting, and the first approach deserves more attention than it has received. Five types of action are discussed here: mediation, population exchange, peace-keeping, international administration, and sanctions. All these are types of action which have been applied in cases of ongoing conflicts; preventive action – a partly separate, larger and more rewarding field – is not covered here.

Mediation

Attempts at inter-ethnic mediation by international bodies have taken many forms, and have been the subject of much interesting advocacy.[21] Two of the most common have been proposals for partition to enable hostile communities to live in separate states, and proposals for federal arrangements within a single state.

The UN has been continuously and deeply involved in attempting to mediate in conflicts with an inter-communal dimension, but with only limited results. Its efforts at mediation in various phases of the Middle East conflict – whether through international conferences, or the 'good offices' function of the Secretary-General – have been less productive of agreements than those of other mediators, especially the USA. The longest running 'good offices' effort of the Secretary-General – the attempt since 1964 to get a confederal structure of government in Cyprus – has served many useful functions, but has not yet succeeded. Similarly, the joint efforts under European Community, UN, and Contact Group auspices to mediate in the Yugoslav conflicts have repeatedly run into difficulties.[22]

International attempts to mediate in communal conflicts frequently revolve around efforts at territorial management, in which the recognition of distinct zones, even of separate states, is seen as the basis of a solution.[23] UNSCOP (the UN Special Committee on Palestine) tried to create separate units in 1947. The resulting UN Partition Plan for Palestine, approved by the General Assembly on 29 November 1947, would have created an Arab state and a Jewish state, each composed of three separate parts. As Avi Shlaim has written: 'The borders of these two oddly shaped states, resembling two fighting serpents, were a strategic nightmare.'[24]

Similarly, in respect of the former Yugoslavia, the Vance–Owen mission in its various incarnations, and the international Contact Group which has largely succeeded it, have proposed complex schemes for partition, albeit within the framework of a loose federal Bosnian state. A principal problem is that such mediation proposals involve setting up under international auspices a series of zones which may reflect (albeit imperfectly) existing ethnic distributions of population, or the interests of major outside powers, or the current state of the battlefield, but also have built-in faults. Such arrangements often lack territorial contiguity, and in an extreme form are sometimes likened to leopard spots. They are often criticised on the ground that the proposed units fail to meet important aspirations of the embattled belligerents; make little economic sense; and fail to provide defensible territory and a sense of security for the inhabitants. The desire for security, which is at the heart of many communal conflicts, militates against the acceptance of any patchwork solution that leaves a group with frontiers that are vulnerable and hard to defend.

It is hard to see what else mediators can do when circumstances make inter-ethnic cooperation within a single political unit hard to achieve. They point out that the belligerents themselves often produce complicated patchwork plans. International mediators, representing not just the individual countries of the international community but also the principles to which those countries subscribe, simply cannot propose the vast population expulsions, or violent changes in existing states and frontiers, which would be necessary to create ethnically homogeneous and militarily defensible states. If they were to advocate such a course they would, with good reason, incur heavy criticism. Sometimes it even seems, and not only to some of the belligerents directly involved, that despite the terrible costs involved, the fortunes of war can have a better chance of yielding defensible territorial units than the machinery of international diplomacy.[25]

There are good reasons why, in mediation as in other matters, international bodies do not necessarily trump individual states. International bodies are often constrained from departing from well-known fixed positions – by their fundamental principles, by their record on the issue at stake, and by the need to maintain whatever agreement there is among their member states. Yet the resolution of conflicts with an ethnic dimension, whether in the matter of Israel–Palestine, or former Yugoslavia, almost always involves making departures from key principles, including that of the non-recognition of any changes of frontiers by force. Such resolution also frequently involves working on limited agreements with limited numbers of parties – something which universal bodies such as the UN are often reluctant to do. Hence the effectiveness of individual states in patching up limited deals, as the USA did in helping to bring about the fragile peace between the Bosnian government and Bosnian Croats in February–March 1994, and as Russia did between the Croatian government and the Serbian rebel forces (Republic of Serb Krajina) in March 1994.

Efforts at mediation of conflicts with an ethnic or communal dimension have to be made, and can open up possibilities for peace. Yet they always involve hovering around the very fine line between the containment of conflict and its exacerbation. Attempts to force hostile parties into a federation they do not want are unlikely to succeed. There are no quick fixes, and no possibility of imposing a *diktat* from outside. Since they necessarily involve reassuring threatened communities, mediation efforts require local knowledge and readiness for a long haul.[26]

Population Exchange

Where efforts to protect minority rights seem doomed to failure, exchange of populations is sometimes proposed as the only way of preventing the continuation of a conflict. The exchange of populations between Greece and Turkey starting in 1912 is a leading example. Mass flights of Greeks from Turkey largely preceded the convention of 30 January 1923 which sought to regulate the exchange process. The convention, widely denounced at the time as inhumane, may well have been 'the best policy in the unhappy circumstances'.[27] The League of Nations Council was deeply involved in the implementation of the convention, and in the various controversies that arose.

Within the UN system, especially the Office of the UN High Commissioner for Refugees (UNHCR), forced population exchange is a taboo subject. The appalling practices associated with so-called 'ethnic cleansing' in former Yugoslavia have forced UNHCR and other organisations to help move threatened people, mainly Bosnian Muslims. This has led to occasional accusations that they are actually assisting ethnic cleansing. In 1994–95 UNHCR conducted internal studies on forced exchange, but remained very strongly opposed.

Peace-keeping

All significant UN peace-keeping operations in the first three decades after 1945 related to territory and people recently freed from colonialism.[28] In practically all these cases there was some element of communal conflict, often combined with dispute about some of the territorial arrangements left by departing colonial powers. In many of these cases the inter-position of lightly-armed UN peace-keeping forces worked reasonably well. There was usually some willingness of the parties involved to stick to an agreed ceasefire, to give consent to the presence of a UN peace-keeping force, and to respect its impartial and neutral character.

The conflicts that have erupted in the former Yugoslavia and former Soviet Union have – because of their violence, their terrible effects on civilians, their creation of refugee flows, and their tendency to spread – created strong and natural demands in the international community for action. Where it has materia-lised at all, such action has taken the form of peace-keeping or some variant thereof. However, peace-keeping has been made particularly difficult by eight characteristics of these conflicts:

(1)   The involvement of a large number of belligerent parties, including both governments and non-state groups, mak-ing peace negotiations difficult.

(2)   Lack of willingness or ability on the part of the leaders of the principal groups involved to stick to the terms of an agreed ceasefire.

(3)   Widespread use of hastily assembled armed forces, often with little professional training and an uncertain com-mand structure; and wide dispersion of light weapons. These factors make the forces involved hard to bring under control as part of a ceasefire, peace or partial dis-armament agreement.

(4)   Rejection by some parties of certain existing borders (in-cluding international ones in some cases), and a com-plex, widely dispersed pattern of military activities, making ceasefire lines hard to establish and monitor.

(5)   The existence of numerous points of friction between the parties involved, arising from the fact that commun-ities at war with each other live in the same regions, some-times even in the same towns and villages.

(6)   Desire to carry out policies – such as forcible border changes, expulsion or killing of members of an ethnic group, massive resettlement of occupied areas with mem-bers of another ethnic group – which by their very nature

are contrary to basic principles of international law in general, and the laws of war (international humanitarian law) in particular.

(7) The creation of human disasters with which the belligerents cannot cope, thus drawing peace-keeping forces into humanitarian activities which result in their dispersion, and their dependence on the cooperation of the warring parties.

(8) A tendency to endure for decades, even generations, thus severely testing the patience and staying power of outside peace-keepers.[29]

These features of recent conflicts have forced UN peace-keeping away from its traditional character; and they have cruelly exposed its limits. This is especially the case in the former Yugoslavia, where there has been very little peace to keep.

Established in February 1992, the UN Protection Force (UNPROFOR) in the former Yugoslavia became the largest UN peace-keeping operation ever. By the end of 1994 it had some 40 000 personnel, which is more than any previous UN peace-keeping operation; and it was costing $1.6 billion a year – nearly half the cost of all 17 peace-keeping operations in place around the world at that time.[30] Its mandates, based on over 60 Security Council resolutions, were more complex than those of any previous UN force.[31] On 31 March 1995, following a crisis over the renewal of the mandate in Croatia and prolonged negotiations, the UN Security Council resolved to transform UNPROFOR in former Yugoslavia into three separately named forces, in each of the three successor states which were the theatre of its main operations: the UN Confidence Restoration Operation in Croatia (UNCRO); the UN Preventive Deployment Force (UNPREDEP) in Macedonia; and, keeping the old name, the UN Protection Force (UNPROFOR) in Bosnia and Herzegovina.[32]

What UN peace-keeping forces have been attempting in former Yugoslavia – a major international presence in the midst of unresolved conflicts and ongoing wars – is historically unprecedented. Their initial, and fundamental, task, laid down in 1992, was 'to create the conditions of peace and security required for the negotiation of an overall settlement of the Yugoslav crisis'.[33] In their operations – especially in the two major tasks of attempting to implement ceasefires in Croatia and in Bosnia – they have encountered extreme difficulties. It has probably been a mistake, and one that led to inflated expectations, for UNPROFOR to carry the name 'Protection Force', and to be classified as a 'peace-keeping force'. In Croatia, UN peace-keeping forces have monitored a ceasefire between the government and the Serb-held areas. However, President Franjo Tudjman of Croatia, hostile to the *de facto* emergence of a state within a state comparable to that in northern Cyprus, repeatedly threatened to refuse consent to a renewal of UNPROFOR's mandate, and in May 1995 defied the UN by successfully recapturing western Slavonia.[34] Meanwhile in Bosnia, UNPROFOR has helped monitor and implement local ceasefires, including between the Muslims and Croats, but it has not stopped the Muslim–Serb war. Its most effective performance has been in humanitarian assistance, including to besieged areas. For example, getting over 12 000 flights to Sarajevo is an impressive achievement.[35] This role in itself poses a problem: it requires forces to be widely dispersed, and to operate with the permission of the dominant forces in the area – in many cases the Bosnian Serbs. Hence it becomes very difficult for the UN forces to take, or encourage NATO to take, tough action against the parties. Indeed, critics argue that, in a communal conflict, a peace-keeping and humanitarian role tends to buttress the military *status quo*.

International Administration

The reluctance of the UN to take over responsibility for government in a quasi-trustee role is particularly evident in divided societies, including Bosnia and the UN-protected areas of Croatia. However, there have been important civil affairs and police components in the work of UNPROFOR. In addition, in Bosnia-Herzegovina there is the office of the UN Special Coordinator for Sarajevo, established in April 1994 to help restore essential public services in the Bosnian capital; and the European Union Administrator for Mostar, who assumed his responsibilities on 23 July 1994. These outside officials in Sarajevo and Mostar have had limited but very different administrative roles. In both cases the experience has been difficult and the achievements modest. Neither these nor any other administrative arrangements under negotiation constitute anything like a prospective government.

The historical record of trusteeship systems under international auspices is not encouraging: indeed, the problems of some divided societies – including Palestine, Iraq, and Ruanda-Urundi (now Rwanda and Burundi) – may well have been made worse in the period of the League of Nations mandate system. Except in cases of regional hegemony, old-fashioned forms of the direct exercise of dominance are out of fashion.[36]

The contemporary importance of the question of administration has been well identified by Boutros-Ghali:

> Another feature of such [intra-state] conflicts is the collapse of state institutions, especially the police and judiciary, with resulting paralysis of governance, a breakdown of law and order, and general banditry and chaos. Not only are the functions of government suspended, its assets are destroyed or looted and experienced officials are killed or flee the country. This is rarely the case in inter-state wars. It means that international intervention must extend beyond military and humanitarian tasks and must include the promotion of national reconciliation and the re-establishment of effective government.[37]

What is emerging is not a formal doctrine of trusteeship, but rather a modest, tentative and pragmatic international involvement in aspects of government in many countries, in collaboration with local and national authorities, and often in connection with an ongoing UN peace-keeping operation. If unavoidable, this seems also to be an inadequate role for international organisations. It obviously provides an incomplete answer to the problems of the deeply divided state, the genocidal state (as in Rwanda in 1994), and the failed state. It leaves open the possibility that, faced with communal conflicts in their neighbourhood, some regional powers may assume an administrative burden that the international community as a whole is unwilling to carry.

Economic Sanctions and Arms Embargoes

At least in theory, global international organisations have a special capacity to organise economic sanctions and arms embargoes, which generally need to be near-universal if they are to be effective. The UN has imposed non-forcible sanctions under Article 41 of the Charter in several cases of conflict where there has been an ethnic or communal dimension. There have been general economic sanctions against Rhodesia (1966–79), and Serbia and Montenegro (1992–). There have also been embargoes on the supply of arms to South Africa (1977–94); former Yugoslavia (1991–); Somalia (1992–); Liberia (1992–); and Rwanda (1994).

In former Yugoslavia, such measures have been imperfectly implemented, and their results have, at best, been mixed. The general economic sanctions against Serbia and Montenegro may have been a factor in the progressive diminution of Serbia's support for Serb forces in Bosnia and Croatia in 1994–95; and the prospect of their being ended was evidently an inducement to Belgrade to consider changing course. On the other hand, being a plainly partisan measure, aimed at one side only, they reinforced Serb doubts about UN impartiality.

The effects of the arms embargo against the countries of former Yugoslavia have been more controversial. With the exception of the short war in Slovenia in 1991, the conflicts in former Yugoslavia have been prolonged by the general availability of weapons, and the large numbers of people trained in their use. The Yugoslav system of General People's Defence, which had been implemented in 1969, had always involved a risk of misuse in internal conflict. In 1976 I wrote: 'The Yugoslav defence system rests on fragile social and political foundations. If those foundations fail, the idea of General People's Defence might be quickly forgotten; or, worse, it might be perversely misused for civil war.'[38] Although the wide availability of arms was indeed a problem from 1991 onwards, so was the arms embargo. The Yugoslav experience confirms that embargoes on the supply of arms tend to favour one side – in this case the well-armed Serbs. Hence the increasingly strong calls for Bosnia to be enabled to defend itself, and the evidence of blind eyes being turned to numerous violations of the arms embargo, not only in respect of Bosnia. Like other aspects of the international response, the arms embargo was perceived as ineffective, yet far from impartial.

DILEMMAS OF RECOGNITION POLICY

Diplomatic recognition, whether by individual states or by international institutions, is an important and controversial issue in ethnic/communal conflicts. Acts of recognition have had several consequences. The prospect of recognition can force the pace of state creation by putting pressure on would-be states to get their claims in while the music of recognition is being played. An act of recognition implies a degree of obligation on the part of states and international organisations to maintain respect for the newly recognised state and its international borders, even if there has not always been deep determination to act on this. Once recognised, a state may feel entitled to insist on retaining all its territory, however strongly it is disputed. Above all, recognition can have the effect of transforming other states' legal and political perceptions of a conflict: what was previously a civil war or communal conflict may come to be viewed as an international war. A state trying to recover its old territory may suddenly be seen as an aggressor.

Lord Carrington and Javier Pérez de Cuéllar in December 1991 warned of the hazards of early and selective diplomatic recognition of some of the Yugoslav republics in advance of an overall settlement. As Lord Carrington put it in a letter to Hans van den Broek:

> There is also a real danger, perhaps even a probability, that Bosnia-Herzegovina would also ask for independence and recognition, which would be wholly unacceptable to the Serbs in that republic in which there are something like 100 000 JNA [Yugoslav People's Army] troops, some of which have withdrawn there from Croatia. Milosevic has hinted that military action would take place there if Croatia and Slovenia were recognized. This might well be the spark that sets Bosnia-Herzegovina alight.[39]

There can be no question of attributing the ensuing tragedy in Bosnia entirely to the acts of recognition that took place in January 1992. However, recognition was politically explosive, both in the countries and institutions carrying out acts of recognition, and in the states being recognised. Recognition of a new entity is especially controversial where, as in former Yugoslavia, the old state still exists, at least in rump form, and has not accepted its own collapse; where there are large minorities that adhere to an outside state and reject the borders or even the existence of the new entity in which they find themselves;

and where promises by emergent states in the field of human rights are not backed up by performance. Yet it is understandable that states sometimes see a strong case for early recognition of new entities. In an unstable situation, in which the central state or imperial power has collapsed, there is a need to keep some control on events. Where recognition is conditional upon certain commitments (for example, about human rights, treatment of minorities, or respect for frontiers), it can have special attractions. In respect of Croatia, there was a serious belief that the process of European Community recognition, which finally took effect on 15 January 1992 even before Croatia had met EC conditions for protection of minorities, might actually assist the process of concluding and implementing the ceasefire between Croatia and Serbia. This ceasefire accord, concluded on 2 January, was indeed implemented, however inadequately, better than its 14 predecessors.

Should there be a reversion to old and well-established criteria for diplomatic recognition? Principal among these are some coherence as a political and social entity, and a capacity for self-defence. The experience of European decolonisation, in which the successor states achieved recognition and UN membership reasonably smoothly, contributed to a relative decline of these older criteria. The EU and UN experience with former Yugoslavia raises doubts about whether international institutions are necessarily better at making judgements on these matters than individual states. The traditional criteria for recognition need to be revived, perhaps with some changes, including more emphasis on human rights and minority protection.

ATTEMPTS TO DEVELOP CRITERIA FOR INVOLVEMENT

As great powers tire of heavy commitments to distant and puzzling conflicts, it is likely that the Security Council's attitude will become more parsimonious. Since 1991, the Council has in fact limited its involvement in a number of conflicts with an ethnic dimension, including several in the former Soviet Union. Already in 1992, *An Agenda for Peace* indicated an interest in placing a greater part of the burden of peace-keeping onto regional powers and organisations.[40] In May 1994 the Council specified six factors that must be taken into account when a

new operation is under consideration. These were: the existence
of a threat to international peace and security; whether regional bodies are ready to assist; the existence of a ceasefire;
a clear political goal which can be reflected in the mandate;
a precise mandate; and reasonable assurances on the safety of
UN personnel.[41] Several of these would be hard to satisfy in
many communal conflicts, including that in former Yugoslavia. An even stronger note of caution was struck at about the
same time in the Clinton administration's unveiling of Presidential Decision Directive 25, on 'multilateral peace operations'.[42] PDD 25 raised questions as to whether, had it applied
earlier, many existing UN operations would have been undertaken, or would have secured US participation. As Mats Berdal
has said, 'strict adherence to the criteria of "no open-ended
commitments" and continuing public support are bound to
limit the scope for UN action in a world where domestic, religious and ethnically motivated hatreds are the major sources
of conflict.'[43] Since PDD 25 appeared, the US has moved still
further away from support for UN peace-keeping. The new
Republican majorities in the House and Senate are the inheritors of a long-standing American distrust of any mode of over-
seas military involvement other than the quick victory based
on overwhelming force. The proposals of the Senate Budget
Committee, announced in February 1995, threatened even
more serious cutbacks in support for UN peace-keeping than
those previously discussed.[44]

GENERAL ISSUES AND CONCLUSIONS

The conflicts of the post-Cold War era, not least the communal conflict aspects of them, present exceptionally difficult
challenges to the international community and its institutions,
especially the UN. How are those challenges to be understood,
addressed, and acted upon especially in the light of the Yugoslav disasters?

(1) The international community has faced periods of such
    conflict before – including, in this century, in the Balkans
    around the time of the two World Wars, and in former
    European colonies around the time of decolonisation.

The international system managed to endure these periods of conflict, sometimes with great difficulty and cost, and to prevent intensely disruptive regional phenomena from leading to a general process of fission.

(2)   While conflicts with a communal dimension can have tendencies to spread within a country or region, it is probably wrong, in a new version of the domino theory, to view them as a universal threat.

(3)   The use of armed force in the hands of states and would-be states still has some role in processes of state formation. Issues, even frontiers, are sometimes decided by these means.

(4)   The historical record suggests that the management of communal conflicts is inherently difficult, whether it be attempted by states, empires, regional or global organisations. The UN should not be judged harshly merely for running into difficulties similar to those encountered by other bodies.

(5)   The UN system was not designed to address problems of communal conflict, but rather the very different challenge of the excessively well-organised and aggressive state, exemplified by Nazi Germany. However, this does not make it impossible to address such problems effectively: the UN's history is replete with innovations. The UN has in fact spent a great deal of its existence dealing with this very issue.

(6)   The performance of the UN in tackling such conflicts suggests that it does not trump individual states and alliances, and has some institutional defects:

(a)   The collective character of UN decision-making is not necessarily appropriate to the management of complex and fast-moving situations. States differ in their views on and interests in specific conflicts; and may vote for all kinds of resolutions, for a variety of reasons, in ignorance or indifference. While decisions for specific immediate action may be possible, especially if it is of an essentially humanitarian character, it is more difficult to get agreement on long-term goals and strategy.

(b)   States providing personnel for multilateral peace-keeping in such conflicts may not have sufficient interest, determination and local knowledge to take risks, accept sacrifices, and stay involved over the long term. National contingents may reflect diverging policies and practices; and there may even be ethnic tensions within and between them, hampering efficiency. For such reasons, UN forces are often seen as ineffectual compared to those of determined local parties.

(c) The UN's Charter and past practices drive it to respond to crises in one of two basic ways: *either* by taking sides in a Chapter VII enforcement operation, *or* by resorting to its more normal modes of operation – impartiality, ceasefires, mediation, peace-keeping. Yet complex communal conflicts, as in Yugoslavia, Somalia, Angola and Rwanda, may require elements of both approaches: for example, the simultaneous use of sanctions against Serbia and maintenance of a supposedly impartial peace-keeping operation in various parts of former Yugoslavia. The combination of the two, and especially the transfer from peace-keeping to enforcement mode, has proved difficult.

(d) Whereas the UN is bound by its Charter and other principles, including the non-acquisition of territory by force, the settlement of communal conflicts sometimes involves deals between parties which, in greater or lesser degree, conflict with some of those principles.

(e) The UN lacks a strong tradition of analysis and debate, reinforcing the difficulty of addressing such problems.

(7) In discourse in the UN and elsewhere, recent cases of communal conflict have contributed to a growing flexibility about the meaning of 'self-determination'. Full sovereign statehood is not necessarily the only possible goal of movements for self-determination; even where it is the goal, the nation may need to be defined not so much as an ethnic group, but more as all the inhabitants of a given area. There is a need to revive more modest ideas of the state as being based on geography, values and procedures, history and sentiment, administrative

convenience, and the capacity to mediate relations between citizens of very different interests, classes, regions, and ethnic groups.

(8)   As compared to regional organizations and individual states, the UN does have some significant advantages in addressing conflicts with a communal dimension:

    (a)   Its reputation for impartiality, however tarnished, makes it a possible interlocutor and provider of services.

    (b)   Notwithstanding such cases as Cyprus and Lebanon, a UN presence has some capacity to discourage competitive national interventions in a conflict.

    (c)   It has, in the Security Council, clearer and more effective decision-making machinery than that of many international bodies.

    (d)   It can bring huge resources to bear.

    (e)   There is only one UN, and it is often more acceptable to refer a problem to it than a regional body.

(9)   In several ongoing conflicts, and most strikingly in former Yugoslavia, the UN has become involved in a historically novel response: maintaining a large presence, partly for humanitarian assistance purposes, and partly to assist the negotiating process, in the middle of a continuing war. Somalia, Angola and Rwanda offer parallels. This radical departure from traditional peace-keeping is caused by the difficulty of getting lasting ceasefires in communal conflicts. In these conflicts, the UN has faced a cruel dilemma in the 1990s. If it takes little or no action, it risks being accused of ineffectiveness, or of unjustifiable selectivity in choosing which problems to tackle. If it does get more deeply involved in military action, it risks falling prey to hostage-taking, accusations of colonial oppressiveness, and the imposition of an unbearable burden on contributing states. UN forces may sometimes be able to do little more than reduce the number of casualties, assist victims, help broker ceasefire accords (often local rather than general) and limit the likelihood of the conflict spreading to other states. To the extent that their presence is based on consent of the parties, they are perpetually vulnerable to pressure for their missions to be changed and their mandates

modified. In the Balkans and elsewhere, UN forces end up in unheroic if still important roles. It is not surprising that there is much dissatisfaction with the UN's role in such ongoing conflicts, and a belief that it must be possible to find better answers than those found so far.

(10) As the limits of the UN Security Council's capacity to provide effective overall direction of operations relating to communal conflicts are exposed, there is bound to be pressure on the UN to establish systems of delegated authority to individual states or regional bodies in the management of UN peace-keeping operations. To a modest extent, as much by drift as formal decision, and with many difficulties and denials along the route, this has begun to happen in several recent cases, not least former Yugoslavia.

(11) The UN is in danger of severe over-commitment. The very universality of the organisation makes it hard to refuse involvement, and the scope of problems in Yugoslavia and elsewhere has led to a requirement for forces of substantial size. The various methods for limiting involvement – devising general criteria, encouraging regional action, and being prepared to cut losses when UN efforts fail – have not prevented an accretion of responsibilities. The main limit is a crude and unsatisfactory one: the reluctance of states to provide the money and the troops needed for operations. There is a widespread perception that former Yugoslavia has had massive (if still inadequate) resources devoted to it, and that the UN has not succeeded in maintaining a proper balance between the various crises that demand its attention.

(12) Because of the pressures on the existing system of obtaining troops for UN action, it is natural that there are several proposals for UN rapid reaction forces – whether composed of individual volunteers, or of national contingents held on a genuinely stand-by basis for participation in UN operations. However, such proposals should not feed illusions that all the UN needs is faster mobilization and more muscle. Nor should they deflect attention from the fundamental requirement for the UN to find some means of being selective, and decisive, about its involvements.

(13)   The difficult problems of selectivity thrown up in the post-Cold War period mean that Security Council decisions are inevitably controversial and contested. An unavoidable consequence is that the case for enlarging the Security Council, to secure its legitimacy as a body broadly representative of the international community, is strengthened. Any such enlargement, especially an increase in the number of permanent members with veto power, presents hazards for its capacity to reach decisions.

(14)   A further consequence of the UN's unavoidable selectivity is that there has been some revival of a tendency for regional powers to handle problems of communal conflict more or less independently of the UN, whether acting unilaterally or through regional organisations. There may even be a revival of certain notions of 'spheres of influence' – always a contested concept in international relations.

(15)   There remains a risk that the issue of ethnic and communal conflict will be the undoing of the UN. The UN has achieved remarkable results in many situations, including in Mozambique. Yet its record in Angola, Rwanda, Somalia, and former Yugoslavia is not encouraging. Its combination of denunciatory resolutions and ineffective actions is reminiscent of the conduct of democracies before the outbreak of the Second World War. Its reputation could easily crash like that of the League of Nations. It is perennially faced with the unenviable choice between continuing a presence perceived as ineffectual, or staging a withdrawal perceived as humiliating. Yet the UN has proved to be a more robust organisation than the League, with an astonishing capacity to survive setbacks, including in its management of communal conflict. It has begun to develop some capacity, as shown in *Supplement to An Agenda for Peace*, for careful examination of its own modes of action. It deserves continued support, not just because of the sheer difficulty of the problems of communal conflict, but also because it has achieved some results and may yet achieve more. In the matter of communal conflict, as also more generally, it needs to avoid creating false expectations of a new era of collective security. There are rare occasions when, to

put out a fire in Utah, it *is* necessary to go to Oklahoma for the fire engine. However, if this is perceived as the rule rather than the exception – and if the states involved do not have a common strategic appreciation and a serious commitment to the operation – it will never work.

NOTES

1. This is a heavily revised and updated version of the author's 'Ethnic Conflict: Threat and Challenge to the UN', in Anthony McDermott (ed.), *Ethnic Conflict and International Security* (Oslo: NUPI, 1994). Another version of this paper, based on the 1995 E. H. Carr Memorial Lecture, appears in *Review of International Studies*, vol. 21, no. 4 (October 1995).

2. Jan Christian Smuts, *The League of Nations: A Practical Suggestion* (London: Hodder and Stoughton, 1918), p. 25.

3. The eleventh of the Fourteen Points, Washington, DC, 8 January 1918. *Foreign Relations of the United States, 1918*, Supplement 1, *The World War*, Vol. I, p. 15.

4. Cited in Robert D. Schulzinger, *American Diplomacy in the Twentieth Century* (New York: Oxford University Press, 1984), p. 121.

5. See esp. Benedict Anderson, *Imagined Communities: Reflections on the Origin and Spread of Nationalism* (London: Verso, 1983).

6. Dr Danilo Türk, Permanent Representative of Slovenia to the UN, addressing UN Security Council, *Security Council Official Record*, 3492nd meeting, 19 January 1995, pp. 7–8.

7. Apart from other works cited in this text, in the United Kingdom this tradition includes E. H. Carr's *Nationalism and After* (London: Macmillan, 1945); Alfred Cobban, *The Nation State and National Self-Determination*, rev. edn. (London: Collins Fontana Library, 1969); Elie Kedourie, *Nationalism in Asia and Africa* (London: Weidenfeld & Nicolson, 1971); and Hugh Seton-Watson, *Nations and States: An Enquiry into the Origins of Nations and the Politics of Nationalism* (London: Methuen, 1977).

8. See especially R. W. Seton-Watson, *The Southern Slav Question and the Habsburg Monarchy* (London: Constable, 1911), pp. 46–7. This book carries the hopeful printed inscription: 'To that Austrian Statesman who shall possess the genius and the courage necessary to solve the Southern Slav question, this book is respectfully dedicated.' In the copy in the Bodleian Library, Oxford, a reader has handwritten here: 'Marshall Tito'. Alas!

9. See e.g. Daniel Patrick Moynihan, *Pandaemonium: Ethnicity in International Politics* (Oxford: Oxford University Press, 1993); and Walker Connor's collected articles from several decades in his *Ethnonationalism: The Quest for Understanding* (Princeton, NJ: Princeton University Press, 1994).

10. Hans J. Morgenthau, *Politics Among Nations*, 4th edn. (New York: Knopf, 1967), pp. 97–158: this is Part III, 'National Power'. See also his discussion of nationalism on pp. 321–4. The equivalent passages in the 6th edn. are at pp. 117–83 and 349–52.

11. Louis Henkin, *How Nations Behave: Law and Foreign Policy*, 2nd edn. (New York: Columbia University Press, 1979), p. 1n.

12. Boutros Boutros-Ghali, *An Agenda for Peace: Preventive Diplomacy, Peacemaking and Peace-keeping* (New York: UN, June 1992), para. 11.

13. Boutros-Ghali, statement in opening a seminar on ethnic conflict at National Defense University, Washington DC, 8 November 1993, UN doc. SG/SM/5152 (New York: UN, 1993), pp. 3 and 5.

14. Ibid., p. 5.

15. Cited in Owen Harries, 'The Collapse of "The West"', *Foreign Affairs*, vol. 72, no. 4 (September/October 1993), p. 49.

16. Quoted in Andrew Rosenthal, 'Bush Urges UN to Back Force to Get Aid to Bosnia', *New York Times*, 7 August 1992, pp. 1 and 8; cited in a chapter by Jack Snyder which is severely critical of the 'ancient hatred' view, 'Nationalism and the Crisis of the Post-Soviet State', in Michael E. Brown (ed.), *Ethnic Conflict and International Security* (Princeton, NJ: Princeton University Press, 1993), p. 79.

17. Secretary of State Warren Christopher, 'New Steps Toward Conflict Resolution in the Former Yugoslavia', opening statement at a news conference, Washington DC, 10 February 1993; published in *US Department of State Dispatch*, vol. 4, no. 7 (15 February 1993), p. 81.

18. For a critical evaluation of the European Community and US record on self-determination with respect to former Yugoslavia, and of the work of the Badinter Commission, see Kamal S. Shehadi, *Ethnic Self-Determination and the Break-up of States*, Adelphi Paper 283 (London: Brassey's for International Institute for Strategic Studies, December 1993), pp. 28–31.

19. For an account of such efforts, see especially a paper by Prof. Valery Tishkov, who was in charge of the nationalities issues in the Yeltsin government in February–October 1992 as Chairman of the State Committee for Nationalities Policy, 'The Burden of the Past: Experiences with Ethnic Mediation and Governance in the Former Soviet Union', in Anthony McDermott (ed.), *Ethnic Conflict and International Security* (Oslo, 1994), pp. 70–83.

20. Boutros-Ghali, statement at seminar on ethnic conflict, Washington DC, 8 November 1993, p. 3.

21. For a discussion of economic and legal pressures by outsiders to help mediate ethnic tensions within states, see Jenonne Walker, 'International Mediation of Ethnic Conflicts', in Brown, *Ethnic Conflict*, pp. 165–80.

22. For a succinct account of the UN Secretary-General's efforts over Cyprus, see Thomas Franck and Georg Nolte, 'The Good Offices Function of the UN Secretary-General', in Adam Roberts and Benedict Kingsbury (eds.), *United Nations, Divided World: The UN's Roles in International Relations*, 2nd edn. (Oxford: Oxford University Press, 1993), pp. 155–7. They also refer to the difficulties encountered in the Middle East (pp. 163–4) and former Yugoslavia (pp. 169–72).

23. For a useful general survey, see John Coakley (ed.), *The Territorial Management of Ethnic Conflict* (London: Cass, 1993). Cases considered include Belgium, Canada, Czechoslovakia, Pakistan, Sri Lanka, the former Soviet Union, and Tanzania.

24. Avi Shlaim, *The Politics of Partition: King Abdullah, the Zionists and Palestine 1921–1951* (Oxford: Oxford University Press, 1990), p. 101. See also the map of the UN Partition Plan on p. 102.

25. These conclusions are echoed in IISS, *Strategic Survey 1993–1994* (London: Brassey's, May 1994), p. 99. It describes the complex ethnic patchwork proposal for Bosnia, painstakingly constructed in early 1993 by the UN mediators, as 'a piece of laboured artificiality, a construct imposed from the outside'.

26. These points are all made in John Chipman, 'Managing the Politics of Parochialism', in Brown, *Ethnic Conflict*, esp. at p. 261. The chapter has a notably *de haut en bas* managerial tone, opening (p. 237) with a reference to 'overindulgence in the domestic and international politics of parochialism'.

27. The view expressed in C. A. Macartney *et al.*, *Survey of International Affairs 1925*, vol. II (London: Oxford University Press, 1928), p. 258.

28. The exception that proved the rule was DOMREP, the Mission of Representative of the Secretary-General in the Dominican Republic, 1965–66. It consisted of two persons, or at a generous count four.

29. Many of the above points can be found in Boutros Boutros-Ghali, *Supplement to An Agenda for Peace*, UN doc. A/50/60 of 3 January 1995, e.g. at paras. 12 and 13.

30. At 31 December 1994 UNPROFOR had 39 789 military and civilian police personnel, plus over 4000 civilian personnel. It had suffered 131 fatalities since it commenced operations in March 1992. Figures from UN Department of Public Information, New York, January 1995.

31. From 25 September 1991 to 31 December 1994 there were 81 UN Security Council resolutions on former Yugoslavia. Some, however, dealt with separate matters (e.g. admission of new members, and establishment of the War Crimes Tribunal) and were not directly part of the mandate of UN peace-keeping forces.

32. SC Res. 981 of 31 March 1995, establishing UNCRO in Croatia and defining its mandate in very broad terms, which left detail to be added in further difficult negotiations; SC Res. 982 of 31 March 1995, extending UNPROFOR's mandate in Bosnia and Herzegovina, and deciding that 'all previous resolutions relating to UNPROFOR shall continue to apply'; and SC Res. 983 of 31 March 1995, renaming UNPROFOR within Macedonia as UNPREDEP and reaffirming its mandate.

33. SC Res. 743 of 21 February 1992, establishing UNPROFOR.

34. Franjo Tudjman wrote to Boutros Boutros-Ghali on 12 January 1995 informing him 'that the UNPROFOR mandate is hereby terminated in Croatia effective March 31, 1995'. Copy on file with author. As noted above, on 31 March 1995 a revised mandate for the renamed UN force, UNCRO, was approved by the Security Council. It had been the subject of prolonged and difficult negotiation, in which the US government played the lead role.

35. From the start of the humanitarian airlift on 30 June 1992 up to

26 March 1995, there were 12 181 flights to Sarajevo, which delivered 151 202 tonnes, of which 136 652 were food, and the rest non-food items (shelter materials, medical supplies etc.). Figures in note from UNHCR to author, 28 March 1995. In April 1995 Serb threats forced a curtailment of the airlift to Sarajevo.

36. For general discussions, see Gerald B. Helman and Steven R. Ratner, 'Saving Failed States', *Foreign Policy*, no. 89 (Winter 1992–93), pp. 3–20; and Peter Lyon, 'The Rise and Fall and Possible Revival of International Trusteeship', *Journal of Commonwealth and Comparative Politics*, no. 31 (March 1993), pp. 96–110.

37. *Supplement to An Agenda for Peace*, para. 13.

38. Adam Roberts, *Nations in Arms: The Theory and Practice of Territorial Defence* (London: Chatto & Windus for IISS, 1976), p. 217. See also p. 136. When a Serbo-Croat edition of the book was proposed, these were among the passages that Yugoslav colleagues indicated would have to be cut. I was not able to agree these cuts, and the project never went ahead.

39. Letter from Lord Carrington, Chairman of the Conference on Yugoslavia, writing from London to Mr Hans van den Broek, Minister of Foreign Affairs of the Netherlands (at that time President of the European Community Council of Ministers), 2 December 1991. On 10 December 1991 UN Secretary-General Javier Pérez de Cuéllar wrote in similar vein to Hans van den Broek. Remarkably, it was Hans-Dietrich Genscher, Vice-Chancellor and Minister for Foreign Affairs of the Federal Republic of Germany, who responded, in a short letter to Pérez de Cuéllar of 13 December. Pérez de Cuéllar, in a letter of 14 December, sent a strong and detailed response reiterating that 'early selective recognitions could result in a widening of the present conflict'. Copies on file with author.

40. *Agenda for Peace*, paras. 11, 16, 27, and 60–65.

41. Statement by the President of the Security Council, UN doc. S/PRST/1994/22, 3 May 1994.

42. *The Clinton Administration's Policy on Reforming Multilateral Peace Operations*, US Department of State Publication 10161 (Washington DC: 1994). This document was unveiled on 5 May 1994. This and the UN Security Council presidential statement mentioned in the preceding note are briefly summarised and discussed in Adam Roberts, 'The Crisis in UN Peacekeeping', *Survival*, vol. 36, no. 3 (Autumn 1994), pp. 108–9.

43. Mats Berdal, *Whither UN Peacekeeping?*, Adelphi Paper 281 (London: Brassey's for IISS, October 1993), p. 74.

44. Overall, the Senate draft report proposes to reduce US spending on international affairs from about $21 billion a year at present, down to about $17.5 billion. Peace-keeping is one of the major targets for such cuts. See Eric Pianin and Thomas W. Lippman, 'Republicans Float Proposal to Slash Foreign Spending', *International Herald Tribune*, Paris, 17 February 1995, p. 2.

Index